OXFORD

THE SON

AND OTHER POI

The Song of Roland is the mos̲̲ ̲ ̲ ̲ ̲ ̲ ̲ ̲ ̲ ̲ ̲ ̲ ̲ epic poem of the
European Middle Ages and the best-known medieval French epic.
The earliest version of the poem dates from the turn of the eleventh
and twelfth centuries at the time of the First Crusade. Loosely based
on the historical massacre of Charlemagne's rearguard at Rencesvals
in 778, the poem narrates the heroic actions and death of Roland,
Charlemagne's nephew and captain of the rearguard. The earli-
est surviving version of the poem is translated here with two other
medieval epics featuring Charlemagne and Roland: the comic *Charle-
magne's Journey to Jerusalem and Constantinople* and the Occitan
Daurel and Beton.

SIMON GAUNT is Professor of French Language and Literature at
King's College London. His books include *Marco Polo's* Le Devise-
ment du Monde: *Narrative Voice, Language and Diversity* and
*Martyrs to Love: Love and Death in Medieval French and Occitan
Courtly Literature*.

KAREN PRATT is Professor emerita at King's College London
having been Professor of Medieval French Literature. She is the
editor of *The Arthur of the French: The Arthurian Legend in Medieval
French and Occitan Literature* with Glyn Burgess, and *Roland and
Charlemagne in Europe: Essays on the Reception and Transformation of
a Legend*.

OXFORD WORLD'S CLASSICS

The Song of Roland
and Other Poems of Charlemagne

Translated with an Introduction and Notes by
SIMON GAUNT *and* KAREN PRATT

OXFORD
UNIVERSITY PRESS

OXFORD
UNIVERSITY PRESS

Great Clarendon Street, Oxford, OX2 6DP
United Kingdom

Oxford University Press is a department of the University of Oxford.
It furthers the University's objective of excellence in research, scholarship,
and education by publishing worldwide. Oxford is a registered trade mark of
Oxford University Press in the UK and in certain other countries

Translations and editorial material
© Simon Gaunt and Karen Pratt 2016

The moral rights of the authors have been asserted

First published as an Oxford World's Classics paperback 2016

Impression: 1

Published in the United States of America by Oxford University Press
198 Madison Avenue, New York, NY 10016, United States of America

British Library Cataloguing in Publication Data
Data available

Library of Congress Control Number: 2016935436

ISBN 978-0-19-965554-0

Printed in Great Britain by
Clays Ltd, St Ives plc

CONTENTS

Introduction   vii

Note on the Texts and Translations   xxvi

Select Bibliography and Further Reading   xxix

Maps   xxxii

THE SONG OF ROLAND   3

DAUREL AND BETON   135

CHARLEMAGNE'S JOURNEY TO
   JERUSALEM AND CONSTANTINOPLE   197

Explanatory Notes   225

Glossary   234

Index of Proper Names   235

INTRODUCTION

THE SONG OF ROLAND, like other great epic poems in the European tradition such as *The Iliad*, *Beowulf*, *The Nibelungenlied*, and *El Cantar del mio Cid*, offers a particularly heady mixture of history, legend, and poetry. Charlemagne (768–814) was an influential historical character, who was crowned Holy Roman Emperor in 800 and presided over a huge empire and a rich cultural renaissance. However, the great warlord and pious crusading figure who appears in later medieval literature is the product of much legendary embellishment. He did not actually have a nephew called Roland, yet this figure (probably originally a Frankish warrior whose feats were celebrated in *cantilena* or short epic songs) plays an ever more prominent role in 'historical' documents from the late 820s onwards, as oral legend influenced 'history' writers. Thus, in Einhard's *Life of Charlemagne* (828–9), Hruodlandus, prefect of the Breton march (the border between Charlemagne's Francia and Brittany), was killed in an ambush by Basques as Charlemagne's army was returning to France after a military campaign in Spain. It is the epitaph (preserved in an eleventh-century manuscript) of another casualty in this disaster, a certain Eggihard, which gives us the date of 15 August 778 for Roland's death. And another late eleventh-century document, the *Nota Emilianense*, mentions Charlemagne's twelve 'nephews' who died at the hands of Saracens (Spanish Muslims) in the rearguard at Rencesvals, a mountain pass in the Pyrenees, thus providing the scenario for *The Song of Roland*.

In the version of the medieval French *Roland* we have translated here, which was probably composed at the turn of the eleventh and twelfth centuries, so around the time of the First Crusade (1096–9), the legend of Rencesvals has become far more elaborate: now Roland, with his faithful companion Oliver by his side, is the foremost of Charlemagne's twelve peers; he is the great king's nephew, and one of the principal agents in the expansion of the Carolingian Empire. Furthermore, Roland dies not at the hands of the Basques in a surreptitious ambush, but overwhelmed by hordes of Saracens. The Saracens are able to attack the rearguard of the Frankish army, now represented significantly also as a Christian army with an archbishop

(Turpin) as one of its principal warriors, as a result of the treachery of another high-ranking Frankish noble, Ganelon, who is Roland's step-father and Charlemagne's brother-in-law. At Rencesvals, Roland fights at the head of Charlemagne's famous twelve peers, leading the united ranks of 20,000 Frenchmen with prodigious bravery and against impossible odds: he is the last man left alive on the battlefield. He does not, however, die as a result of wounds inflicted by 'pagans' (as the text calls them), but rather because his temples burst as he blows his oliphant (an elephant tusk horn), thereby alerting Charle-magne that the rearguard has been attacked. Roland has previously quarrelled with his beloved friend Oliver, who has unsuccessfully urged him to blow his horn, thereby summoning the main portion of the army back. However, his dying gesture at least ensures that Charlemagne, in the role of overall protector, can bury those who fell at Rencesvals and avenge their deaths. The second half of the poem narrates the defeat of the Saracen king Marsilie, then the great army of the emir Baligant who arrives to reinforce the Spanish Muslims, and finally the punishment of Ganelon, who is tried and gruesomely dismembered as befits a traitor.

The *Roland* narrates all this with intense and highly emotive lyri-cism. Modern readers may understandably balk at the poem's ques-tionable ideology: it states unequivocally that pagans must either be converted or killed (lines 101–2) and celebrates violence in explicit terms: one by one bodies are pierced and dismembered, brains are mashed up, knights are cleaved in two with swords, which even cut right through them into the flesh of the horses they are riding. Yet few can fail to be moved by Roland and Oliver's final exchange after a blinded and mortally wounded Oliver strikes Roland in error, or by Roland's solitary and desolate tour of the battlefield to gather up one by one the bodies of his fallen comrades. The laconic yet haunting evocation of the sound of Roland's horn echoing up the narrow mountain passes, creating a tangible if fragile line of communication between Roland and his beloved uncle and king, as the high peaks cast dark shadows over the treacherous landscape, or the calamitous description of houses collapsing throughout France as the earth trembles out of grief at Roland's imminent death are indeed the stuff of legends. Roland is taken up to heaven by the archangel Gabriel himself and his loss marks the death not just of a man, but also of a heroic age in which men were larger than life, and life was lived so much more intensely. As with all other epic poems, the past is a screen onto which contemporary ideals are projected, and the ideals this narrative espouses are those of the warrior chivalric classes and of militant Christianity during the First Crusade.

If the *Roland* is the most intense evocation we have of the legend of Roland centuries after the death of this 'historical' figure, we have plenty of evidence that stories about him were widespread and popular. They may well have grown up around the pilgrimage routes to Compostela, and the town of Blaye on the Gironde (lines 3689, 3938) no doubt benefited materially from being the supposed burial place of Roland and Oliver. In the eleventh and twelfth centuries the name Roland became common throughout western Europe, and brothers of Rolands were often called Oliver. Further testimony to the popularity of the legend are the numerous visual representations of Roland, for example in the sculptures at Verona Cathedral and the stained glass windows of Chartres Cathedral (though the latter depict the legend of Charlemagne as presented in the *Pseudo-Turpin* (a Latin chronicle dated *c.*1140 supposedly penned by the archbishop himself)). The audience of the *Roland*—who would have heard the poem sung, recited, or read aloud—were surrounded by so much supporting evidence for the 'historicity' of the story, that it is likely that they not only knew the outcome in advance, but also received the epic as true history. The repeated references in the *Roland* to what is written in the French annals (lines 1443, 1685, etc.) serve to bolster this impression.

Although in modern times its status has changed from history to legend, the *Roland* certainly had, and continues to have, immense symbolic power, even though we have very little evidence that it circulated widely in the form in which it is generally known today: the Oxford *Roland*, so called because the sole surviving copy of this version is preserved in the Bodleian Library's manuscript Digby 23. The Digby manuscript is the earliest witness to a French version of the story; it dates from 1125 to 1150 and therefore just a few decades after the Oxford poem's composition. The manuscript was made in England and the language is the French of the elite post-conquest ruling classes of England, generally known as Anglo-Norman. The six other manuscript versions of the *Roland* in French do not derive directly from the Oxford *Roland*, but from a similar version of the text, and they all preserve later reworkings: three of these manuscripts are from France and three from Italy; their versions date from the later twelfth century through to the late thirteenth, and the manuscripts themselves were copied between the mid-thirteenth and the early fifteenth centuries; some passages are rewritten, often eliminating the Oxford *Roland*'s lyricism, and in some manuscripts the assonanced verse of the earlier text (discussed later) is transposed into rhyme; most of these other manuscripts also have quite extensive additions, mainly expanding on the sections devoted to Ganelon and to Aude, Oliver's sister and Roland's fiancée, who has only a walk-on part in the Oxford *Roland* before dropping dead from grief when she learns of his death. While seven surviving manuscripts of a medieval text do not amount to widespread dissemination (the *Romance of the Rose* survives in over 300 manuscripts), references to the *Roland* in a wide range of other works (including lyrics, romances, and historical documents), as well as visual representations and adaptations of the story in other languages, suggest that the legend had a vibrant and popular oral as well as written tradition. In the late nineteenth and early twentieth century considerable scholarly ink was spilt over whether the *Roland* (generally conflated with the Oxford *Roland*) should best be regarded as a unique work of literature—the product of one author according to the 'individualists'—or as the outcome of generations of oral retellings of a popular story, in which case the surviving text—however magnificent—would be but an avatar of a living performance (the 'traditionalist' theory).

The critical consensus nowadays is to view the Oxford *Roland* as a story moulded by centuries of oral development, but then given a complex literary treatment at the time of the First Crusade by a gifted poet, who included oral stylistic devices not to aid him in oral recomposition or improvisation, but to facilitate the poem's aural reception. Its complexity and relationship with the other versions suggest that it partakes in a written culture of composition and manuscript dissemination, but that it was intended to be read aloud in such a way as to encourage intense emotional engagement on the part of the audience. However, while the critical conflict between the 'individualists' and the 'traditionalists' has nowadays largely been resolved, it can still offer us insights into the development of French national culture in the nineteenth century.

The nineteenth century saw the rise and consolidation of the modern nation states in Europe, each of which identified—during the course of the century—a national epic onto which to project its cultural and political origins. Just as ancient Greece adopted Homer as the singer of the spirit of its culture, so modern nations each needed their very own epic poem. France lagged somewhat behind other countries in this respect: *Beowulf* was first transcribed in 1786, with selections translated into modern English in 1805, and then editions and translations appeared thick and fast from 1814 onwards. The version of the *Roland* held in the Bibliothèque du roi (subsequently the Bibliothèque nationale de France) in Paris first received public attention in 1832, but it was the identification of the 'original' in the Bodleian Library in Oxford by the young scholar Francisque Michel in 1835 that caused real excitement in France. The *Roland*'s status as the French national epic was established immediately following Michel's publication of an edition in 1837, which led to his being made a *chevalier de la Légion d'honneur* the following year. As the debate between the traditionalists and the individualists hotted up later in the century, positions polarized. Was the *Roland* an expression of the spirit of the French people and their feelings for 'France the fair' (*douce France*), as the great Parisian medievalist Gaston Paris (1839–1903) would have it? Or was it, as his student Joseph Bédier (1864–1938) argued, the work of the first great poet of the French literary tradition? Thus Turoldus (mentioned at the very end of the poem in line 4002, though not nowadays thought to be the author) was identified as an illustrious predecessor to Corneille and Racine. The patriotic fervour of both scholars was equally intense, even if it became invested in rather different models of French culture. All the same, the intensity of the commitment to the *Roland* as the expression of something quintessentially French translated itself frequently into French political and cultural life. Gaston Paris gave public recitations of the *Roland* during the siege of Paris in 1870; Joseph Bédier wrote propaganda pamphlets for the French government during the First World War, incorporating language that was borrowed unmistakably and liberally from the *Roland* with a view to vaunting the heroism of French soldiers and encouraging them to further bravery. Bédier's heroic language seems poignantly inappropriate to the context of trench warfare, but the young French men and boys about whom he was writing would all have read the *Roland* at school.

Subsequent criticism of the *Roland* has been less invested in its status as national epic, indeed it has often highlighted aspects of the poem that undermine any simplistic account of its French proto-nationalism. The poem has elicited divergent views on its ideological underpinning (is it fundamentally Christian, imbued with the ideals of the First Crusade, or rather a reflection of chivalric values deriving from Frankish, i.e. ultimately Germanic, culture?); on its ethics of heroism and action; on the psychology of Roland and his potential as a tragic hero; on the relative merits of Roland (representing either overweening pride or militant Christianity and perhaps imbued with the folly of the cross) and Oliver (a Christian fighter, whose prowess is less flamboyant than Roland's, and whose moderation as a tactician is perceived by some as superior and by others as inferior to Roland's self-sacrificial heroism); on the nature of Ganelon's treachery; and on the political implications of Charlemagne's style of kingship. Recent criticism has focused on the representation of Christian–Muslim relations and in particular on the extent to which the central conflict between Christians and Saracens narrated by the poem deflects attention away from other key aspects of the poem's world view, which sets the racial and religious conflict against a backdrop of exchange and commerce between the two sides. Indeed, as we shall see, the poem's stylistic parallelism draws our attention to similarities with, as well as differences from, the Muslim world.

While the *Roland* retains the power to generate interpretative debates, its status as a great work of literature rests upon its style and the mesmerizing power of its poetry. The style owes much to techniques that were probably drawn from orally transmitted epic poetry, though the precision of their deployment in the Oxford *Roland*, the density of the patterning they generate, and the poem's meticulous attention to detail in the description of weapons, human anatomy, horses, and so on, make it unlikely that the text we have was in its present form the result of oral composition or improvisation. The poem is written in decasyllabic assonanced *laisses*, which is to say uneven stanzas of ten-syllable lines, which, rather than rhyming, end with assonance on the final stressed vowel. The Oxford manuscript is not always metrically regular, and there is some debate as to whether editors should regularize the metre throughout, or accept that occasionally the poet could have a rather rough-and-ready approach to form. The most common structure of individual lines deploys a strong caesura, or pause, after the fourth syllable, thus creating two hemistichs of four and six syllables, as in the following extract:

Dist Oliver: | 'Paien unt grant esforz,
De noz Franceis | m'i semblet aveir mult poi.
Cumpaign Rollant, | kar sunez vostre corn!
Si l'orrat Carles, | si returnerat l'ost.'
Respunt Rollant: | 'Jo fereie que fols,
En dulce France | en perdreie mon los...' (lines 1049–54)

Oliver said: 'The pagans have a huge army,
We Frenchmen seem to me so few in number.
Roland, companion, pray blow your horn.
Charles will hear it and the army will return.'
Roland replies, 'I'd be foolish to do so.
I would lose my reputation in France the fair...'

The *Roland* poet exploits the caesura generally to create dense patterns of repetition, both locally and across the entire poem, particularly in the (normally) four-syllable first hemistich. Thus 'Dist Oliver' repeats line 1039, 'Cumpaign Rollant' is repeated in line 1059, 'Si l'orrat Carles' in line 1060, 'Respont Rollant' in line 1062, and so on. Some of the most densely used of these four-syllable 'formulae' are specific to the *Roland*, for example, 'En Rencesvals' and 'Se truis Rollant' ('if I find Roland'), found in the series of parallel *laisses* (71–8) in which the twelve Saracen peers announce their murderous intentions when they find Roland in Rencesvals. Others seem more generic, such as 'Son cheval broche' ('he spurs his horse', line 1125 and so on). It is likely that the deployment of formulae in this way derived from the mnemonic devices of oral poets and performers, but in the Oxford *Roland* the effects are intensely lyrical and elegiac, provoking an emotional response from the audience. When echoed particularly intensely on a local level, formulae can culminate in *laisses similaires*: a sequence of three or more *laisses* in which the same event is narrated repeatedly, with variation. The most celebrated examples of these *laisses similaires* are the two horn scenes—in which first Oliver asks Roland to blow his horn before battle commences to summon back Charlemagne's army, but to no avail, and then Roland declares his intention to sound his horn, but this time with Oliver arguing against it, since battle has already been joined—and the scene just before Roland dies, in which he tries to break his famous sword, Durendal, to prevent it from falling into Saracen hands. In the horn scenes, repetition may not imply three requests, but is instead an effective device for slowing down the action and zooming in (cinematographic terms are very appropriate here) on key episodes in the narrative. In the death scene, there is some ambiguity as to whether Roland has three attempts at breaking his sword, or whether the three stanzas give us a slightly different perspective on a single event, though Charles does later find three slabs of stone damaged (line 2875). In any event, the three laments that Roland addresses to his sword as he brings it crashing down on solid rock each begins with the same four-syllable hemistich ('E! Durendal', line 2304), which echoes across the three strophes. This is accompanied by incremental repetition with variation, which enables this key episode (depicted in the Charlemagne window in Chartres) to be examined from a range of different ideological viewpoints with shifting emphases, as Roland laments first his sword as an emblem of his own heroic prowess in the service of Charlemagne, secondly as the instrument with which he conquered all the lands of Charlemagne's empire, and finally as the receptacle of the sacred relics which underpin their Christian mission. The effects of repetition are perhaps most moving in *laisses similaires* such as these, but they are exploited throughout the poem, particularly during intense moments of drama in the counsel scenes, or in the descriptions of battle.

Another technique exploited to the full in the *Roland* is parallelism. On a local level, this is exemplified by the series of *laisses parallèles* (48–50), which depict Ganelon receiving, Judas-like, various gifts from his new pagan allies. On a larger scale, parallels are drawn between counsel scenes (including nominations), horn scenes, and Charlemagne's dreams. In some cases, echoes between different episodes suggest causal links—Ganelon nominates Roland to the rearguard because he has already been nominated by his stepson for a dangerous mission; Roland prepares to blow his horn because (whether rightly or wrongly, depending on one's view of the heroic ethos) he did not blow it earlier. The two sets of dreams, on the other hand, emphasize the active role of the Christian God in the outcome of the battle between good and evil, and He is called on again to intervene during the judicial combat connected with Ganelon's trial. Repetition and parallelism in counsel scenes draw our attention to the similarities between the so-called pagans and Christians, who share the same social organization and heroic ethos, and whose religion and codes of honour even betray uncanny parallels (note in particular the 'trinity' of gods falsely ascribed to the 'pagans'). Yet their absolute and fundamental difference is starkly asserted with simple, symmetrical lines like Roland's famous assertion that 'The pagans are wrong and the Christians are right' (line 1015).

A further key feature of the style of the *Roland* is the use of parataxis, which is characterized by sequences of discrete clauses or phrases, simply juxtaposed or linked by neutral syntactic markers with little semantic value such as 'Et' ('and') and 'Si' ('and', 'indeed', or 'then'). This is not to say that the *Roland* never uses subordinate clauses, but they are relatively rare other than in direct speech. Consider the following example:

> Rollant est proz e Oliver est sage,
> Ambedui unt meveillus vasselage.
> Puis que il sunt as chevals e as armes,
> Ja pur murir n'eschiverunt bataille:
> Bon sunt li cunte e lur paroles haltes.
> Felun paien par grant irur chevalchent. (lines 1093–8)

> Roland is brave and Oliver is wise;
> Both are extraordinarily valiant knights.
> Once they are mounted and fully armed
> They will never leave the field, fighting to the death.
> Worthy are these counts and noble their words.
> The treacherous pagans ride forward, full of ire.

What we see here is a sequence of two independent clauses (the first of which is one of the most famous lines in the poem), each of which is coterminous with a decasyllabic line, followed by a couplet that involves subordination and therefore more complex syntax, followed by two independent clauses, each of which is again coterminous with the line. The predominance of clauses that are not linked by subordination or logical/causal connectives makes the style of the *Roland* at times declarative, at times elegiac. When this is combined with the use of the historic present, this can make the narrative have a more immediate impact on the audience (as in lines 1093–4) or have the effect of seemingly quickening the pace (as in lines 1097–8). Interestingly, parataxis is a lot less dominant in direct speech, which suggests that the poet makes a deliberate choice to differentiate stylistically between narrative and dialogue.

The *Roland* belongs to a medieval French genre known as the *chanson de geste*, also referred to simply as the epic: there are some 120 or so extant texts, surviving in several hundred manuscripts, most of which have received very little or no critical attention. One of the consequences of this—and also precisely because the Oxford *Roland* has received so much attention—is that it is often assumed that this work is typical or emblematic of the genre as a whole. Yet the later versions of the *Roland*, which differ from the Oxford text in terms of both style and ideology, are far more typical of the medieval French epic genre: they have more developed, articulated, and intricate narratives; they give more space to women and to political intrigue; and they use the lyrical techniques we have just described less frequently and less intensely than the Oxford *Roland*. Bertrand de Bar-sur-Aube, a late twelfth-century poet and author of two *chansons de geste*, helpfully offered a classification of the Old French epic into three types or cycles: the *geste du roi*, the *geste de Garin de Monglane* (also known as the *Guillaume* cycle), and the *geste de Doon de Mayence*. The term *chanson de geste* itself plays upon the multiple meanings of *geste* in Old French, which can mean 'gesture' (therefore 'action' or 'deed'), but also something like 'kin-group', and finally 'story' or 'legend'. The *Roland* plays on all three meanings (see lines 788, 1443, 2095, and 3742), which leads us to multiple translations of the word.

So what are these three *gestes* outlined by Bertrand de Bar-sur-Aube? The *geste du roi* comprises poems about Charlemagne and his heirs, particularly their feats as Christian warriors. The Guillaume cycle focuses on the loyal eponymous hero, who helps to bolster Carolingian power after Charlemagne's death. For example, in the central text of the cycle—*Le Couronnement de Louis*—Charlemagne's weak son Louis needs to turn repeatedly to Guillaume to shore up his authority. The *geste de Doon de Mayence* is somewhat more eclectic and is also known as the 'rebel baron' cycle. In these epics, which include *Raoul de Cambrai*, *Girart de Vienne*, and *Girart de Roussillon*, an initially loyal vassal rebels against his lord following mistreatment, and this rebellion spirals into endless wars of attrition and bloodthirsty vendettas. In *Raoul de Cambrai*, for example, Raoul burns down the convent at Origny where the abbess is Marsent, mother of his boyhood companion Bernier, who refuses to follow him into rebellion because of his father's allegiances. As with many later *chansons de geste*, *Raoul de Cambrai* is haunted by the *Roland*: Raoul wears a helmet taken by Roland from a Saracen in battle, while the evocation of companionship invites comparison with the friendship of Roland and

Oliver. Whereas Roland's violence is directed against the Saracen Other, in *Raoul de Cambrai* we are treated to a graphic description of the scene of the burning of the abbey at Origni as a horrified Bernier looks on, with collapsing roofs, psalters in flames on women's breasts, and searing evocations of the smell of burning flesh. Raoul then eats a hearty meal (even though it is a fast day) and plays chess beside the smouldering ruins of the abbey. Appalled references to this scene in other texts indicate that the *chansons de geste* were not always perceived as glorifying or aestheticizing violence, and it is tempting to see a gradual disintegration of the epic world view working across the three types of *gestes* identified by Bertrand de Bar-sur-Aube: thus the *geste du roi* represents a golden age of epic heroism over which the mighty king Charlemagne presided, guaranteed by the presence of the most heroic of epic heroes, Roland; things then start to fall apart after Roland's loss and Charlemagne's demise since his son Louis is clearly not up to the job; finally the rebel baron epics offer us a vision of social disorder and moral decrepitude, in some cases even associated with Charlemagne's kingship. However, one might argue that the seeds of the disintegration of the epic ideal are already present in the *Roland*. After all, the loss of the French rearguard at Rencesvals is not just down to the wicked Saracens, but is caused first and foremost by Ganelon's treachery, and therefore by squabbling in the French ranks. Moreover, Roland's heroic behaviour is questioned by his brother-in-arms, Oliver, and even Ganelon's guilt has to be decided by God. The *Roland*, despite its crusading zeal, may well have offered audiences matter for debate.

Considering the *Roland* in the broader context of the Old French epic cycles puts the poem in a rather different light. It is but one of a body of texts that builds on and feeds the legend of Charlemagne some 300 years after he died. Interest in Charlemagne offers a French counterpart to the British fascination with Arthur that was crystallized by Geoffrey of Monmouth in his *History of the Kings of Britain* (*c*.1138). Of course, Arthur was equally popular on the Continent, but in England the legendary king offered the Anglo-Norman rulers a vision of a glorious past kingdom, which they could aspire to recreate. Charlemagne's 'Frankish' empire offers the French a similar myth, at a point when the French king was relatively disempowered and the lands directly controlled by the crown were restricted to the area immediately around Paris, the Île-de-France. But just as Arthur was sometimes treated satirically or humorously, so Charlemagne was not always treated as the dignified but fierce and heroic elderly king he is in the *Roland*. In the two poems we have chosen to translate along with the *Roland* in this volume, Charlemagne is a corrupt figure in *Daurel and Beton*, then a comic figure in *Charlemagne's Journey*. We hope that the interest of this selection will be threefold: first these additional poems offer a different perspective on the legend of Charlemagne; second, they offer a different approach to epic idealization; third, the young hero of the *Roland* appears in both of these poems, but in a less central role, and while his presence confirms his legendary status, it also underlines the extent to which it is a mistake to take the *Roland* as emblematic of the entire genre of the *chanson de geste*.

Daurel and Beton is one of a handful of surviving epics written in Occitan (Old Provençal), the language spoken in what is now southern France. Composed in the late twelfth or early thirteenth century, the poem survives in just one fourteenth-century manuscript, which is incomplete, leaving us with no clear sense of how the story will end. The poem opens with the Duke of Antona, Bovis, pledging his companionship to his poor vassal Guy, with whom he promises to share his worldly goods, and, should he marry and then die, to whom he will pass on his wife. Summoned by Charlemagne, Bovis is then married to the great king's sister, Ermenjart, while Guy looks on seething with rage and envy. Shortly afterwards, Guy murders Bovis while the two men are hunting, making it look like an accident following instructions given by the dying Bovis himself, who remains loyal to his friend even in full knowledge of his betrayal. Guy's subterfuge fools no one, however, particularly not Ermenjart, who had intuited Guy's treachery and who relies on Charlemagne to punish the traitor. Her brother, however, is bought off (Judas-like) by Guy, who offers him wagonloads of gold and silver so that he can pay off his mercenary soldiers, and Charlemagne promptly forces Ermenjart to marry her husband's murderer. Guy now has murderous designs on Bovis's baby son, Beton, who is rescued from the traitor's clutches by Daurel, Bovis's trusty minstrel. Daurel substitutes his own infant son for Beton, and Guy murders him, thinking him to be Beton. Daurel then leaves for foreign parts with the real Beton, unaware that his wife has committed suicide on learning of their son's death. There follows a lengthy interlude as Beton grows up in Babylon (Cairo) at the court of the Saracen emir, where he is presented as Daurel's son. The boy Beton becomes a skilled minstrel and knight, and so the emir and his family become increasingly incredulous that such a paragon of courtly and chivalric worth could be the son of a mere minstrel. Their suspicion that Beton is in fact a high-ranking noble is, of course, proved correct and when the truth is eventually revealed by Daurel, Beton is betrothed to the emir's daughter, who, like other Saracen princesses in medieval epics, will convert to Christianity on marriage. But with his true identity now known, Beton is keen to return to France to avenge his father. This he does, and the poem breaks off just as Beton, having dispatched Guy and been reunited with his mother, is hatching a plot to take revenge on Charlemagne.

Daurel and Beton is remarkable for the attention it pays to the growing up of a child and to the character of a minstrel, since Daurel is very much the ethical mainstay of the text once Bovis is dead. *Daurel*'s narrative style is far looser than that of the *Roland* with classic epic formulae only really being deployed in the battle scenes, which by no means predominate. Its versification is irregular, moving between ten- and twelve-syllable lines, and there is some evidence that the surviving text is a reworking of an earlier poem that had a different division of the *laisse*. All in all, this is a significantly less sophisticated work than the *Roland*. Yet *Daurel* has moments of high drama that match the most intense episodes of the *Roland* and interestingly several of these involve women. For example, when Ermenjart is married to Guy against her will she unleashes against Charlemagne a furious tirade of the most acerbic invective found anywhere in medieval literature, implies he is colluding in his own sister's rape in exchange for money, and then casts her wedding ring into the fire. Another high (or low) point comes as Guy tortures Beton's wet nurse Aicelina by having her breasts beaten with specially sharpened hawthorn switches 'until a hundred spines are embedded in her flesh | [and] blood and milk are running together down her body' (lines 921–2), an image worthy of medieval hagiography. The world over which Charlemagne presides in *Daurel and Beton* is corrupt and starkly brutal. When Daurel tells the emir that he is the 'greatest king there has ever been' (line 1215), this may be read as implicit but rather pointed and devastating criticism of Charlemagne (who claims this accolade for himself in *Charlemagne's Journey*!). Yet, Roland, who significantly is Beton's godfather, has an unsullied reputation in the midst of all this: when Beton sends a messenger to Charlemagne at the end of the surviving fragment to demand reparation for his father's death and the king's collusion with Guy, he has him declare 'May God save and protect Roland and Oliver' (line 2161) before insulting and chastising Charlemagne because 'he sold his sister for silver and shiny gold' (line 2166). The presence of Roland here is but one of a series of implicit invitations to read *Daurel and Beton* against the *Roland* and an extremely negative view of Charlemagne emerges. Perhaps the difference in perspective on the great *French* monarch (whose home in *Daurel* is Paris, not Aix/Aachen) can be attributed to the poem's Occitan provenance, since Occitania was culturally and linguistically distinct from northern France, and also in some areas politically pitted against the French crown, throughout much of the Middle Ages. Be that as it may, *Daurel and Beton* shows that the *chansons de geste* are far from univocal in their presentation of Charlemagne.

This variety is also exemplified by the Old French work in 870 alexandrines arranged in fifty-five assonanced *laisses* called by some critics the *Pèlerinage de Charlemagne* and by others *Le Voyage de Charlemagne à Jérusalem et à Constantinople*. We have opted for *Charlemagne's Journey to Jerusalem and Constantinople*, not only because this title is closer to the scribal incipit in the only manuscript witness, but also because the term pilgrimage is so problematic as an interpretative key to the work, and could only be used ironically. For, as the incipit makes clear, Charles's main reason for heading eastwards is not religious, but rather to test his wife's assertions about a rival Byzantine ruler.

This unusually short epic poem was copied by an Anglo-Norman scribe in the late thirteenth or early fourteenth century in the miscellaneous (containing items in Latin and French) manuscript London, British Library, Royal, 16. E. VIII (folios 131ra–144ra), now lost. Modern editors therefore have to rely on an 1836 edition prepared by Francisque Michel, which was then corrected by other scholars before the manuscript was definitively mislaid between 1879 and 1880. Although the existence of only one known manuscript might suggest that the poem was not particularly popular, there were medieval adaptations in both Welsh and Norse (three different versions). There is an unresolved critical debate as to whether the original poet was insular or Continental (Anglo-Norman authorship might explain the criticism of the French Charlemagne as relic hunter), and a range of dates from the late eleventh to the thirteenth centuries has been

proposed for the original work. In our view, the *Journey* was probably
produced in the late twelfth century as a humorous response to the
late eleventh-century *Descriptio qualiter* (see below). A late twelfth-
century date would also fit the narrative's presentation of Charle-
magne as having problematic relations with women, as we have
already witnessed in *Daurel*; for example, in *Girart de Vienne* (*c.*1180)
the king provokes war with his loyal vassal, when, overcome with lust
for a rich widow he had promised to Girart, he weds her himself.

Another similarity with *Girart de Vienne*, in which enmity between
young Roland and Oliver is eventually resolved when the former is
betrothed to the latter's sister Aude, is that the *Journey* is presented as
a prequel to the *Roland*, the tragic events of which are referred to
explicitly in *laisse* 15. However, many of the knights who fight in the
Battle of Rencesvals play a less than heroic role in the *Journey*, which
combines characters from the *Roland* and from the *Guillaume* cycle in
creating a new set of twelve peers for the king (see Index of Proper
Names). Moreover, Charlemagne, despite receiving special favour
from God, fails to live up to the reputation established for him by the
Roland.

The real Charlemagne visited neither Jerusalem nor Constantin-
ople, but by the tenth century his legend had expanded to include
these journeys (see the chronicle of Benedict of St Andrea, dated
*c.*968) and they appear in his 1165 canonization *Vita* (along with his
feats in Spain as related in the *Pseudo-Turpin*). Probably the most
relevant text for our interpretation of the *Journey* though is the
Descriptio qualiter, a Latin document designed to authenticate relics
held at the royal abbey of Saint-Denis. In the *Descriptio*, the Greek
emperor Constantine, in response to an angelic dream-vision, calls on
Charlemagne to save Jerusalem from the Muslims. The Holy Roman
Emperor is thus clearly a superior Christian champion to his eastern
counterpart, who proves unable to help the patriarch of Jerusalem.
After liberating the Holy Land, Charlemagne stops off in Constan-
tinople, but is reluctant to accept Constantine's gifts, fearing that his
men might be seduced by Byzantine luxury (there are echoes of this
in the *Journey*, in which the French have fewer scruples). Although
his barons advise him to refuse the offerings, the king eventually
accepts the presents as visible evidence of God's mercy which he can
take back to France. When relics of the passion are miraculously
revealed, Charles takes them home to Aachen, where he establishes

a feast day in their honour. These precious objects were then later donated by Charles the Bald to Saint-Denis, where a Lendit (a feast, accompanied by a very lucrative fair) was established. By the time of the composition of the *Journey*, the monks of Saint-Denis, their royal patrons, and their venal ambitions were ripe for satire. What is a matter of scholarly debate, however, is whether this twelfth-century comic narrative is a parody of the Old French epic (i.e. critical of the genre, and more specifically of the *Roland*), or merely appropriates ironically epic style, characters, motifs, and poetic techniques in order to poke fun at the relic-grabbing emperor of clerical propaganda, leaving the dignity of the founding father of the *cycle du roi* uncompromised.

The first few *laisses* of the *Journey* make it clear that despite a vague reference to dreams (line 71, no doubt rewriting humorously Charlemagne's hotline to God in the *Roland*) and a professed pious desire to see Jerusalem, Charles's main motivation for leaving France is to measure himself against a ruler his wife has described flatteringly. Epic diction and idealizing epithets are used to describe his preparations; the goods taken (line 73) are reminiscent of those used as bargaining tools between Charlemagne and Marsilie in the *Roland*; and the latter text's iconic seven years during which Charles had campaigned in Spain are echoed in the *Journey* by the seven years' worth of provisions the emperor of the Franks will require while abroad (line 74). Other echoes of the *Roland* are their somewhat fanciful travel through foreign lands, their arrival in fine weather (compare the formula 'Clers fut li jurs' (*Roland*, 1002) with 'Li jours fu beaus e clers' (*Journey*, 109), and the well-known heroic description of Charles's fierce demeanour 'Karles out fer le vis' (line 128). However, expectations of heroic derring-do are undermined by the fact that Charles and his retinue are dressed as pilgrims, mounted on mules (which they incongruously spur on as if they were war horses), and instead of exhibiting noble, courteous behaviour they gawp like curious tourists at the splendours of Jerusalem. Even worse, Charles, oblivious to the religious significance of the thirteenth seat in the church of the Paternoster, flops down into it, along with his 'peers', who claim the seats of Christ's Apostles. The fact that a Jew decides, on seeing the emperor, that he has beheld God himself and therefore wishes to convert forthwith to Christianity, enhances rather than defuses the humour of the situation, and makes us all the more aware of the ironic discrepancy between the pious, fierce defender of Christendom from the *Roland* and the insensitive, arrogant braggart of the *Journey* (which is why we have chosen to translate *fer* in the later work as 'proud' rather than 'fierce').

The patriarch of Jerusalem's reaction to Charlemagne's behaviour further enhances the *Journey*'s satire on the propagandist scenario promoted by the *Descriptio*. The patriarch not only bestows on the unworthy Charles his famous epithet 'the great' (line 158), he also generously accedes to Charles's unsubtle request for holy relics with which he might 'enluminer' France (line 161). The implication is that Charles is more concerned to enhance the reputation of his homeland than to encourage deeper faith in French Christians, no doubt a veiled criticism of contemporary Capetians, given that the relics listed include those of which Saint-Denis boasted (with others added for comic good measure). So, an undeserving Charlemagne is not only rewarded with the most precious objects known to Christendom, but he is also told that this is a mark of God's favour, according to whose plan he will henceforth act. The divine miracles which the relics proceed to work during the rest of the narrative are another example of the poet's creation of humour through incongruity, repetition, and exaggeration.

Charles's stay in Jerusalem is marked by lavish demonstrations of pomp and luxury. Unsurprisingly therefore, the Latin church he establishes there is associated with commerce. The poet's criticism of such mercantile activity is evident when, invoking Christ's expulsion of the moneylenders from the temple, he states that 'God is still in his heaven and will punish this behaviour' (line 213). The intended target of this remark may well be the monks of Saint-Denis and their over-commercialized Lendit celebrations.

When Charles eventually remembers his wife's words and leaves for Constantinople, he manages to defeat King Hugo the Strong, not heroically in battle, but by carrying out a number of excessive, destructive boasts with the aid of the relics. There is none of the dignity of the *Roland* here, in which the eponymous hero's sword Durendal contains holy fragments, and in which God sends angelic warnings and holds back the sun in order to help Charles avenge his nephew's death against the Saracen foe. Instead, we witness rather coarse epic heroes entering the sophisticated 'other' world of Byzantine romance and responding aggressively to the abundant hospitality offered by the courtly eastern emperor. Then the relics enable the French to fulfil a series of outrageous, often insulting, postprandial boasts, uttered after consuming too much wine. This is probably a humorous rewriting of the heroic *gab* or boast, with which many an epic hero provokes the enemy before entering combat. In a series of *laisses parallèles* in the *Journey*, Charlemagne, Roland, and Oliver make outrageous claims respectively for their martial prowess, horn-blasting abilities, or sexual exploits with the king's daughter. The great fighter and cleric Archbishop Turpin then claims to be an expert equestrian juggler, and although some of the boasts of other 'peers' recall biblical scenes of punitive destruction, the context and intention of their proposed Herculean feats are too trivial to raise them above the level of circus acts. It is particularly disturbing, perhaps, to see Oliver associated with courtly language on the one hand, but raw sexual aggression on the other, and none of the French emerges from this episode with his heroic reputation intact. Once King Hugo has learnt from his informer of his guests' verbal sparring, he threatens the French with death if they cannot fulfil their boasts. He even, rather shockingly, supplies his daughter so that Oliver can attempt first, although Oliver's reputation is partially preserved when the situation is apparently resolved amicably with the girl, even if there is some ambiguity as to what actually happens (see explanatory note to line 725). What is more surprising, though, is that God helps some of the French carry out their inglorious tasks, thus saving all their lives, although Charles and his 'doughty' barons receive an angelic warning not to insult people in the future, are forced to take refuge all together in a tree (stupidly not having anticipated the consequences of making a river flood), and inconsiderately cause huge damage to King Hugo's palace.

The ambiguous presentation of Charlemagne as an unworthy favourite of God is equalled by that of King Hugo with his golden plough, ingenious automata, and the exotic wonders associated with his palace. Although he is able to reduce the French to quivering wrecks, he does resort to some underhand spying and is ultimately trumped by his rather fortunate rivals. Eventually, Charles receives confirmation of his superiority to Hugo when their simultaneous crown wearing demonstrates that the Byzantine ruler is shorter than Charles. In this comically literal way, the great western Emperor is able to satisfy himself concerning his wife's taunts, while we laugh at the boorish Frankish ruler who equates social/moral status with physical height.

While it is likely that the *Journey*'s main aim is to satirize contemporary misuse of holy relics and the fanciful narratives which underpin their translation, this is often achieved by parodying the style and diction of French epic in general, and occasionally the *Roland* in particular. These parodic elements range from close allusion to the *Roland* (its characters, iconic oliphant, and angelic visitations) to the incongruous inclusion, exaggeration, and repetition of epic motifs, character traits, and laudatory formulae, all in order to create humour. The effect is that the Charles of the *Journey* fails to live up to the reputation of the venerable hero of the *cycle du roi*. However, whereas Charlemagne in *Daurel* seems an irredeemably tainted figure, it is unlikely that the portrayal of him as a great crusading leader and favourite of God in the *Roland* was totally undermined by the comic narrative of his inglorious journey to the East: to poke fun at the idealized Charlemagne of the *Roland* only has a point if he is also taken seriously.

NOTE ON THE TEXTS AND TRANSLATIONS

SINCE all three texts have survived in only one manuscript each, modern editions do not differ substantially one from the other.

For the *Song of Roland* we have translated Frederick Whitehead's edition, correcting it occasionally in the light of Ian Short's emendations (see Select Bibliography).

For *Daurel and Beton* we have used Charmaine Lee's edition, with occasional references to Arthur Kimmel.

For *Charlemagne's Journey to Jerusalem and Constantinople*, our translation is based on the diplomatic edition published by Paul Aebischer in 1965 (2nd edn. 1971), with the occasional emendation taken from his critical edition or from the editorial notes provided by Madeleine Tyssens in her 1977 translation into modern French. Glyn Burgess offers an even more conservative text than Aebischer in his 1998 edition/translation into English, and as such it resembles closely our source text, although we differ frequently in editorial decisions and English renderings.

In this volume we offer line-by-line translations of the Old French and medieval Occitan originals, since some indication of form is the only way of conveying their narrative dynamic and lyricism. We have not, however, attempted to adhere to a rhyme scheme or form of versification that imitates closely the original, as such translations tend to sacrifice accuracy to metre, and also often date very quickly.

While endeavouring to give as accurate a translation as possible, we have prioritized a number of key stylistic features of the originals in our translations:

1. The rhythm of the individual line, paying particular attention to euphony, number of stressed syllables, caesurae, and the placing of words at the beginning and end of the line.
2. Patterns of repetition. This is particularly important in the *Roland*, as its lyricism derives in part at least from the repeated use of a restricted lexis and so-called epic formulae. Wherever possible we have retained repeated collocations in all three poems.
3. Parataxis. The *Roland* famously uses parataxis extensively in narrative or descriptive sections and this can be quite startling for English

readers. Parataxis is also an important feature of *Daurel* and the *Journey*. Previous translations of the *Roland* have tended to supply conjunctions, relative pronouns, and demonstratives to alleviate the effect of parataxis, while editors have often used punctuation liberally (particularly colons and semicolons) for similar reasons. We have preferred, however, to retain parataxis wherever possible, as this helps to convey the starkness of the poem in French. This in turn has required a certain amount of repunctuation in relation to the editions used.

4. Tense usage. Old French and Occitan narratives frequently use the historic present to create immediacy and pace; they also often switch more rapidly between past and present tenses, and between simple past and present perfect, than is currently usual in either French or English. Whereas some modification to tense usage in translation is unavoidable due to the norms of modern English, we have retained the Old French and Occitan tenses as much as possible, again to give a better sense of the original.

5. Lexis. We have deliberately used the occasional archaism in order to defamiliarize both the direct speech and the narrative voices of the poems. All three works contain a fair amount of technical and specialized vocabulary, particularly relating to warfare, precious stones, land tenure, social rank, and so on. Some of this terminology is explained in the Explanatory Notes, but we also provide a Glossary of some frequently repeated unusual terms.

6. Proper names. The *Roland* in particular displays an astonishing array of proper names. The poet names a considerable number of Frankish and Saracen knights, as well as providing much Spanish topographical detail and some very exotic 'pagan' place names. Many of the Saracen names and places mentioned may well be fictitious, building on the radicals *mal* ('evil' or 'bad') or *fals* ('false' or 'duplicitous'). The symmetrical way in which characters on both sides are named before, during, and after the Battle at Roncevaux contributes to the poem's use of repetition and parallelism, while the reappearance in *Daurel* and the *Journey* of characters from the *Roland* provides different perspectives on these epic heroes. Since the spelling of proper names in the originals is not consistent, we have standardized their spelling across all three poems. Our Index of Proper Names identifies the characters as far as possible and attempts to locate the places mentioned, though, as noted above, many of the Saracen names are invented.

Our translation of the *Roland* is an entirely joint endeavour. Simon Gaunt took the lead on translating *Daurel* while Karen Pratt was the lead translator for the *Journey*. We would like to thank the following for their expert advice and encouragement: Ruth Harvey, Sarah Kay, Linda Paterson (who heroically gave some very helpful feedback on *Daurel*), Simone Ventura, and all our academic predecessors, on whose shoulders we have been standing.

SELECT BIBLIOGRAPHY
AND FURTHER READING

Editions and Translations

THE SONG OF ROLAND

La Chanson de Roland, ed. T. Atkinson Jenkins (Boston, New York, Chicago, and London: D. C. Heath, 1924)—despite its age, the notes to this edition are a mine of information.

La Chanson de Roland, ed. Frederick Whitehead (Oxford: Basil Blackwell, 1942)—the standard anglophone edition with a good glossary, but no translation; Whitehead offers a more conservative edition of the Oxford manuscript than Segre or Short.

The Song of Roland: An Analytical Edition, ed. Gerard J. Brault (Philadelphia: Pennsylvania University Press, 1978), 2 vols—informative edition with a commentary and translation of the Oxford text into English.

La Chanson de Roland, ed. Cesare Segre (Geneva: Droz, 1989), 2 vols—a magisterial critical edition which uses the other versions of the text to correct the Oxford manuscript; volume ii has extensive notes and textual variants.

La Chanson de Roland, ed. Ian Short (Paris: Livre de Poche, 1990)—a critical edition, which uses other manuscripts to correct the Oxford text and has a facing-page modern French translation; minimal notes.

The Song of Roland, trans. Glyn S. Burgess (London: Penguin, 1990)—a translation of Whitehead's text, including some extracts from the original.

The Song of Roland: The French Corpus, ed. Joseph J. Duggan et al. (Turnhout: Brepols, 2005), 3 vols—an edition of all the different versions of the *Roland* and a revised version of Short's edition of the Oxford manuscript with far more extensive notes.

DAUREL AND BETON

Daurel and Beton, trans. Janet Shirley (Felinfach: Llanerch Publishers, 1997)—translation into English prose.

Daurel et Beton, ed. Arthur S. Kimmel (North Carolina Studies in the Romance Languages and Literatures, 108; Chapel Hill: University of North Carolina Press, 1971)—English-language edition with a prose translation.

Daurel et Beton, ed. Charmaine Lee (Biblioteca medievale, 19; Parma: Pratiche, 1991)—has a facing Italian translation, also available at http://www.rialto.unina.it/narrativa/daurel.htm.

CHARLEMAGNE'S JOURNEY TO JERUSALEM AND CONSTANTINOPLE

Le Voyage de Charlemagne à Jérusalem et à Constantinople, ed. Paul Aebischer (Geneva: Droz, 1965; 2nd edn. 1971)—contains a diplomatic transcription of the manuscript, a critical edition, and textual notes.

The Pilgrimage of Charlemagne (Le Pèlerinage de Charlemagne); Aucassin and Nicolette (Aucassin et Nicolette), ed. Glyn S. Burgess and Anne Elizabeth Cobby (New York: Garland, 1988)—includes a facing prose translation in English.

Le Pèlerinage de Charlemagne, ed. Glyn S. Burgess (British Rencesvals Publications, 2; Edinburgh: Société Rencesvals British Branch, 1998)—includes a facing prose translation in English.

Le Voyage de Charlemagne à Jérusalem et à Constantinople, trans. Madeleine Tyssens (Ktêmata, 3; Ghent: Story-Scientia, 1978)—very informative notes.

Further Reading

Please note, these are suggestions for further reading in English only. There is also an extensive critical literature on the *Roland* and other *chansons de geste* in French, German, Italian, and Spanish.

Benton, John, '"Nostre Franceis n'unt talent de fuïr": The *Song of Roland* and the Enculturation of the Warrior Class', *Olifant*, 6 (1979), 237–58—an interesting article on the ideology of the Frankish warrior class and its use in the modern period.

Cobby, Anne Elizabeth, *Ambivalent Conventions: Formula and Parody in Old French* (Faux Titre, 101; Amsterdam and Atlanta: Rodopi, 1995)—a detailed study of parody and its effects.

Daniel, Norman A., *Heroes and Saracens: An Interpretation of the Chansons de Geste* (Edinburgh: Edinburgh University Press, 1984)—a readable and lively account of the representation of Saracens in the *chansons de geste*.

Duggan, Joseph J., *La Chanson de Roland: Formulaic Style and Poetic Craft* (Berkeley and Los Angeles: University of California Press, 1973)—a careful and judicious study of the Oxford *Roland*'s style.

Gabriele, Matthew, and Stuckey, Jace (eds.), *The Legend of Charlemagne in the Middle Ages: Power, Faith, and Crusade* (New York: Palgrave Macmillan, 2008)—a useful collection of essays on the development of the medieval legend of Charlemagne, including one on the *Journey* and the *Descriptio qualiter*.

Gaunt, Simon, 'The *Chanson de Roland* and the Invention of France', in R. Shannan Peckham (ed.), *Rethinking Heritage: Cultures and Politics in Europe* (London and New York: IB Tauris, 2003), 90–101—looks at the *Roland*'s reception in the modern period, particularly in nineteenth- and early twentieth-century France (so, for example, Gaston Paris and Joseph Bédier).

Gilbert, Jane, 'The *Chanson de Roland*', in Simon Gaunt and Sarah Kay (eds.), *The Cambridge Companion to Medieval French Literature* (Cambridge: Cambridge University Press, 2008), 21–34—an interesting introduction to the Oxford *Roland* and to other versions, also treats the text's use in the modern period.

Haidu, Peter, *The Subject of Violence: The Song of Roland and the Birth of the State* (Bloomington: Indiana University Press, 1993)—a stimulating account of political tensions in the Oxford *Roland* and of their implications.

Hunt, Tony, 'The Tragedy of Roland: An Aristotelian View', *Modern Language Review*, 74 (1979), 791–805—a provocative but interesting reading of the text as tragedy.

Kay, Sarah, 'Ethics and Heroics in the *Song of Roland*', *Neophilologus*, 62 (1978), 480–91—a brief but excellent account of warrior ethics in the Oxford *Roland*.

——*The* Chansons de Geste *in the Age of Romance: Political Fictions* (Oxford: Clarendon Press, 1995)—the best general study in English of the *chansons de geste*, with a particularly good section on *Daurel*.

Kinoshita, Sharon, *Medieval Boundaries: Rethinking Difference in Old French Literature* (Philadelphia: Pennsylvania University Press, 2006)—includes an excellent chapter on the Oxford *Roland*'s representation of Christian–Muslim relations in Spain.

Taylor, Andrew, *Textual Situations: Three Medieval Manuscripts and Their Readers* (Philadelphia: University of Pennsylvania Press, 2002)—includes an informative and interesting chapter on the Oxford manuscript of the *Roland*.

Van Emden, Wolfgang, *La Chanson de Roland* (London: Grant and Cutler, 1996)—a student guide to the Oxford *Roland*.

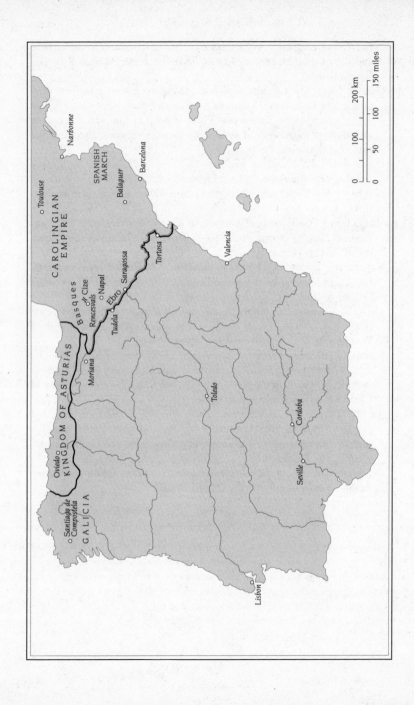

Narbonne

Toulouse

CAROLINGIAN EMPIRE

SPANISH MARCH

Barcelona

Balaguer

Valencia

Basques
Cize
Roncesvals
Napal
Ebro
Saragossa
Tortosa
Tudela

Moriana

KINGDOM OF ASTURIAS

Oviedo

Toledo

Córdoba

Santiago de Compostela

GALICIA

Sevilla

Lisbon

0   50   100
0   100   200 km
150 miles

These maps show the Carolingian Empire and the Iberian Peninsula during the life of Charlemagne, the historical period in which the action of our three epics is set. We have included the key identifiable place-names mentioned. However, as our texts were composed some three to four hundred years after the eighth century, their depiction of European political organization does not reflect any one particular point in time, often conflating the political geographies of different periods.

THE SONG OF ROLAND
AND OTHER POEMS OF CHARLEMAGNE

THE SONG OF ROLAND

1

Charles the king, our emperor great,
Has been a full seven years in Spain.
As far as the sea he conquered this haughty land.
Not a single castle remains standing in his path,
There is not one wall or town still left to be razed   5
Except Saragossa, which sits perched on a mountain;
King Marsilie, who holds God in contempt, rules there.
He serves Mohammed and prays to Apollo.
But he cannot prevent disaster overtaking him.   AOI*

2

King Marsilie was staying in Saragossa.   10
He has sought out the shade of an orchard
And reclines on a slab of pale marble.
Around him gather more than twenty thousand men.
He summons from among them his dukes and counts:
'Listen, my lords, what misfortune is upon us.   15
The emperor Charles, from France the fair,
Has come into this land to confound us all.
I have no army to face him in battle,
Nor do I have men capable of routing his:
Now counsel me as my wise men should,   20
And save me from slaughter and from shame.'
Not one pagan present says a word in reply,
Save Blancandrin from Castel del Valfunde.

3

Blancandrin was among the wisest of pagans.
His bravery made him an exceptional knight.   25

He was most worthy when it came to serving his lord
And he said to the king: 'Do not be dismayed.
Send instead to Charles, the proud and the arrogant,
Tokens of faithful service and sincerest friendship.
30 Give him bears and lions and hunting dogs,
Seven hundred camels and a thousand moulted hawks,
Four hundred mules laden with gold and silver,
Fifty carts in which it will be carted away:
More than enough to pay his mercenaries.
35 He's already waged war a good while in this land:
He ought now to go home to Aix, in France;
You will follow him there at Michaelmas,
And you will then adopt the Christian faith.
With your lands and goods, you'll become his vassal.*
40 If he requires hostages, then send some to him,
Ten or twenty, enough to secure his trust.
Let us send him the sons our wives have borne:
I'll send my own, even though he may die.
It's far better that they should lose their heads over there
45 Than that we lose our honour or our dignity,
Or that we should be reduced to beggary.'   AOI

4

Said Blancandrin: 'I swear by my right hand
And by the beard that flows down to my chest,
You'll soon see the French army routed;
50 The Franks will return to France, to their own land.
Once each has returned to his beloved hearth,
Charles will be at Aix, in his chapel,
Holding a magnificent feast for Michaelmas.
Then the day will come, the deadline will pass,
55 Yet he'll hear no word from us, nor any news.
The king is fierce and his heart cruel.
He'll have our hostages' heads cut from their bodies:
It's far better that they should lose their heads over there
Than that we lose our fine, resplendent Spain
60 Or that it should be us who bear the pain and suffering.'
The pagans say: 'That may well be the case.'

5

King Marsilie had finished taking counsel.
So he summoned Clarin of Balaguer,
Estamarin and his brother in arms Eudropin,
And Priamun and Guarlan the bearded,   65
And Machiner and his uncle Matthew,
And Joüner and Malbien from the Levant,
And Blancandrin, who was to deliver his message.
Thus he addressed his ten most treacherous men:
'My lords, barons, you will go to Charlemagne.   70
He is at Cordoba, besieging the citadel.
You'll carry olive branches in your hands,
Which usually signify peace and humility.
If you are clever enough to negotiate a treaty,
I shall give you gold and silver aplenty,   75
As much land and as many fiefs as you would like.'
The pagans say: 'That will be ample for us.'   AOI

6

King Marsilie had finished taking counsel.
He said to his men: 'My lords, you will go hence.
You will carry olive branches in your hands,   80
And you will ask King Charlemagne on my behalf
For the sake of his God to take mercy on me.
He will see that before this very month is out
I shall follow him with a thousand of my trusty men
And I shall adopt the Christian faith.   85
I shall become his vassal, loyally and faithfully.
If he wants hostages, he will certainly have some.'
Said Blancandrin: 'You will have a very good case.'   AOI

7

Marsilie had ten white mules brought forward
Which had been sent to him by the King of Suatilie.   90
Their bridles are of gold, their saddles inlaid with silver.
Those who were to deliver the message mounted them,

Carrying olive branches in their own hands.
They came to Charles, who rules over France.
95 Yet he cannot help but be taken in by them.   AOI

8

The emperor's demeanour is jubilant and joyful.
He has taken Cordoba and torn down its walls,
With his catapults he has smashed its towers.
His knights now have vast amounts of booty,
100 Gold and silver, and expensive equipment.
There is not a single pagan left in the town
Who has not been either killed or converted.
The emperor has now entered a great orchard,
He is accompanied by Roland and Oliver,
105 Duke Samson and Anseïs the fierce,
Geoffrey of Anjou, the king's standard-bearer;
And also present were Gerin and Gerer;
Alongside these men there were many others.
There are fifteen thousand men from fair France.
110 These knights are sitting on white brocaded silk,
Some amusing themselves at the gaming tables.
The wisest and most mature are playing chess
While the agile young warriors are fencing.
In the shade of a pine, beside a wild briar,
115 A chair of state has been erected, made of solid gold,
And there sits the king who rules France the fair.
His beard is white and his hair is all hoary;
He is a fine figure of a man, with a fierce countenance.
If anyone seeks him, there is no need to point him out.
120 The messengers dismounted and stood before him.
They greeted him warmly and courteously.

9

Blancandrin was the very first to speak
And he said to the king: 'Hail in the name of God,
Whom in His glory we should adore.
125 This is noble King Marsilie's message to you:

He has long sought salvation through the true faith.
He wishes to give you a great deal of his wealth:
Bears and lions, hounds trained for hunting,
Seven hundred camels and a thousand moulted hawks,
Four hundred mules laden with gold and silver,   130
Fifty carts in which you will cart it all away.
There will be so many pure gold bezants
That you will easily be able to pay your mercenaries.
You have been in this land for far too long:
You really ought to return to Aix, in France;   135
My lord assures you that he will follow you there.'
The emperor stretches out his hands towards God,
Lowers his head and begins to reflect.   AOI

10

The emperor kept his head bowed;
When he did speak it was not at all in haste,   140
His custom is always to speak when he is ready.
When he raises his head, his expression was most fierce;
He said to the messengers: 'You have spoken very well.
King Marsilie is in fact my sworn enemy.
These words you have just delivered to me,   145
How far can I place my trust in them?'
'If hostages are required,' said the Saracen,
'Then you can have ten, fifteen, or even twenty.
Even though he may die, I shall include one of my own sons;
And you shall have, methinks, even more noble men.   150
When you have returned to your royal palace,
During the great feast of Michaelmas.*
My lord will follow you there, he assures you;
Entering your baths, which God made for you there,
He intends to be baptized a Christian.'   155
Charles replies: 'Indeed, he may yet be saved.'   AOI

11

The evening was fine and the sun shone brightly.
Charles orders the ten mules to be stabled.

The king has a tent erected in the great orchard,
160 Thus providing lodgings for the ten messengers.
Twelve servants have catered for their every need.
They remain there all night until daybreak.
The emperor has risen in the early morning.
The king has heard mass and matins.
165 Under a pine tree the king has gone to sit.
He summons his barons to help him reach a decision:
In all he does he seeks counsel from the men of France.   AOI

12

The emperor goes to sit under a pine tree,
He summons his barons to help him reach a decision:
170 Here come Duke Ogier, Archbishop Turpin,
Richard the Old and his nephew Henry,
And from Gascony brave Count Acelin,
Tedbald of Rheims and his cousin Miles,
And Gerer and Gerin were present too;
175 Count Roland also came along with them,
And Oliver, the brave and the noble.
There are more than a thousand Franks from France.
Ganelon, who committed the treachery, came too.
Now begins the council that turned out badly.   AOI

13

180 'My lords, barons,' said the emperor Charles,
'King Marsilie has sent his messengers to me,
He wants to give me a great deal of his wealth,
Bears and lions, hounds trained for hunting,
Seven hundred camels and a thousand moulted hawks,
185 Four hundred mules laden with Arabian gold,
And with all this more than fifty carts.
However, his message to me is to return to France.
He will then follow me to Aix, to my abode,
And there he will seek salvation by adopting our faith.

Becoming a Christian, paying homage to me for his marches.*   190
But I am not sure what his true intention is.'
The French say: 'In this case we must be wary.'   AOI

14

The emperor had finished speaking.
Count Roland, who cannot agree to the proposal,
Leaps to his feet, and steps forward to contradict him.   195
He said to the king: 'Believe Marsilie at your peril!
It has been a full seven years since we came to Spain;
I conquered both Noples and Commibles for you;*
I have captured Val-Terne and the land of Pine
And Balaguer, Tudela, and Seville;   200
King Marsilie behaved most treacherously:
He sent fifteen of his pagans to you,
Each one carrying an olive branch.
They delivered exactly the same message to you.
You sought the counsel of your Frenchmen,   205
They advised you to behave somewhat recklessly.
You sent two of your counts to the pagan,
One was Basan and the other Basilie.
He cut off their heads in the hills near Haltilie.
Pursue the war that you have undertaken,   210
Take your assembled troops to Saragossa,
Spend the rest of your days besieging it,
And avenge those men the traitor had murdered.'   AOI

15

The emperor kept his head bowed,
He stroked his beard and twisted his moustache.   215
He neither agrees nor disagrees with his nephew.
The French remain silent, except for Ganelon:
He leaps to his feet and stepped before Charles;
With fiery passion he begins his speech thus,
Saying to the king: 'Believe a fool at your peril,   220

Whether me or another, unless it's in your interests.
Since King Marsilie has sent you the message
That he'll be your vassal, placing his hands together,
And will hold the whole of Spain from you as a fief,
225 And will then adopt the faith that we observe,
Anyone who advises you to reject this treaty
Does not care, my lord, what kind of death we suffer.
It is not right that an arrogant man's advice should prevail,
Let us reject the foolish and side with the wise!'   AOI

16

230 After this Naimon steps forward to speak,
There was no better vassal in the whole court.
He said to the king: 'You have clearly heard
What Count Ganelon has replied to you.
There is some sense in it if properly understood.
235 King Marsilie has been defeated in war:
You have deprived him of all of his castles,
With your catapults you've smashed his fortifications,
Burned down his towns and defeated his men.
Since he asks you to have mercy on him,
240 It would be a sin if one were to pursue him further...*
Since through hostages he wishes to secure your trust,
This great war must not escalate further.'
The French say: 'The duke has spoken well.'   AOI

17

'My lords, barons, whom shall we send there,
245 To Saragossa, to King Marsilie?'
Duke Naimon replies: 'By your leave, I shall go.
Pray give me now the glove and the staff.'
The king replies: 'You are a wise man,
By this beard and by this moustache of mine,
250 Never will you go so far away from me.
Go and sit down since no one has called on you.'

18

'My lords, barons, whom shall we send there,
To the Saracen who holds Saragossa?'
Roland replies: 'I am very happy to go there.'
'Under no circumstances,' said Count Oliver,   255
'Your heart is too bellicose and fierce:
I would be afraid that you would pick a fight.
With the king's approval, I am willing to go.'
The king replies: 'Be silent, both of you.
Neither you nor he will set foot there.   260
By this beard that you see growing white,
Woe betide anyone who nominates the twelve peers.'
The French are quiet; see how they have been silenced.

19

Turpin of Rheims steps forward from the ranks
And said to the king: 'Leave your Franks in peace.   265
You have been in this land for seven years;
They have experienced great pain and suffering.
My lord, give me the staff and the glove,
And I shall go to the Spanish Saracen
And I shall discover something of his attitude.'   270
The emperor replies in an angry fashion:
'Go and sit down on that white brocaded cloth.
Speak no more, unless I command otherwise.'   AOI

20

'Noble knights,' said Charles the emperor,
'Now select for me a baron from my kingdom*   275
To take a message for me to Marsilie.'
Said Roland: 'Let it be Ganelon, my stepfather.'
The French say: 'Yes, for he would be good at this.
If you reject him, you will not send a wiser man.'
At this Count Ganelon was extremely distressed: 280
He casts off from his shoulders his great marten fur cloak

And now stands there in his brocaded silk tunic.
His eyes flashed and his expression was very fierce;
He was a fine figure of a man with a broad chest.
285   He was so handsome that all his peers look at him.
He said to Roland: 'You fool, are you raving mad?
Everyone knows that I am your stepfather,
And yet you have nominated me to go to Marsilie.
If it is God's will that I come back alive,
290   I shall instigate against you such a great vendetta
That it will continue for the rest of your life.'
Roland replies: 'I hear nothing but arrogance and stupidity.
Everyone knows that I am immune to threats.
But a messenger needs to be a wise man:
295   With the king's approval, I am ready to go in your place.'

21

Ganelon replies: 'No, you won't go in my place.   AOI
You are not my vassal and I am not your lord.
Charles orders me to do this service for him
So I shall go to Saragossa to see Marsilie.
300   There I'd prefer to behave somewhat recklessly
Rather than leave my great wrath unassuaged.'
When Roland heard this, he began to grin.*   AOI

22

When Ganelon sees that Roland is grinning at him,
He is so annoyed that he nearly explodes with rage—
305   He very nearly goes out of his mind.
And he says to the count: 'Now we are sworn enemies!*
You have falsely pronounced sentence upon me.
Just emperor, take note of me standing before you,
My wish is to fulfil your every command.'

23

310   'I know that I have to go to Saragossa,   AOI
Whoever goes there cannot expect to return.

And what is more, I am married to your sister,
And I have a son with her, none could be more handsome.
I speak of Baldwin, who is going to be a worthy man.
I bequeath to him my land and my fiefs.   315
Look after him; I shall never set eyes on him again.'
Charles replies: 'You are far too soft-hearted.
Since I command it, you will have to go.'

24

The king then said: 'Ganelon, step forward   AOI
And receive the staff and the glove.   320
As you have heard, the Franks have assigned this task to you.'
'My lord,' said Ganelon, 'this is all Roland's work:
I shall bear him ill will for the rest of my life,
And Oliver, because he is his companion.
To the twelve peers, because they love him so much,   325
I hereby issue a challenge, my lord, as you are my witness.'
The king said: 'You are too quick to anger.
Now you must certainly go, since I command it.'
'I can go there, but I shall have no protection,   AOI
No more than had Basilie and his brother Basan.'   330

25

The emperor offers him his right-hand glove,
Yet Count Ganelon would rather have been elsewhere:
As he was about to take it, he dropped it on the ground.
The French say: 'Good Lord, what can this mean?
From this embassy we shall suffer great losses.'   335
'My lords,' said Ganelon, 'you will hear more of this.'

26

'My lord,' said Ganelon, 'give me leave to depart.
Since I must go, there is no point in delaying.'

The king said: 'Go, in the name of Jesus and my own.'
340 With his right hand he has absolved and blessed him,
Then he handed him the staff and the letter.

27

Count Ganelon goes off to his lodgings;
He begins now to put on his armour,
The very best that he was able to obtain:
345 He has attached spurs of gold to his feet,
And has girded his sword Murgleis at his side.
He has mounted Tachebrun, his warhorse:
The stirrup was held for him by his uncle Guinemer.
Then you would have seen so many knights weeping,
350 All saying: 'Much good it did you to be a great knight.
You have been at the royal court for a long time;
You were always called a noble vassal.
Whoever nominated you for this mission
Will not be protected or saved by Charlemagne.
355 Count Roland should never have suggested this,
For you are born of a very noble family.'
Then they say to him: 'My lord, take us with you.'
Ganelon replies thus: 'God forbid that I should do so.
It is better that I alone die than so many good knights.
360 You are going to return to fair France, my lords.
Pray pass on my warmest greetings to my wife,
And to Pinabel, my friend and kinsman,
And to Baldwin, my son, whom you know.
Serve him and acknowledge him as your lord.'
365 He begins his journey and has set off on his way.   AOI

28

Ganelon rides forth; under a tall olive tree
He has caught up with the Saracen messengers.
Yet, note how Blancandrin has slowed down to meet him.
With great cunning each addresses the other:

Said Blancandrin: 'Charles is an amazing man, 370
Who conquered Apulia and the whole of Calabria.
To reach England he crossed the salty sea,
Where he imposed a poll tax for the Holy See.
What does he want from us here in our kingdom?'
Ganelon replies: 'Such is his disposition. 375
There will never be a man to equal him.' AOI

29

Said Blancandrin: 'The Franks are very noble men,
But these dukes and these counts do great harm
To their lord in giving him such advice;
They are bringing upon him and others distress and ruin.' 380
Ganelon replies: 'This is true of none of them
Except for Roland, who will yet suffer shame for it.
Yesterday morning, the emperor was sitting in the shade,
His nephew approached; he had put on his hauberk,
And had been on a raiding trip around Carcassonne. 385
He was holding in his hand a scarlet apple;
"Here, fair lord," said Roland to his uncle,
"I present you with the crowns of all living kings."
His arrogance must eventually be his undoing,
For every day he exposes himself to mortal danger. 390
If someone kills him, then we shall all be at peace.' AOI

30

Blancandrin said: 'Roland is utterly merciless.
His aim is to force all races into submission
And he disputes the ownership of all lands.
With which people does he hope to achieve all this?' 395
Ganelon replies: 'With the help of the French.
They love him so much that they will never let him down.
He rewards them with so much gold and silver,
Mules and warhorses, brocaded silk and armour.
The emperor himself has all that he desires. 400
He will win for him all the land from here to the Orient.' AOI

31

Ganelon and Blancandrin rode together for so long
That they finally swore an oath to each other
To do all they could to bring about Roland's death.
405 They continued to ride along highways and byways
Until in Saragossa they dismount under a yew tree.
There was a chair of state in the shade of a pine tree,
Covered in brocaded silk from Alexandria.
There sat the king who held the whole of Spain.
410 All around him were twenty thousand Saracens;
Not a single one of them spoke or said a word,
Because of the news they were keen to hear.
Then Ganelon and Blancandrin step forward.

32

Blancandrin came before Marsilie,
415 He was holding Count Ganelon by the hand.
And he said to the king: 'Hail, in the name of Mohammed,
And of Apollo, whose holy laws we observe.
We delivered your message to Charles.
He raised both his hands towards the heavens,
420 Praised his god and made no other reply.
Here is one of his noble barons he has sent you.
He is from France and is a most powerful man.
From him you will learn whether you will have peace or not.'
Marsilie replies: 'Now let him speak! We'll heed him!'   AOI

33

425 Yet Count Ganelon had thought things through carefully;
He begins to speak with great cunning
Like someone who is very adept at it.
And he said to the king: 'Hail, in the name of God,
Whom in His glory we should adore.
430 This is noble Charlemagne's message to you,

That you should adopt holy Christianity;
He intends to give you half of Spain as a fief.*
If you do not wish to accept this pact,
You will be captured and bound by force
And you will be taken to his capital in Aix. 435
In that place you will be sentenced and put to death;
There you will die in shame and degradation.'
King Marsilie was deeply alarmed by this.
He was holding a spear with golden pennons;
If he had not been stopped, he would have struck him. AOI 440

34

King Marsilie's face has changed colour,
He has shaken the shaft of his spear.
When Ganelon saw this, he reached for his sword
And has already unsheathed it the length of two fingers.
He addressed it thus: 'You are very fine and shiny; 445
I shall have borne you for so long at the royal court.
May the Emperor of France never once say
That I died alone in a foreign land
Without first making the best knights pay for you.'
The pagans say: 'Let us break up the fight.' 450

35

The noblest Saracens eventually persuaded
Marsilie to sit back down on his chair.
Said the caliph: 'You have harmed our cause
By going to strike this Frenchman;
You should have listened to and heeded him.' 455
'My lord,' said Ganelon, 'I shall have to put up with it.
I shall not refrain, for all the gold created by God
Nor all the riches this country possesses,
From delivering to him, if I am allowed to do so,
The message that Charlemagne, the powerful king, 460
Sends to him, his mortal enemy, through me.'

He was clad in a cloak lined with sable
And covered in brocaded silk from Alexandria.
He casts it to the ground and Blancandrin picks it up.
465 Yet he did not wish to relinquish his sword:
He held it in his right hand by its golden pommel.
The pagans say: 'Here indeed is a noble baron.'   AOI

36

Ganelon has stepped towards the king,
And said to him: 'You are wrong to get angry,
470 For Charles, ruler of France, sends this message
Requiring you to adopt the Christian religion;
He will give you half of Spain as a fief,
And Roland, his nephew, will have the other half;
You will have a very arrogant partner.
475 If you do not wish to accept the terms of this pact,
He will come and besiege you in Saragossa;
You will be captured and bound by force,
And you will be taken straight to his capital at Aix.
You will have neither palfrey, nor warhorse,
480 Nor mule, whether male or female, upon which to ride;
You will be thrown onto a lowly packhorse.
There you will be sentenced and put to death.
Our emperor sends you this very letter.'
He has placed it in the pagan's right hand.

37

485 Marsilie is so angry the colour has drained from his face.
He breaks the seal and has cast off the wax.
He looks at the letter and saw what is written:
'The message from Charles, who rules over France,
Is that I should remember his pain and anger
490 With respect to Basan and his brother Basilie,
Whose heads I cut off in the hills below Haltilie.
If my aim now is to save my own skin,
Then I must send my uncle the caliph to him.

Otherwise, he will be my sworn enemy.'
After this, Marsilie's son addressed him,   495
And said to the king: 'Ganelon has spoken like a fool;
He has gone so far that he deserves to die now.
Hand him over to me, and I will see him justly punished.'
When Ganelon heard this, he brandished his sword;
He goes to lean against the trunk of the pine.   500

38

The king has gone right into the orchard;
He takes his finest men along with him:
White-haired Blancandrin came too,
And Jurfaleu, Marsilie's son and heir,
And the caliph, his uncle and his confidant.   505
Said Blancandrin: 'Summon the Frenchman!
He has sworn to me to act in our best interests.'
The king said: 'Then you shall bring him here.'
He took Ganelon gently by the right hand,
And leads him into the orchard to the king.   510
There they hatch the treacherous, unlawful plot.   AOI

39

'Fair lord Ganelon,' Marsilie has addressed him thus,
'I behaved somewhat recklessly towards you
When I nearly struck you in a fit of great anger.
By these sable furs, I guarantee before the law,   515
(Just the gold on them is worth more than five hundred pounds),*
That before tomorrow evening full reparation will be paid.'
Ganelon replies: 'I do not refuse in the least.
If it pleases God, may He reward you well for it.'   AOI

40

Thus spoke Marsilie: 'Ganelon believe me truly*   520
I would really like us to be very close allies.

Pray tell me all about Charlemagne.
He is very old and his days are numbered.
I think he is over two hundred years old.
525 He has toiled his way through so many lands,
Taken so many blows on the boss of his buckler,
Reduced so many powerful kings to beggary,
When will he ever tire of campaigning?'
Ganelon replies: 'Charles is not like that.
530 There is no one who sees him and gets to know him well
Who does not say that the emperor is brave.
I cannot praise and recommend him to you enough
To do justice to his integrity and goodness.
Who could describe adequately his great worth?
535 He shines with such God-given courage
That he would rather die than abandon his barons.'

41

Said the pagan: 'There is much to amaze me
About Charlemagne, who is white-haired and old:
I think he is two hundred years old and more.
540 He has toiled his way through so many lands,
Taken so many blows from lances and spears,*
Reduced so many powerful kings to beggary,
When will he ever tire of campaigning?'
'Not,' said Ganelon, 'while his nephew is alive.
545 You'll find no better vassal under heaven's canopy.
His companion Oliver is a most fearsome warrior.
The twelve peers, whom Charles holds so dear,
Make up the vanguard with twenty thousand knights.
Charles feels secure for he fears no man.'   AOI

42

550 The Saracen spoke thus: 'I am truly amazed
About Charlemagne, who is white-haired and hoary:
I think he is over two hundred years old.

He has gone conquering through so many lands,
Taken so many blows from fine, razor-sharp spears,
Killed and beaten in the field so many powerful kings,   555
When will he ever tire of campaigning?'
'Not,' said Ganelon, 'while Roland is still alive.
You'll find no better vassal from here to the Orient.
His companion Oliver is a most fearsome warrior.
The twelve peers, whom Charles loves so much,   560
Make up the vanguard with twenty thousand Franks.
Charles feels secure; he fears no man alive.'   AOI

43

'Ganelon, fair lord,' said King Marsilie,
'You could never see finer troops than mine;
I can muster four hundred thousand knights.   565
Should I join battle with them against Charles and the French?'
Ganelon replies: 'Not on this occasion, you must not.
You will suffer very great losses amongst your pagans.
Abandon foolishness and stick to good sense:
Pray give the emperor so much wealth   570
That no Frenchman can fail to be amazed.
Thanks to the twenty hostages you will send to him,
The king will return to France the fair.
He will leave his rearguard behind him.
In it, I think, will be his nephew, Count Roland,   575
And valiant Oliver, such an excellent courtier.
Take my word for it, the counts are dead men walking.
Charles will witness his great pride toppled,
He will lose the will to wage war against you.'   AOI

44

'Ganelon, fair lord,' thus spoke King Marsilie,   580
'How shall I be able to get rid of Roland?'
Ganelon replies: 'I can easily tell you how:
The king will be at the highest pass of Cize.

He will have left his rearguard behind him;
585 In it will be his nephew, powerful Count Roland
And Oliver, in whom he places so much trust.
With them they have twenty thousand Franks.
Send a hundred thousand of your pagans against them;
Let them join battle with them first of all.
590 The French troops will be wounded and weakened.
I am not saying your men won't also be slaughtered.
Then launch an equally large force against them.
Roland will not escape alive from one or the other.
Thus you will have performed a noble feat of chivalry.
595 You will live in peace for the rest of your days.'   AOI

45

'If someone could bring about the death of Roland,
Then Charles would lose his right-hand man,
And those amazing troops would lose the will to fight.
Charles would never be able to muster such great forces;
600 Our great homeland would be for ever at peace.'
When Marsilie hears this, he kisses him on the neck.
Then he begins to open his treasure chests.   AOI

46

Then Marsilie said: 'What's the point of speaking further?
Promises are meaningless *without a sworn oath.**
605 You must swear to me to betray Roland.'
Ganelon replies: 'Let it be as you wish!'
On the relics embedded in his sword Murgleis
He swore treachery, thus committing the heinous crime.   AOI

47

A chair of state made of ivory stood there.
610 Marsilie has a book brought before them,

Containing the holy teachings of Mohammed and Tervagant.
This oath was sworn by the Spanish Saracen:
That if he finds Roland present in the rearguard,
He will attack him along with all of his men,
And, if possible, Roland will definitely die there.   615
Ganelon replies: 'May your wish be fulfilled.'   AOI

48

Now a pagan called Valdabrun stepped forward,*
Who had helped to bring up King Marsilie;*
Smiling brightly he said to Ganelon,
'Here, take my sword; no man owns one finer: 620
Between its quillons there are more than a thousand mangons.
Fair lord, I give it to you as a token of friendship,
Since you are helping us deal with Roland the brave,
Ensuring that we find him present in the rearguard.'
'This will certainly be done,' replies Count Ganelon.   625
Then they kissed each other on the face and the chin.

49

Next a pagan called Climborin stepped forward;
Smiling brightly he said to Ganelon:
'Here, take my helmet; I have never seen a finer one.
Pray help us to deal with Roland the marquis,   630
By advising us how we can bring shame upon him.'
'This will certainly be done,' Ganelon replied.
Then they kissed each other on the mouth and the face.   AOI

50

Now Queen Bramimunde stepped forward:
'I love you dearly, my lord,' she said to the count,   635
'For my lord and all of his men esteem you greatly.
I shall send two brooches to give to your wife,

Generously fashioned from gold, amethysts, and jacinths.
They are worth more than all the wealth of Rome.
640 Your emperor never saw their equal in quality.'
He has taken them, stuffing them down his boot. AOI

51

The king summons Malduit his treasurer:
'Has all the payment for Charles been prepared?'
And he replies: 'Yes, my lord, and it is generous:
645 Seven hundred camels laden with gold and silver,
And twenty of the noblest hostages under the sun.' AOI

52

Marsilie grabbed Ganelon by the shoulder
And said to him: 'You are extremely brave and wise.
By the faith that you believe guarantees salvation,
650 Make sure that you do not turn against us.
I wish to give you a huge amount of my wealth:
Ten mules laden with the purest Arabian gold;
No year will pass without my giving you the same.
Pray take the keys to this great city;
655 Present its immense wealth to Charles,
Then have Roland nominated to the rearguard.
If I can find him in a pass or defile,
I shall launch a deadly attack on him.'
Ganelon replies: 'Methinks I am delaying too much.'
660 Then he mounts his steed and sets off on his way. AOI

53

The emperor is approaching his homeland.
He has arrived at the town of Galne.
Count Roland has just captured and destroyed it:
Since that day it lay waste for a hundred years.

The king is awaiting news from Ganelon   665
And the tribute to be paid by Spain, that great land.
In the morning around dawn, just as the day was breaking
Count Ganelon arrived at their encampment.   AOI

54

The emperor has risen early in the morning,
The king has heard mass and matins.   670
He was standing on the green grass in front of his tent.
Roland was there, and also brave Oliver,
Along with Duke Naimon and many others.
Ganelon arrived, the treacherous perjurer.
With great cunning he begins to speak   675
And said to the king: 'Hail in the name of God!
I bring to you here the keys of Saragossa.
I have arranged for huge wealth to be brought to you
And twenty hostages; make sure they are guarded well!
And this is brave King Marsilie's message to you: 680
With regard to the caliph, you must not blame him;
I myself saw four hundred thousand armed men,
Clad in hauberks, some with helmets fastened,
With swords girded on, their golden pommels incised,
Accompany him all the way out to sea.   685
They were fleeing Marsilie because of Christianity,
Which they do not wish to practise or adopt!
Before they had sailed four leagues from the coast
They were overtaken by high winds and storms:
There they drowned; you will never see them again.   690
If he had still been alive, I would have brought him here.
As for the pagan king, my lord, believe me
You will see before this very month is out
Him follow you to the kingdom of France
And he will adopt the religion that you observe.   695
Placing his hands together he will become your vassal;
From you he will hold the kingdom of Spain as a fief.'
Thus spoke the king: 'Thanks be to God!
You have done well; you will be richly rewarded for this.'

700 Throughout the army they sound a thousand bugles.
The Franks break camp and have their packhorses loaded;
They are all now on their way to France the fair.   AOI

55

Charles the Great has laid waste to Spain,
Captured its castles and taken its towns by force.
705 The king announced that he was done with war.
The emperor is riding towards France the fair.
Count Roland has fastened the standard to his lance,
On a hilltop he has raised it towards the sky.
The Franks pitch camp throughout the countryside.
710 The pagans are riding through the widest valleys,
Clad in hauberks and *double-thickness byrnies*,
Helmets fastened and swords girded on,
Shields hanging from their necks and lances at the ready.
Within a wood, high in the mountains, they stop.
715 Four hundred thousand wait for the break of day.
Oh God! How dreadful that the French are not aware!   AOI

56

The day comes to an end and night has fallen.
Charles, the mighty emperor, was fast asleep.
He dreamt that he was at the highest pass of Cize.
720 In his hands he was holding his lance made of ash.
Count Ganelon has grabbed it from his grasp.
He has smashed and shaken it with such violence
That splinters fly off towards the heavens.
Charles is still sleeping; he does not wake at all.

57

725 After this he dreamt another dream:
That he was in France, in his chapel at Aix;
A most vicious boar bites him in the right arm.

He saw a leopard approaching from the Ardennes,
It attacks his very person with great ferocity.
From within the hall a hound came rushing down,   730
Approaching Charles in leaps and bounds;
First of all it bit off the boar's right ear,
Then ferociously fights with the leopard.
The French say that this is indeed a great battle,
But they do not know which one of them will win.   735
Charles is still sleeping; he did not wake at all.*   AOI

58

Night passes and dawn spreads its bright light.
Throughout the army the bugle peals *ring out*.
The emperor is riding at a furious pace.
'My lords, barons,' said the emperor Charles,   740
'Look at the passes and narrow defiles;
Pray decide for me who will be in the rearguard.'
Ganelon replies: 'What about Roland, my stepson?
You have no vassal who equals him in courage.'
When the king hears this, he looks fiercely at him,   745
And then he says to him: 'You are the devil incarnate:
A lethal madness has entered your very soul.
And who will be ahead of me in the vanguard?'
Ganelon replies: 'Ogier of Denmark:
You have no knight better able to do it than he.'   AOI 750

59

Count Roland, when he heard himself nominated,
Then spoke in the manner of a true knight:
'My lord, stepfather, I should be very grateful to you;
You have nominated me to the rearguard.
Charles, the King of France, will not lose,   755
If I can help it, a single palfrey or warhorse,
Nor mule, male or female, which he could ride.
Nor will he lose a single nag or packhorse

Which has not first been paid for with the sword.'
760 Ganelon replies: 'You speak the truth, as I well know.'   AOI

60

When Roland hears that he will be in the rearguard,
He was furious and spoke to his stepfather thus:
'Ah, vile wretch, low born and evil villain,
Did you think that I would drop the glove on the ground
765 As you did the staff in the presence of Charles?'   AOI

61

'Just emperor,' said Roland the brave,
'Give me the bow you are holding in your hand.
If I can help it, people will not be able to reproach me
For letting it fall, as happened to Ganelon,
770 From his right hand, when he received the staff.'
At this the emperor kept his head bowed.
He stroked his beard and twisted his moustache;
He cannot stop the tears from falling down his cheeks.

62

After this Naimon steps forward to speak—
775 There was no better vassal than him at court—
And he said to the king: 'You have heard him loud and clear:
Count Roland is absolutely furious.
He has been nominated to the rearguard;
None of your knights can ever change this situation.
780 Give him the bow that you yourself have flexed
And then find people to give him strong support.'
The king gives it to him and Roland has accepted it.

63

The emperor addresses his nephew Roland:
'My lord, fair nephew, now be in no doubt,

Half of my army I shall leave behind for you; 785
Keep them with you; this will be your salvation.'
Thus speaks the count: 'I shall do no such thing;
May God confound me if I taint my family's name.*
I shall keep twenty thousand very brave Franks.
Ride through the passes with complete confidence: 790
You should never fear anyone while I am alive.'

64

Count Roland has climbed onto his warhorse. AOI
His companion Oliver rides to meet him.
Along came Gerin and brave Count Gerer,
And then came Oton, followed by Berenger. 795
Astor came too and Anseïs the fierce.
Along came old Gerard of Roussillon,
And mighty Duke Gaifier has also arrived.
The archbishop said: 'By my head, I shall go too!'
'And I shall go with you,' rejoined Count Gautier, 800
'I am Roland's man; I must never fail him!'
Between them they choose twenty thousand knights. AOI

65

Count Roland addresses Gautier del Hum thus:
'Select a thousand Franks from France, our homeland,
And station yourselves in the passes and in the hills, 805
So that the emperor loses not one of his men there.' AOI
Gautier replies: 'Certainly I owe it you to do this.'
With a thousand Frenchmen from France, their homeland,
Gautier goes on patrol in the passes and in the hills;
He will not come back down in response to bad news 810
Until seven hundred of their swords have been drawn.
King Almaris from the kingdom of Belferne
On that day launched a terrible attack against them.

66

High are the hills and the valleys dark with shadows,
The rocks are sinister, the passes full of danger. 815

That day the French suffered greatly as they journeyed:
You could hear the clamour from fifteen leagues away.
Once they arrive in their great homeland,
They could see Gascony, the land of their lord.
820 Then they remember their fiefs and their domains,
And their young girls and their noble wives:
Every single one of them is moved to tears.
Of all of them Charles suffers the greatest distress:
He has left his nephew at the main pass into Spain;
825 He is overcome by pity; he cannot help but weep.   AOI

67

The twelve peers have remained in Spain,
They have twenty thousand Franks in their company;
They are not afraid, nor do they fear death.
The emperor is returning to France;
830 Under his cloak he gives way to his emotion.
Duke Naimon rides up alongside him
And says to the king: 'What are you worried about?'
Charles replies: 'It is wrong to ask me about this.
My distress is such that I cannot help but vent it.
835 France is going to be ruined by Ganelon!
Last night I had a dream sent by angels,
In which the spear in my hands was shattered
By him who nominated my nephew to the rearguard.
I have left him in hostile border country;
840 Oh God, if I lose him, I shall never replace him!'   AOI

68

Charles the Great cannot help but weep.
A hundred thousand Franks feel great pity for him
And, on account of Roland, terrible fear.
Treacherous Ganelon has betrayed him;
845 The pagan king has rewarded him with fine gifts:
Gold and silver, silk cloth and brocades,

Mules and horses, camels and lions.
Marsilie summons his barons from all over Spain,
Counts, viscounts, both dukes and almaçors,*
The amirafles and the sons of the counts: 850
He musters four hundred thousand men in three days.
In Saragossa he orders his drums to be beaten;
They raise an image of Mohammed on the highest tower:
There is no pagan who does not worship and adore it.
Then they ride off most eager for battle   855
Across friendly territory, the valleys and the mountains.
They spotted the pennons of the men of France.
The rearguard led by the twelve companions
Will not fail to engage them in combat.

69

As for Marsilie's nephew, he has ridden forward,   860
Mounted on a mule that he urged on with a stick.
Smiling, he said to his uncle in a friendly tone:
'Fair king, my lord, I have served you for so long
And have suffered as a result both pain and distress,
Have fought battles and known victory in the field: 865
Pray grant me a reward, the first blow against Roland.
I shall kill him with my razor-sharp spear.
If it is Mohammed's wish to protect me
I shall liberate all the territory within Spain
From the Spanish passes as far as Durestant.*   870
Charles will be weary and his Franks will give in;
You will have no more wars for the remainder of your life.'
King Marsilie consented by handing him the glove.   AOI

70

Marsilie's nephew is holding the glove in his hand;
He addresses his uncle with very confident words: 875
'Fair king, my lord, you have granted me a great boon.
Pray select for me twelve of your barons

And I shall fight against the twelve companions.'
Falsaron is the very first to reply,
880 He was brother to King Marsilie:
'Fair nephew, my lord, let you and me go together,
We shall engage in this combat well and truly.
Those in the rearguard of Charles's great army
Are condemned to die at our hands.'   AOI

71

885 Then King Corsablix comes forward to join in:
He is a Berber and expert in the black arts.
He speaks in the manner of a true vassal:
'For all God's gold, I don't wish to be a coward.
888a [*If I find Roland, I shall not fail to fight him.*
888b *I am the third, now select the fourth.*']*
Now Malprimis of Brigal rushes forward:
890 He runs faster on foot than the speed of a horse.
Before Marsilie he shouts at the top of his voice:
'I too shall take myself off to Rencesvals;
If I find Roland, I shall not fail to slay him.'

72

Here comes an amirafle from Balaguer:
895 A fine figure of a man with a bright, fierce face;
As soon as he is mounted on his horse,
He exhibits great pride in bearing his arms.
He has a fine reputation for exceptional courage:
Had he been a Christian, he would have been a great hero.
900 Before Marsilie this man has shouted out:
'To Rencesvals I too shall take myself off;
If I find Roland, that will be the end of him,
And of Oliver and of all twelve of the peers;
The French will die in pain and degradation.
905 Charles the Great is very old and senile;
He will be very weary of waging this war,

And Spain will be liberated once and for all.'
King Marsilie thanked him very much indeed.   AOI

73

An almaçor from Moriana then comes forward:
There is no one more treacherous in the whole of Spain.   910
Before Marsilie he has uttered his boast:
'To Rencesvals I shall lead my company of men:
Twenty thousand of them with shields and lances.
If I find Roland, I guarantee to kill him,
Causing Charles to lament every day of his life.'   AOI 915

74

The next to come forward is Turgis of Tortosa;
This man is a count and the town belongs to him.
His aim is to inflict great slaughter on the Christians.
He goes to join the others before Marsilie.
He spoke thus to the king: 'Never lose heart!   920
Mohammed is more powerful than Saint Peter of Rome:
If you serve him, the honour of victory will be ours.
I shall go to Rencesvals to fight Roland;
No one will be able to protect him from death.
See here my sword, which is mighty and long;   925
I intend to pit it against Durendal;
You are bound to hear which one prevails.
The French will die if they risk battle against us.
Charles the old will suffer grief and shame:
Never again will he wear a crown on his head.'   930

75

Then Escremiz of Val-Terne comes forward:
He is a Saracen and that region belongs to him.
Before Marsilie he shouts out from the crowd:
'I shall go to Rencesvals to destroy their arrogance.
If I find Roland, he will not escape with his head,   935

Nor will Oliver, who is the leader of the others;
The twelve peers are all condemned to death.
The French will die, causing France to be bereft,
Charles will not have many good vassals left.'   AOI

76

940 Then a pagan called Estorgant comes forward,
     Along with Estramarit, one of his companions:
     These two are treacherous, deceitful traitors.
     Thus spoke Marsilie: 'My lords, come forward.
     You will travel through the passes to Rencesvals
945 And you will help to lead my troops.'
     And they reply: 'We are at your command!
     We shall attack Oliver and Roland;
     The twelve peers will have no protection against death,
     For our swords are strong and razor-sharp;
950 We shall stain them crimson with warm blood.
     The French will die and Charles will grieve for them.
     We shall make you a gift of their great homeland.
     Accompany us, royal lord, and you will witness this yourself.
     We shall hand over to you the defeated emperor.'

77

955 Margarit of Seville now rushed forward:
     He rules the territory as far as Cazmarine.
     His good looks make him popular with the ladies:
     No woman can see him without her face lighting up;
     When she sees him she cannot help but smile.
960 None of the pagans equals him in chivalry.
     He pushes through the crowd and shouts above the others,
     Saying to the king: 'Do not lose heart at all!
     I shall go to Rencesvals to slay Roland,
     Nor will Oliver escape with his life;
965 The twelve peers will end up being slaughtered.
     Behold my sword with its golden hilt—

The Emir of Primes sent it to me as a present—
I promise you it will be bathed in crimson blood.
The French will die and France will be dishonoured.
Charles the old with his hoary beard   970
Will suffer grief and rage every day of his life.
Within a year we shall have captured France;
We shall be able to sleep in the town of Saint-Denis.'
The pagan king bows deeply towards him.   AOI

78

Next comes Chernuble of Muneigre: 975
His flowing hair reaches down to the ground;
For sport, to amuse himself, he can carry a heavier load
Than four mules can carry when fully loaded.
It is said that in the land from which he hails
The sun never shines and wheat cannot grow,   980
Rain does not fall there, nor does dew gather.
There is not one stone which is not entirely black.
Some people say that devils live there.
Chernuble said: 'I have girded on my mighty sword;
In Rencesvals I shall stain it crimson.   985
If I find Roland the brave in my path,
If I don't attack him, I'm not worthy of your trust.
I shall beat Durendal with my own sword.
The French will die and France will be bereft.'
Their talking ended, the twelve peers assemble;   990
They take with them a hundred thousand Saracens
Who are eager and keen to join battle.
They go to arm themselves under some pine trees.

79

The pagans arm themselves with Saracen hauberks,
The majority of them have three layers of mail.   995
They fasten their fine helmets from Saragossa,
Gird on swords of steel from Viana;

They have splendid shields, spears from Valencia,
And pennons coloured white, blue, or red.
1000 Leaving behind their mules and all their palfreys
They mount their warhorses, and ride in close formation.
The day was fine and the sun shone brightly:
Every bit of their equipment gleamed in the light.
They sound a thousand bugles to add to the effect.
1005 The din is incredible and the Frenchmen heard it.
Said Oliver: 'My lord, companion, in my view
We shall have the opportunity to fight some Saracens.'
Roland replies: 'May God grant it to us!
It is our clear duty to be here for our king:
1010 For his lord a man should suffer great hardship
Enduring both extreme heat and extreme cold,
And be willing to sacrifice his skin and hair.
Let every man make sure he inflicts great blows,
So that no shameful song is sung about us.
1015 The pagans are wrong and the Christians are right.*
No bad example will ever be set by me.' AOI

80

Oliver is standing on the brow of a lofty hill.
He looks to his right, into a lush valley
And watches the advance of the pagan army.
1020 Then he told Roland, his companion, about it:
'I can see the glint of burnished metal coming from Spain,
With so many gleaming hauberks, so many shiny helmets;
These men will inflict great distress on our Frenchmen.
Ganelon was in the know, the villain, the traitor,
1025 When he nominated us in the emperor's presence.'
'Hold your tongue, Oliver,' Count Roland replies,
'He is my stepfather, I will not have you speak of him.'

81

Oliver has climbed to the top of a hill,
Now he can see clearly the kingdom of Spain,

And the hordes of Saracens who are gathered there.   1030
Their helmets shine, with jewels set in gold,
As do their shields and their burnished hauberks,
And their lances with pennons affixed.
He is incapable even of counting the divisions:
There are so many of them the number eludes him.   1035
For his part, Oliver is deeply troubled by this.
As soon as he could, he ran down the hill.
Having reached the French, he's told them everything.

82

Said Oliver: 'With my own eyes I have seen pagans;
No man alive has ever seen more of them.   1040
In the front line are a hundred thousand shield-bearers
With their helmets fastened and shiny hauberks donned.
Spears held straight, their burnished lances glisten.
You face such a battle as has never been seen before.
My lords, fellow Frenchmen, may God give you strength,   1045
Stand fast in the field so that we are not vanquished!'
The French reply: 'Cursèd be him who flees.
Not a single man will hesitate to die for you.'   AOI

83

Oliver said: 'The pagans have a huge army,
We Frenchmen seem to me so few in number.   1050
Roland, companion, pray blow your horn.
Charles will hear it and the army will return.'
Roland replies: 'I'd be foolish to do so.
I would lose my reputation in France the fair.
Very soon with Durendal I'll be dealing mighty blows.   1055
The blade will be bloody right up to the golden hilt.
These false pagans will regret coming to these passes.
I swear to you, they are all condemned to death.'   AOI

84

'Roland, companion, pray blow your oliphant.
1060 Charles will hear it and make the army turn back.
Along with his barons the king will save us.'
Roland replies: 'May it never please God
That my family should be reviled on my account
Or that fair France should ever fall into disrepute.
1065 I would rather strike many blows with Durendal,
My mighty sword, which I've girded at my side.
You will see its blade all dripping with blood.
These treacherous pagans will regret mustering here.
I swear to you, they are all destined to die.'   AOI

85

1070 'Roland, companion, blow your oliphant,
And Charles will hear it as he rides through the pass.
I swear to you, the Franks will soon turn back.'
'God forbid'—this is Roland's reply to him—
'That people should say that because of any man alive
1075 Or on account of any pagan I'd ever blow my horn.
Never will my relatives be reproached for this.
When I'm in the thick of the great battle
And I have struck one thousand seven hundred blows
You will see the blade of Durendal dripping with blood.
1080 The French are brave and will fight valiantly.
Nothing can protect these men of Spain from death.'

86

Said Oliver: 'I can see no reproach in this.
I've seen for myself these Saracens from Spain.
The valleys and the mountains are swarming with them,
1085 And so are the hillsides and the plains all around.
Great are the forces of this race of foreigners
And our band of men is very small indeed.'

Roland replies: 'My thirst for battle grows.
Let it not please Our Lord God or His angels,
That on my account France should ever lose its worth.   1090
I would rather die than be covered in shame.
The mightier our blows, the greater our emperor's love.'

87

Roland is brave and Oliver is wise;
Both are extraordinarily valiant knights.
Once they are mounted and fully armed,   1095
They will never leave the field, fighting to the death.*
Worthy are these counts and noble their words.
The treacherous pagans ride forward, full of ire.
Said Oliver: 'Roland, just take a look at them!
These men are close by, whereas Charles is far off.   1100
You would not deign to blow your oliphant,
Yet if the king were here, we would suffer no losses.
Look up there towards the Spanish passes.
You can see that the rearguard is in dire straits.
Those who take part in it will never form another.'   1105
Roland replies: 'Don't say such dreadful things.
Cursèd be the heart that turns coward in the breast.
We shall hold our ground on the field of battle.
We shall be the ones to hack and to hew.'   AOI

88

When Roland sees that battle is inevitable,   1110
He grows more ferocious than a lion or leopard.
He cries out to the French, and calls to Oliver:
'My lord, companion, do not speak thus, my friend.
The emperor, who entrusted these Frenchmen to us,
Singled out these twenty thousand men: 1115
He knew there was not one coward among them.
For his lord a man must suffer great torment,
Enduring both harsh cold and searing heat,

And be willing to sacrifice his blood and flesh.
1120 You strike with your lance and I with Durendal,
      My mighty sword, given to me by the king.
      If I die here, then whoever possesses it next
      Can say that *this sword* belonged to a noble warrior.'

                              89

      Elsewhere Archbishop Turpin is to be found:
1125 He spurs his horse and climbs to the top of a hill.
      He calls out to the French, with a rousing speech:
      'My lords, barons, Charles left us here;
      It is our clear duty to be ready to die for our king.
      Help us now in our defence of Christianity!
1130 You will soon go into battle, there is no doubt about it,
      For with your own eyes you can see the Saracens.
      Proclaim your mea culpa; pray for God's mercy!*
      I will absolve you for the salvation of your souls.
      If you die, you will become holy martyrs:
1135 You will have a seat in paradise on high.'
      The French dismount, prostrating themselves,
      And the archbishop blesses them in God's name.
      He commands them to strike penitential blows.

                              90

      The French get to their feet and stand tall;
1140 They are fully absolved and cleansed of their sins,
      And in God's name the archbishop blessed them.
      Then they climbed onto their swift warhorses;
      They are armed in the manner of knights
      And are fully equipped to go into battle.
1145 Count Roland calls out to Oliver:
      'My lord, companion, as you were well aware
      Ganelon has betrayed each and every one of us:
      He has done so for gold, wealth, and money.
      The emperor should avenge us by rights.

King Marsilie has struck a deal involving us, 1150
But he will have to pay for it at the point of a sword.' AOI

91

Roland has ridden through the Spanish passes
On Veillantif, his fine and swift warhorse.
He is fully armed and cuts a most dashing figure.
Thus the great warrior advances, brandishing his lance, 1155
Constantly turning its point towards the sky.
There is a pure white pennon fastened to its tip,
Whose gold fringes trail down as far as his hands.
He is a fine figure of a man, with a bright, smiling face.
He is closely followed by his companion 1160
And the men of France proclaim him their protector.
He sizes up the Saracens with a fierce look,
But with humility gazes tenderly on the French,
As he says a few well-chosen words to them:
'My lords, barons, advance slowly but surely! 1165
These pagans are riding for a bloody fall.
Before nightfall we shall have fine, precious booty,
No king of France ever had such rich spoils.'
On hearing this, the armies rush to join battle. AOI

92

Oliver speaks: 'The time for discussion is over. 1170
You did not deign to blow your oliphant,
And so Charles is not here with you now.
He knows nothing of this and our lord is not at fault;
The men who are with him should bear none of the blame.
Now pray ride as hard as you possibly can! 1175
My lords, barons, stand firm on the battlefield!
By God, I beseech you to prepare yourselves
To strike, parry, and wield mighty blows.
Let us not forget Charlemagne's war cry.'
On hearing this, the French cried out as one. 1180
If you had heard them then shouting 'Monjoie!',

You would have known what true bravery was.
Then they charge forward, oh God, so very boldly:
Vigorously spurring their horses to advance at top speed,
1185 They start their attack. What else should they do?
Yet the Saracens were not afraid of them.
Just look at how the Franks and pagans clash!

93

It is none other than Aëlroth, Marsilie's nephew,
Who is the first to ride out before the troops,
1190 Insolently insulting our Frenchmen as he does so:
'Today you treacherous French will join battle with us.
You've been betrayed by your supposed protector:
The king who left you here in the passes is a fool!
Before nightfall fair France will lose her glorious name,
1195 And Charlemagne will lose his right-hand man.'
When Roland hears this, oh God, he was so outraged.
He spurs on his horse, letting it gallop freely;
The count goes to strike him as brutally as he can:
He shatters his shield and rips open his hauberk.
1200 He cleaves his chest, shattering several bones.
From his back he completely severs his spine.
He thus casts out his soul with the point of his lance,
Driving it in deeply, toppling his body backwards.
With his lance level he knocks him dead from his horse,*
1205 And in so doing he has broken his neck in two.
Yet he will not refrain, he says, from speaking:
'You utter scoundrel, Charles is no fool,
Nor did he ever have betrayal in his heart.
He was right to leave us behind here in the passes.
1210 Today fair France won't lose her glorious name.
Franks, strike now; we have drawn first blood!
Right is on our side; these swine are in the wrong.'   AOI

94

Now here's another duke, his name is Falsaron;
This man was brother to King Marsilie:

His was the land that belonged to Dathan and Abiram.   1215
A more dastardly scoundrel never walked this earth.
His eyes were separated by an extremely wide brow:
It measured a good six inches or more across.
When he saw his nephew slain, he was wild with grief.
He rides forward from the ranks, heedless of danger,   1220
As he does so he screams the pagan war cry.
He hurls terrible abuse at the French:
'Today fair France will lose her reputation!'
When Oliver hears this, his rage knows no bounds.
He drives his horse on with his golden spurs.   1225
He valiantly rides forward to strike him down:
He shatters his shield and smashes his hauberk,
Ramming into his body the tails of his pennon.
With his lance level, he knocks him dead from his saddle.
He looks down, sees the swine lying on the ground,   1230
Then addressed him with these ferocious words:
'I am immune to your threats, you vile wretch!
Franks, strike now, for we will easily vanquish them!'
He shouts out 'Monjoie!', which is Charles's war cry.   AOI

95

Now here's a king, whose name is Corsablix;   1235
He is a Berber, hailing from a foreign land.
He called upon the other Saracens to listen:
'This battle can be ours for the taking,
For the Frenchmen are few in number.
Those here before us we should hold in deep contempt;   1240
Whatever Charles does, not one of them will survive.
Today is the day on which they are destined to die.'
Archbishop Turpin cannot help but hear this;
No man on earth is more worthy of his hatred.
He drives his horse on with his spurs of pure gold,   1245
He has gone to strike him down with all his might:
He shatters his shield, his hauberk is smashed.
He plunges his mighty lance into his body,
Thrusting it in so completely he is knocked backwards.

1250 With his lance level he strikes him dead on the ground.
     He looks behind him, sees the swine lying there,
     Yet he cannot refrain from speaking out loud:
     'Pagan churl, everything you have said was a lie:
     My lord Charles always offers us his protection.
1255 Our Frenchmen are not minded to flee.
     We shall stop every one of your companions in his tracks;
     I have news for you, you must suffer the agony of death.
     Frenchmen, strike: each one of you must do your duty!
     We have drawn first blood, thanks be to God.'
1260 He shouts 'Monjoie!' to encourage them to stand firm.

96

     And Gerin is now striking Malprimis of Brigal,
     Whose fine shield does him no good at all;
     He completely shatters its crystal boss,
     Sending half of it flying down to the ground.
1265 He pierces his hauberk through to his flesh,
     Thrusting his fine lance right into his body.
     The pagan falls to the ground in a heap,
     Then Satan carries off this man's soul.   AOI

97

     And his companion Gerer strikes the amirafle:
1270 He shatters his shield and rips his hauberk to shreds,
     He plunges his fine lance straight into his belly,
     Driving it home, so that it comes out the other side.
     With his lance level he knocks him dead to the ground.
     Said Oliver: 'This battle we are fighting is noble!'

98

1275 Duke Samson goes to strike the almaçor.
     He shatters his shield, decorated with golden flowers;

His fine hauberk is of no use as protection:
He slices into his heart, his liver, and his lungs,
Striking him dead, whether anyone cares or not.
The archbishop said: 'This is a mighty warrior's blow.' 1280

99

And Anseïs now allows free rein to his horse
Thus he goes to strike Turgis of Tortosa:
He shatters his shield just underneath its golden boss,
He smashed through both layers of his hauberk,
He thrusts the point of his fine lance into his body, 1285
Driving it home, so that the steel comes out the other side;
With his lance level, he knocks him dead on the battlefield.
Thus Roland spoke: 'This is a valiant man's blow!'

100

And Engeler, the Gascon from Bordeaux,
Spurs his horse on and gives him free rein. 1290
He goes to attack Escremiz of Val-Terne:
He shatters the shield at his neck, smashes it to pieces.
He ripped to shreds the ventail of his hauberk,
Then he strikes him squarely in the chest.
With his lance level, he knocks him dead from his saddle. 1295
Afterwards he said to him: 'To hell with you!' AOI

101

And Gautier strikes a pagan by the name of Estorgant,*
Catching the very top edge of his shield
So that he slices off all the red and white panels.
He has ripped to shreds the skirts of his hauberk; 1300
He drives his fine, razor-sharp lance into his body,
So that he knocks him dead from his swift mount.
Then he said to him: 'No one can protect you now!'

102

And as for Berenger, he strikes Estramarit:
1305 He shatters his shield, his hauberk is smashed.
He drives his sturdy lance right into his body,
Striking him dead in the midst of a thousand Saracens.
Of the twelve pagan peers, ten are now slain;
No more than two of them have been left alive:
1310 These two are Chernuble and Count Margarit.

103

Margarit is an extremely valiant knight,
Handsome and strong, swift and nimble;
He spurs on his horse, goes to strike Oliver:
He smashes his shield under its pure gold boss,
1315 He thrusts his lance, but it just misses his ribs.
God protects Oliver, for his body is untouched:
The shaft shatters, yet he is not knocked to the ground.
He rides straight past with no one to stop him;
Then he sounds his bugle to muster his men.

104

1320 A glorious pitched battle is now in full swing.
Count Roland is by no means hanging back:
He strikes with his lance as long as the shaft stays intact.
Only after fifteen charges has it shattered and broken:
Then he unsheaths Durendal, his mighty sword;
1325 He spurs on his horse, and goes to strike Chernuble:
He shatters his helmet, encrusted with shining gems,
Slicing through his coif and even scalping him.
He even sliced right into his eyes and his face,
Through the fine chain mail of his gleaming hauberk,
1330 Then through his entire body down to his groin.
His sword has even cut through the gilded saddle:
It finally comes to a halt only in the horse's flesh.

And he slices through its spine, not needing to find the joints.
He strikes him dead in the meadow's luxuriant grass.
Afterwards he said: 'Vile wretch, rue the day you came here!   1335
Mohammed will never come to your aid now.
Today's battle will not be won by a churl like you.'

105

Count Roland is riding around the battlefield,
He holds Durendal, which keenly slices and cleaves:
He is cutting a huge swathe through the Saracens.   1340
You should have seen him piling up their bodies,
Their bright blood lying everywhere on the ground.
His hauberk and both his arms are bathed in blood
As are his brave horse's neck and withers,
Nor does Oliver tarry when it comes to the attack: 1345
The twelve peers are all beyond reproach.
And the Frenchmen strike and hack away:
Pagans are dying, while some simply faint.
The archbishop said: 'Victory to our brave warriors!'
He shouts out 'Monjoie!', which is Charles's war cry.   AOI 1350

106

And Oliver now rides further into the fray.
His lance is shattered, only a stump is left,
Yet he goes to attack the pagan Malun:
He smashes his shield, which is decorated with golden flowers,
Makes both his eyes pop right out of his head,   1355
And splatters his brain down at his feet;
He knocks him dead to join all seven hundred of their men.
After this he has killed Turgis and Esturgus:
His broken lance splits right down to his hands.
Roland said: 'Companion, what are you doing?   1360
In such a battle I am not impressed by a stick:
Iron and steel should now show their worth.
Where is your sword, which is called Halteclere?

Its hilt is of gold and its pommel of crystal.'
1365 'I have not had time to draw it,' replies Oliver,
'Because I was far too busy fighting.'   AOI

107

My lord Oliver has drawn his mighty sword,
In answer to his companion Roland's urgent pleas,
And like a true knight he has shown him its blade:
1370 He strikes a pagan, Justin of Val-Ferree:
He has split his head completely in two,
Sliced through his torso and gleaming byrnie
Down to his fine, jewel- and gold-encrusted saddle,
And he has even cut into the horse's spine.
1375 He knocks him stone dead in the grass before him.
Thus spoke Roland: 'Brother, that's more like you!
The emperor loves us because we strike such mighty blows.'
Shouts of 'Monjoie!' can be heard all around.   AOI

108

Count Gerin is sitting astride Sorel, his horse,
1380 And his companion Gerer upon Passecerf.
They give their mounts free rein, both eagerly spur them on,
And go to attack a pagan called Timozel,
One on his shield, the other on his hauberk:
Their two lances break as they enter his flesh.
1385 They knock him dead and he bites the dust.
I neither know, nor ever once heard tell
Which of these two was the swifter.*
Esperveres was there too, the son of Burel,
And he was killed by Engeler of Bordeaux.
1390 Then the archbishop killed one of them, Siglorel,
The magician who had once been to hell:
Jupiter had taken him there by magic.
Thus spoke Turpin: 'This man did us wrong!'
Roland replies: 'This wretch has been vanquished.
1395 Oliver, my brother, I rejoice in these mighty blows!'

109

The battle, meanwhile, has become even bloodier:
Pagans and Franks alike exchange marvellous blows.
One side attacks, their opponents defend themselves.
Many lances are shattered and dripping with blood,
So many pennons and standards ripped to shreds.   1400
Many good Frenchmen die in the flower of their youth:
Never again will they see their mothers or their wives,
Nor the Frenchmen who await them at the pass.   AOI

110

Charles the Great weeps for them and laments.
But what good is this? No one can help them now.   1405
Ganelon served him ill on that day
When he went to Saragossa to betray Charles's kin.
Later, as a result, he was killed and dismembered:
On trial in Aix, he was condemned to death by hanging,
And with him some thirty of his relatives,   1410
Who did not expect to die in this way.   AOI

111

The battle rages on, taking its dreadful toll.
Oliver is striking mighty blows, and so is Roland,
The archbishop strikes more than a thousand times,
The twelve peers are no less ferocious,   1415
And all the French join together in the attack.
Hundreds and thousands of pagans are dying:
Unless they flee, they have no escape from death,
Whether they like it or not, their lives will end there.
Yet the French are also suffering heavy losses: 1420
Never again will they see their fathers or relatives,
Or Charlemagne, who is waiting for them at the pass.
In France there is a most dreadful tempest:
A storm with thunder and a howling gale.

1425 Driving rain and the most prodigious hail.
      Lightning strikes over and over again.
      And truly the land is rocked by an earthquake:
      From the Mont Saint-Michel to Saintes,
      From Besançon to Wissant harbour,*
1430 There is no building with walls left intact.
      Around midday, complete darkness falls,
      Only the flashes of lightning cast any light.
      All who see this are absolutely terrified.
      Many of them say: 'This is the end of everything,
1435 The end of the world is now upon us.'
      They do not realize, but their words are far from true.
      This marks the universal grief for the death of Roland.

                              112

      The French have now been fighting body and soul:
      Throngs of pagans have died by the thousand.
1440 Of a hundred thousand men, fewer than two thousand survive.
      The archbishop said: 'Our men are very brave.
      There is no king on earth with more or better warriors.
      It is written down in the Frankish annals
      That our emperor has excellent vassals.'
1445 They search the battlefield for their fallen brothers,
      Tears of sorrow and pity streaming down their faces,
      Weeping with heartfelt love for their kith and kin.
      King Marsilie, with his great army, looms before them.   AOI

                              113

      Marsilie is coming up through a valley
1450 With the formidable army he had mustered.
      The king has put his men into twenty divisions.
      Their helmets, with jewels set in gold, are gleaming,
      As are their shields and their shiny byrnies.
      Seven thousand bugles sound the charge;
1455 The deafening din can be heard far and wide.

Roland spoke thus: 'Oliver, my brother and companion,
Perfidious Ganelon has condemned us to death;
His treachery can no longer be concealed.
The emperor will wreak a most terrible revenge.
We will fight a bitter and mighty battle, 1460
Such a battle as has never before been joined.
I will strike here with my sword Durendal,
And you, companion, will strike with Halteclere.
We have borne these swords in so many lands,
We have been victorious with them in so many battles! 1465
No shameful song should ever be sung about them!' AOI

114

Marsilie can see his men being slaughtered.
He now has his horns and trumpets sounded,
Then he rides forth with the great army he has mustered.
Riding in front is a Saracen by the name of Abisme: 1470
He was by far the most wicked of the entire company,
A depraved wretch, capable of the greatest iniquity:
He does not believe in God, the son of Blessed Mary.
He is even darker than the blackest molten pitch
And he prefers murder and treachery 1475
To amassing all the gold of Galicia.
No man ever saw him joking or laughing.
He is bold and quite exceptionally courageous,
Which is why he is favoured by wicked King Marsilie;
He carries the standard under which his troops march. 1480
There'll be no love lost between him and the archbishop:
As soon as he saw him, he wants to strike him.
Turpin talks to himself softly, under his breath:
'This Saracen seems a heretic through and through:
It is far better that I should go and kill him. 1485
I've never had any time for lily-livered cowards!' AOI

115

It is the archbishop who is the first to attack.
He sits astride the horse he captured from Grossaille,

Who was a king he killed on campaign in Denmark.
1490 This warhorse is swift and fleet of foot:*
He has sturdy hooves and lean legs.
His haunches are slim, yet he's broad in the croup.
His flanks are long and he stands many hands tall.
His tail is white but his mane is flaxen.
1495 He has small ears and his entire head is dun.
There is no beast that can equal him in speed.
The archbishop spurs him on with such great courage:
He will not give up until he has attacked Abisme.
He goes now to land a prodigious blow on his shield,
1500 Which is covered in gems: amethysts and topaz,
Diamonds and gleaming carbuncles.
It was a gift from a devil in the land of Val-Metas
And was brought to him by the emir Galafre.
Turpin strikes the shield and he spares it nothing.
1505 After such a blow, it is, methinks, worthless.
He slices through his body from one side to the other,
Knocking him dead onto a piece of wasteland.
The French say: 'What a truly courageous man!
In the archbishop's hands the crozier ensures salvation.'

116

1510 When the French see there are pagans everywhere—
The whole battlefield is swarming with them—
They cry out repeatedly for Roland and Oliver,
For the twelve peers, so they might protect them.
Then the archbishop told them what he was thinking:
1515 'My lords, barons, do not contemplate any dishonour!
By God I beg you, on no account think of fleeing,
So that no worthy man can sing of us in disdain.
It is far better that we should die fighting.
One thing is certain: we will soon meet our ends:
1520 After today none of us will still be alive.
But there is one thing I can promise you:
You are assured of a warm welcome in heaven.
You will sit alongside the Holy Innocents.'

On hearing this, the Franks are filled with joy;
Each and every one of them shouts 'Monjoie!'   AOI 1525

117

Present was a Saracen from Saragossa—
One half of the city belongs to him—
His name is Climborin, who was by no means a worthy man.
He was one who made a pact with Count Ganelon:
He kissed him on the mouth in friendship,   1530
Gave him his helmet with a carbuncle.*
He vowed to shame our great homeland,
And also to deprive the emperor of his crown.
He sits astride his horse, called Barbamouche,
Which is swifter than a sparrowhawk or a swallow.   1535
He spurs him eagerly on, allowing him free rein,
And goes to strike Engeler of Gascony:
Neither shield nor byrnie can offer him any protection.
Climborin thrusts the point of his lance into his flesh,
Driving it home so that the steel comes out the other side: 1540
With his lance level, he knocks him dead on the battlefield.
Afterwards he shouts: 'These men are ripe for the picking!
Attack, my fellow pagans, in order to smash their ranks!'
The French say: 'Oh God, alas for this worthy man!'   AOI

118

Now Count Roland calls out to Oliver: 1545
'My lord, companion, Engeler has been killed;
We have never had a more valiant knight.'
The count replies: 'May God grant me vengeance!'
He drives his horse on with spurs of pure gold;
He wields Halteclere, the steel dripping with blood.   1550
He goes to strike the pagan with all his might:
He swings his sword and the Saracen falls.
His soul is carried off by devilish fiends.
Then Oliver has killed Duke Alphaïen,

1555 And he has decapitated Escababi on the spot,
And he has also unhorsed seven Arabs:
All these men will never be fit to wage war again.
Thus spoke Roland: 'My companion is furious.
His deeds are every bit as praiseworthy as mine.
1560 Charles loves us all the more for blows such as these.'
He shouts as loud as he can: 'Knights, attack!' AOI

119

From the other direction comes a pagan, Valdabrun,
He had helped to bring up King Marsilie.
At sea he is captain of four hundred huge galleys:
1565 All the Saracen sailors are under his command.
Through treachery he once captured Jerusalem,
Where he desecrated the Temple of Solomon.
He killed the patriarch in front of the font.
He was one who made a pact with Count Ganelon:*
1570 He gave him his sword and a thousand gold mangons.*
He sits astride his horse, which he calls Gramimund,
It is swifter than any falcon on the wing;
He drives him forward with his razor-sharp spurs,
And goes to strike the mighty Duke Samson:
1575 He shatters his shield and smashes his hauberk,
Ramming into his body the tails of his pennon,
Knocking him dead from his saddle with his lance level.
'Strike, my fellow pagans, for we can easily vanquish them!'
The French say: 'Oh God, alas for this baron's loss!' AOI

120

1580 When Count Roland sees that Samson is dead
You can be sure that his sorrow was unbearable:
He spurs on his horse, galloping at full tilt,
Wielding Durendal, worth more than its weight in gold;
Our hero strikes his opponent as hard as he can,
1585 Catching his helmet, with its gems set in gold.

He slices through his head, his byrnie, and his body,
Splitting his fine saddle with its jewels set in gold,
Then slicing deep into the horse's back.
He kills them both, regardless of what anyone thinks.
The pagans say: 'This is a most grievous loss for us!'   1590
Roland replies: 'I regard your men as my eternal foes:
On your side there is nothing but pride and injustice.'   AOI

121

Now here's an African, freshly arrived from Africa:
His name is Malquïant, the son of King Malcud.
His armour is made entirely of beaten gold: 1595
More than any one else's it shines brightly in the sun.
He sits astride his horse, which he calls Saltperdut:
No other beast alive can keep up with him.
He goes to strike Anseïs on his shield.
He slices right off the red and blue panels.   1600
He has ripped to shreds the skirts of his hauberk,
Driving into his body the steel and wood of his lance.
The count is slain: his life has come to an end.
The French say: 'What a fateful day for you, my lord!'

122

Archbishop Turpin is riding across the battlefield.   1605
Never has mass been sung by such a fine priest,
One able to commit such valiant feats of arms.
He said to the pagan: 'May God confound you!
My heart bleeds for the man you have just killed.'
He has urged his noble steed to gallop ahead,   1610
Landing a blow on the pagan's Toledan shield,
And striking him down dead on the green grass.

123

Then up comes a pagan called Grandonie,
The son of Capuel, the King of Cappadocia.

1615 He sits astride his horse, which he calls Marmorie.
It is far swifter than any bird on the wing.
He gives him free reign and spurs him forward,
And goes to strike Gerin with all his might.
He smashes his scarlet shield, which flies from his neck,
1620 And then slices his byrnie completely open,
Driving his entire blue standard into his flesh;
Thus he strikes him dead on a rocky outcrop.
He also kills Gerin's companion, Gerer,
And Berenger and Guiun from Saint-Antoine.
1625 Then he goes to strike a powerful duke, Austorie,
Who rules over Valence and land in the Rhône valley.
He strikes him dead, which makes the pagans rejoice.
The French say: 'How quickly our men are falling!'

124

Count Roland held aloft his bloody sword.
1630 He has clearly heard that the French are lamenting.
He is so moved by this, he thinks his heart will break.
He called out to the pagan: 'God damn you to hell!
I'll make you pay dearly for the man you've just killed!'
He spurs on his horse and at once it surges forward,
1635 Whoever ends up paying for it, the two men now clash.

125

Grandonie was a valiant and worthy knight,
Exceptionally strong, and a brave warrior.
Now he has found Roland in his path.
Never having seen him, he still recognized him
1640 From his fierce expression and fine physique,
From his noble countenance and bearing.
He cannot help but be terrified of Roland.
He would like to flee, but there is no escape.
The count strikes him with such force
1645 That he splits his helmet down to the nose guard,

Slicing through his nose, mouth, and teeth,
His entire body and fine Moorish chain mail,
Through the golden saddle's two silver side-bars,
And cleaving deeply into the horse's back.
He killed the two of them once and for all.   1650
And the Spanish army cries out in alarm.
The French say: 'Our protector strikes fine blows!'

125A

The dreadful battle grows even more fierce.*
The French are fighting with their gleaming lances.
There you could have seen such grievous losses,   1655
So many men, wounded and dead, bathed in blood,
Lying face down or up, one on top of the other.
The Saracens can hold out no longer:
Like it or not, they begin to flee the field.
The Franks set out after them, in hot pursuit.   AOI 1660

126

The dreadful battle grows even more intense.
The French are fighting with fury and vigour:
They slice off hands, cut into ribs and spines,
Piercing clothes right through to the living flesh.
Rivers of bright red blood run across the green grass.   1665
The pagans say: 'We will not hold out for long!
May Mohammed curse their great homeland!
Of all peoples, yours is by far the boldest!'
Each and every one of them shouts: 'Marsilie!
Ride swiftly, O king, for we need your help!'   1670

127

Now Count Roland calls out to Oliver:
'My lord, companion, you must surely agree

That the archbishop is an excellent knight:
There is no better fighter in all the world.

1675   He handles his lance and spear with equal dexterity.'
The count replies: 'Let's go then to his aid.'
Hearing this, the Franks have renewed their efforts.
The fighting is hard and the combat is vicious.
The Christians are now under great duress.

1680   If only you had seen Roland and Oliver
Striking and hacking away with their swords!
The archbishop continues to strike with his lance.
We have a good idea of how many they killed,
For it is written down in the records and documents,

1685   And according to the annals more than four thousand.
The first four waves of attack they resisted well,
But the fifth was far harsher and took its toll:
Practically all of these French knights were killed,
All except for sixty, whom God has spared.

1690   Before they die, they'll make their foe pay dearly.   AOI

128

Count Roland sees that he has lost many men.
He calls out to his companion Oliver:
'My lord, dear companion, by God, what do you think?
Just look at all these brave men lying on the ground!

1695   We may weep for our beautiful France the fair,
Bereft as she is now of such fine manhood.
Alas my royal kinsman, if only you were here now.
Oliver, my brother, how can we go about it?
How can we send him news of what has happened?'

1700   Said Oliver: 'I do not know how to send for him.
I would rather die than be the cause of shameful reports.'   AOI

129

Roland spoke thus: 'I shall blow the oliphant.
Charles, who is riding through the pass, will hear it.
I swear to you that the Franks will surely return.'

Said Oliver: 'This would be most dishonourable,   1705
And it would disgrace your entire family.
They would never manage to live down this shame!
When I told you to blow your horn, you would not,
And you will not do so now with my consent.
If you blow your horn, this will not be an act of bravery!   1710
Both your arms are already covered in blood.'
The count replies: 'I have struck many fine blows!'   AOI

130

Roland speaks thus: 'Our battle is vicious.
I shall blow my horn and King Charles will hear it.'
Said Oliver: 'This would not be an act of heroism!   1715
Companion, when I asked, you disdained to do so.
If the king were here, we wouldn't have suffered such losses.
The men who are with him are not to be blamed.'
Said Oliver: 'I swear by the hair on my face,
That if I live to see my noble sister Aude   1720
You will never again lie in her embrace.'   AOI

131

Roland spoke thus: 'Why are you angry with me?'
And he replies: 'Companion, what you did was wrong,
For bravery by definition is not folly.*
Restraint is better by far than recklessness.   1725
Frenchmen have died because of your rashness:
Charles will no longer have the benefit of our service.
If you had believed me, my lord would be here now,
We would have fought and won this battle.
King Marsilie would have been captured or killed.   1730
Your brand of bravery, Roland, has been our ruin!
Charles the Great will never again have our support.
There will be no greater man until the Last Judgement.
You will die here, and France will thereby be shamed.
Today our loyal companionship comes to an end: 1735
Before nightfall our parting will be full of sorrow.'   AOI

132

The archbishop hears them arguing with each other.
He drives his horse forward with spurs of pure gold.
He rode up to them and began to chastise them:
1740 'My lord Roland, and you too, my lord Oliver,
In God's name I beseech you, pray do not argue!
Although blowing the horn can be of little use to us,
Nonetheless it is far better that we should do so.
Let the king come, he will be able to avenge us.
1745 The men of Spain must not be allowed to leave happy.
Our Frenchmen will dismount from their horses here:
They will find our dead and dismembered bodies,
They will place us on biers strapped to packhorses,
And they will weep for us in their pity and grief.
1750 They will bury us in consecrated ground near churches,
Ensuring we are not devoured by wolves, pigs, or dogs.'
Roland replies: 'My lord, you speak very well.'   AOI

133

Roland has placed the oliphant to his lips.
He clasps it tightly and blows it as hard as he can.
1755 The mountains are high, the sound travels far:
Its echo was heard over a good thirty leagues.
Charles heard it, as did all the men with him.
The king speaks thus: 'Our men must be fighting!'
To which Ganelon is quick to reply:
1760 'From anyone else, this would seem an egregious lie.'   AOI

134

Count Roland, despite the pain and suffering,
Despite the great agony, blows his oliphant.
Bright red blood gushes forth from his mouth;
In his head, his temples gradually rupture.
1765 The sound of his horn travels far and wide.
Charles hears it as he is riding through the pass.
Naimon heard it, and the Franks are listening too.

The king spoke thus: 'I can hear Roland's horn.
He would not have sounded it, had he not been fighting!'
Ganelon replies: 'No way are they engaged in battle!   1770
You are already old, and hoary, and white-haired;
When you say such things, you sound just like a child.
You are well aware of Roland's great pride,
Indeed it's amazing that God stands for this.   1775
Once he took Noples without your permission;
The Saracens of the town sallied forth
And fought against your trusty vassal Roland.
With water he then washed their blood from the meadows
So that what he had done might not be seen.
Just one hare will make him blow his horn all day.   1780
Right now he is showing off to his peers.
No race on earth would dare engage him in battle.*
Pray ride on now. Why are you lingering here?
Our great homeland is still a long way off.'   AOI

135

Count Roland's mouth is covered in blood: 1785
In his head his temples have ruptured.
He sounds his oliphant, in pain and agony.
Charles heard it and his Frenchmen take heed.
The king spoke thus: 'That horn doesn't stop sounding!'
Duke Naimon replies: 'A great knight is putting his all into this!   1790
I have no doubt that he is now engaged in battle.
This man, who asks you to hold back, has betrayed him.
Pray don your armour, shout out your war cry.
Go to help the men of your noble household.
You can clearly hear that Roland is in trouble!'   1795

136

The emperor has ordered his horns to be blown.
The French dismount and don their armour:
Hauberks and helmets, and gilded swords.
They have fine shields and long, sturdy lances,

1800 And pennons that are scarlet, white, or blue.
All the barons of the army mount their warhorses;
Urgently they spur them on right through the pass.
Each and every one of them says to his neighbour:
'If only we could reach Roland before he dies,
1805 We would be able to strike mighty blows by his side.'
But what use is this? They've already delayed too long.

137

The early evening light has become brighter:
Their armour and weapons glisten in the sun.
Hauberks and helmets reflect the bright light,
1810 And the shields beautifully painted with flowers,
And the lances, with their golden pennons.
The emperor rides on in a great fury,
With the French, full of sorrow and ire:
Each and every one is in floods of tears,
1815 So fearful are they all for Roland's life.
The king has Count Ganelon taken prisoner,
Handing him over to his household cooks.
He summons the head cook, called Besgun:
'Guard him well, as befits such a felon.
1820 He has betrayed the men of my household!'
He takes him off, escorted by a hundred companions,
Cooks all, of good and evil character.
They rip out his beard and his moustache,
And each one punches him four times.
1825 They beat him soundly with sticks and clubs,
And they put an iron collar around his neck,
Chaining him up as they would a bear.
To add insult to injury, he is mounted on a packhorse.
They guarded him until they hand him back to Charles.

138

1830 High are the hills, shadowy and immense,   AOI
The valleys deep, and the streams run swiftly.

Their bugles are sounding from all sides,
Each one responding to the oliphant's call.
The emperor rides on full of ire,
With the French, who are sorrowful but furious.   1835
Each and every one weeps and laments,
And they pray to God to keep Roland safe
Until the entire army arrives at the battlefield:
They will fight tooth and nail by his side.
But what use is this? It is all for nothing.   1840
They delay too long and can't get there in time.   AOI

139

In a great fury Charlemagne continues to ride,
With his white beard flowing onto his byrnie.
All the French barons spur their horses on frantically
Each and every one loudly bemoans the fact   1845
That they are not now with their captain Roland,
Who is fighting against the Saracens of Spain.
But Roland is wounded, methinks on the verge of death!
Oh God, the sixty still with him are such fine men
That no king nor captain ever had any better.   AOI 1850

140

Roland looks around the slopes and hillsides.
He can see so many Frenchmen lying dead,
And he weeps for them, like a noble knight:
'My lords, barons, may God have mercy upon you!
May He receive all your souls in paradise,   1855
And grant them a bed of holy flowers!
Better warriors than you I have never seen:
You have served me constantly for so long
And conquered so many great lands for Charles!
The emperor has cherished you to no avail!   1860
O land of France, you are such a fair country,
Yet today this terrible catastrophe leaves you bereft.

Frenchmen, barons, I see you dying in my name,
And I am able neither to defend nor protect you.
1865 May God, who is always true, come to your aid!
Oliver, my brother, you above all I must not fail,
I shall die of sorrow if nothing else kills me first.
My lord, companion, let's go to fight some more!'

141

Count Roland has returned to the fray.
1870 He wields Durendal and strikes like a brave warrior.
He has sliced Faldrun of Pui clean in two,
And twenty-four of their most renowned knights.
Never again will any man thirst so much for revenge!
Just as a deer runs before a pack of hounds,
1875 So the pagans are now fleeing before Roland.
The archbishop said: 'You excel yourself!
Valour such as this is befitting for a knight,
Who bears arms and rides upon a fine horse:
And he should be invincible and fierce in battle,
1880 Otherwise he's not worth tuppence-ha'penny;
He'd be better off as a monk, cloistered in a monastery,
Where he can spend his time praying for our sins.'
Roland replies: 'Attack! Show them no mercy!'
On hearing this, the Franks have renewed their efforts,
1885 But the Christians sustained heavy losses.

142

A man who knows no prisoners will be taken
Defends himself ferociously in a battle such as this,
Which is why the Franks are as fierce as lions.
Here comes Marsilie, looking every inch a knight!
1890 He sits astride a horse he calls Gaignun.
He spurs him on and goes to strike Bevon,
Who was the lord of Beaune and Dijon.
He shatters his shield and smashes his hauberk,

Knocking him dead without further ado.
Then he has dispatched Ivoire and Ivon,   1895
Together with Gerard of Roussillon.
Count Roland is not far away from him.
He said to the pagan: 'May God damn you!
You have no right to be killing my companions.
Before we part you'll be hit hard for this,   1900
And today you will learn my sword's name.'
He goes to strike him, every inch a true knight,
And the count has cut off his right hand,
Then he takes the head of Jurfaleu the Blond,
This man was the son of King Marsilie.   1905
The pagans cry out: 'Help us, Mohammed!
Ye gods, help us take revenge on Charles!
He brought these villains into our land.
They will die before they leave the battefield.'
They said to one another: 'Let's get out of here!'   1910
On hearing this, a hundred thousand pagans flee.
Whoever calls them back, they will not return.   AOI

143

What use is this? Marsilie has fled the field,
But still his uncle Marganice remains,
Who rules over Carthage, Alfrere, and Garmalie,   1915
And Ethiopia, one of those accursèd lands.
He governs the race of black men;
They have huge noses and flapping ears,
And here they number more than fifty thousand.
These men ride out ferociously and furiously,   1920
Then they shout out the pagan war cry.
Roland spoke thus: 'We shall be martyred here.
I can see now that we do not have long to live,
But damn anyone who fails first to make them pay!
Strike, my lords, with your polished swords,   1925
Defend yourselves and fight for your lives*
So that fair France should not through us be shamed!
When Charles, my lord, arrives on this battlefield,

He will see so many slaughtered Saracens,
1930 That he'll find fifteen of them dead for each one of us,
And he will not refrain from blessing us for this.'   AOI

144

When Roland sees the accursèd races
Who are blacker than the blackest of ink,
With only their teeth showing any whiteness,
1935 The count said this: 'Now I can see truly
That today we shall die, I am sure of this.
Frenchmen, strike, for with you I return to the fray.'
Said Oliver: 'A curse on him who tarries!'
On hearing this, the French surge forward.

145

1940 When the pagans saw that few Frenchmen remained,
They feel reassured and gain in confidence.
They say to one another: 'The emperor was wrong!'
Marganice was mounted on a sorrel warhorse,
He urges it forward with his golden spurs,
1945 And strikes Oliver from behind in the back.
He shatters his shiny hauberk into his flesh,
And drives his spear right through his chest.
Afterwards he says: 'You have taken a good beating!
Charles the Great will regret he left you in the passes!
1950 He did us wrong, it is not right that he should boast,
For with you alone I have fully avenged our men.'

146

Oliver realizes that he is mortally wounded.
He wields Halteclere, with its gleaming blade.
He strikes Marganice's golden, pointed helmet,
1955 Knocking the decorative flowers and gems to the ground.

He slices his skull in two down to his front teeth,
Lifts his sword again and has struck him dead.
Upon which he said: 'A curse on you, pagan!
I can't deny that Charles has suffered losses here.
But never to your wife, nor to any lady that you know,   1960
In the kingdom from which you hail will you boast
That you took away even a pennyworth of my wealth,
Or did any harm to me, or anyone else.'
Then he cries out to Roland for his help.   AOI

147

Oliver realizes that he is fatally wounded.   1965
His thirst for revenge will never be sated:
He renews his blows now, like a true warrior,
Smashing to bits many lances and bucklers,
Feet and fists, saddles and ribs.
If you had seen him dismembering Saracens,   1970
Piling dead bodies one on top of another,
You would have known what true bravery was.
Nor does he wish to forget Charles's war cry.
He shouts out 'Monjoie!' loud and clear.
He calls out to Roland, his friend and peer.   1975
'My lord, companion, join me in battle now.
Today our parting will be most painful.'   AOI

148

Roland looks Oliver squarely in the face.
It was livid and wan, pale and ashen.
Bright red blood streamed down his body,   1980
Falling to the ground around him in spurts.
'My God!' said the count. 'What shall I do now?
My lord, companion, alas for your heroism!
No man will ever be as valiant as you.
Ah, fair France, how bereft you will be today   1985
Of good vassals, confounded and cast down!

Our emperor will suffer a terrible loss!'
On saying this, he passes out astride his horse.   AOI

149

       See how Roland has passed out astride his horse
1990   And Oliver has been fatally wounded.
       He has bled so much that his eyes are dim:
       He cannot see clearly enough, at any distance,
       To be able to recognize anyone at all.
       So when he comes across his companion,
1995   He strikes him on his bejewelled gold helmet,
       Splitting it from the top to the nose guard,
       But without harming his head in any way.
       When struck thus, Roland stares at him,
       And he asks him gently and softly:
2000   'My lord, companion, did you mean to do this?
       For this is Roland, who has always loved you so!
       You had in no way issued me with a challenge.'*
       Said Oliver: 'Now I can hear you speaking,
       But I cannot see you. May God watch over you!
2005   Did I strike you? I beg you to forgive me!'
       Roland replies: 'I have not been harmed at all.
       I forgive you for this now, and before God.'
       After Roland has said this, each bows to the other.
       See now how they part with such great love.

150

2010   Oliver realizes that death has him in its grasp.
       Both his eyes are swivelling in their sockets,
       He is losing his hearing and is completely blind.
       He dismounts and lies down on the ground.
       As loudly as he can he proclaims his mea culpa,
2015   With his hands together, raised towards the sky.
       He prays to God to let him enter paradise,
       And he blessed Charles and France the fair,

Also his companion Roland, above all other men.
His heart stops beating; his helmet falls forward.
His entire body crumples onto the ground.   2020
The count is dead, for he is no more.
Valiant Roland laments and weeps for him.
Never on earth will you hear a more grief-stricken man.

151

Now Roland can see that his friend is dead,
Stretched out on the ground, with his face down.   2025
He began most tenderly to lament him:
'My lord, companion, alas for your great boldness.
We have spent many days and years together:
You never did me wrong, nor did I ever let you down.
Now you are dead, it pains me to go on living!'   2030
On saying this, the marquis passes out,
Sitting astride his horse called Veillantif.
He is held on by his stirrups of pure gold:
Whichever way he leans, he cannot fall off.

152

As soon as Roland regained consciousness,   2035
Recovered and came round from his faint,
He immediately saw the full extent of the carnage.
The French are dead, he has lost all of them,
Except for the archbishop and Gautier del Hum.
He has come back down from the mountains,   2040
Having fought tooth and nail against the Spanish.
His men are dead, vanquished by the pagans.
He has no choice but to flee down the valleys,
And he calls out to Roland to come to his aid:
'O noble count, most valiant of men, where are you?   2045
I have never been afraid with you by my side.
It's me, Gautier, who defeated Maëlgut,
The nephew of white-haired old Droün.

My bravery meant I used to be your favourite.
2050 My lance is shattered and my shield broken,
My hauberk is coming apart and in pieces,
My body has been pierced by lances all the way through.
I am about to die, but I have made them pay dearly.'
As he was saying this, Roland heard him.
2055 He spurs on his horse and gallops over to him.   AOI

153

Roland is sorrowful and was full of rage.
He starts to strike out in the middle of the fray.
He has thrown twenty men of Spain down dead,
And Gautier six, and the archbishop five.
2060 The pagans say: 'These men are arch-villains.
Make sure, my lords, that they don't get away alive!
Anyone who doesn't attack should be deemed a traitor,
And called a coward if he allows them to escape!'
Then the great noise and shouting begins again,
2065 They are renewing their attack on all sides.   AOI

154

Count Roland was a worthy warrior,
Gautier del Hum is a most excellent knight,
And the archbishop is a noble, experienced man.
None of them wishes at any price to leave the others.
2070 Each strikes pagans in the middle of the fray.
A thousand Saracens dismount from their horses,
And forty thousand remain on horseback.
It seems to me that they dare not approach them,
So they throw lances and spears in their direction,
2075 Javelins and darts, pikes and assegais.*
With the first wave, they have killed Gautier,
Pierced all the way through Turpin of Rheims's shield,
Penetrated his helmet and wounded him in the head,
Smashed his hauberk and ripped it to shreds.

His body has been pierced by spears all the way through. 2080
They kill his warhorse from underneath him.
What sorrow now as the archbishop falls in battle! AOI

155

When Turpin of Rheims realizes he has been felled,
His body pierced by spears all the way through,
This brave man swiftly gets back on his feet. 2085
He looks at Roland, then runs over towards him,
And spoke thus: 'No way am I beaten yet.
Never will a worthy knight be taken alive.'
He draws Almace, his shiny steel sword,
He strikes, in the fray, a thousand blows or more. 2090
Charles said afterwards that he had spared no one,
When he found four hundred bodies piled up around him,
Some with flesh wounds, some pierced through.
There were also those who had been decapitated.
Thus state the annals and an eyewitness to the battle, 2095
The noble Giles, for whom God performs miracles,
And who made the charter at the monastery of Laon.
If you don't know this, you have not understood properly.

156

Count Roland continues to fight heroically,
But he has a fever and is sweating profusely. 2100
His head pounds with a searing pain:
His temples have ruptured from blowing the horn.
But he wants to know if Charles will return:
So he takes up the oliphant and blows it feebly.
The emperor stood stock still, and listened. 2105
'My lords,' he said, 'we are in dire straits!
My nephew Roland will leave us this very day.
I can hear from his horn that he'll not live much longer.
If we wish to be there, we need to ride quickly!
Sound all the bugles you have in this army!' 2110

Sixty thousand of them are blown so loudly
That the hills resound with them and the valleys echo.
The pagans hear them and do not take this lightly:
They say to one another: 'We will soon meet Charles!'

157

2115 The pagans say: 'The emperor is returning.   AOI
      Just hear the bugles of the French sounding.
      If Charles comes, we will suffer great losses.
      If Roland survives, then this war continues,
      And we have lost Spain, this land of ours.'
2120 Four hundred men gather with helmets fastened,
      Believing themselves to be the bravest in battle.
      They attack Roland ferociously and without mercy.
      As for the count, he now has his hands full.   AOI

158

      When Count Roland sees them coming for him,
2125 He gathers his strength, growing fierce and alert:
      As long as he is alive, he will never flee.
      He sits astride his horse, which is called Veillantif,
      Urges it forward with his spurs of pure gold.
      He goes to attack them all in the midst of the fray,
2130 And he has Archbishop Turpin by his side.
      The pagans say to one another: 'Friends, get out of here!
      We have heard the horns of the French army:
      Charles, the mighty king, is returning!'

159

      Count Roland never had any time for a coward,
2135 Nor an arrogant man, nor a low-born churl,
      Nor any knight who was not supremely brave.
      He called out to Archbishop Turpin:
      'My lord, you are on foot, yet I am on horseback.

For your sake I will take my stand here:
We'll face what comes, good or evil, together.   2140
For no man on earth shall I ever leave you.
Today we shall make the pagans pay for this attack.
The best blows of all will be dealt by Durendal!'
Said the archbishop: 'Cursèd be he who does not strike well!
Charles is returning and he will avenge you royally.'   2145

160

The pagans say: 'Woe betide us all!
What a dark day dawned for us today!
We have lost our lords and our comrades.
Brave Charles is returning with his great army:
We can hear the clarion calls of the French.   2150
Their cries of "Monjoie!" make a deafening noise.
Count Roland is of such great ferocity,
That he will never be defeated by mortal man.
Let's aim at him, but then let's leave him be!'
And they do just that: with many darts and javelins,   2155
Spears and lances and pennoned pikes.
They have shattered and smashed Roland's shield,
Piercing his hauberk and ripping it to shreds.
Yet none of these weapons cuts into his skin.
In thirty places, though, they have wounded Veillantif,   2160
And have dispatched him from under the count.
The pagans now flee the field and leave him be.
Count Roland remains there on foot.   AOI

161

The pagans flee the field, angry and distraught.
They hurry towards Spain as fast as they can.   2165
Count Roland has no means left to pursue them.
He has just lost Veillantif, his warhorse.
Like it or not, he remains there on foot.
He went to give aid to Archbishop Turpin.

2170 He unfastened his golden helmet from his head,
      Then removed his shiny, lightweight hauberk,
      And he cut up his tunic into pieces,
      Stuffing the material into his most serious wounds.
      Then he embraced him, clasping him to his chest.
2175 After this he has lain him gently on the green grass.
      Roland beseeched him, very softly:
      'Oh, noble friend, pray give me leave to go now!
      Our companions, whom we held so dear,
      Are now dead; we should not leave them thus.
2180 I want to go to seek and identify each one,
      To lay them out and line them up before you.'
      Said the archbishop: 'Do go, but come back!
      The field is ours, thank God, yours and mine.'

162

      Roland sets off, walking the battlefield alone.
2185 He searches the valleys and he searches the hills.
      There he found Gerin and Gerer his companion,
      And he found Berenger and Oton;
      Further on he found Anseïs and Samson,
      He found old Gerard of Roussillon.
2190 One by one he gathered them, this brave man,
      And with them all he returned to the archbishop,
      Arranging them in rows around his knees.
      The archbishop cannot help but weep.
      He raises his hand and blesses them.
2195 Then he said: 'What a sorry day for you, my lords!
      May God in His glory receive all your souls,
      And place them on a bed of holy flowers in paradise!
      My own death fills me with great anguish
      Since I will never again see our mighty emperor.'

163

2200 Roland sets off again to search the battlefield.
      He has found his companion, Oliver.

He embraced him, clasping him closely to his chest.
As best he can he brings him to the archbishop,
Lays him beside the others on a shield,
And the archbishop absolved and blessed them.   2205
Then their pain and sorrow grow yet more acute.
Roland speaks thus: 'Fair companion Oliver,
You were the son of the powerful Duke Rainier
Who held the march in the Vale of Runers.
When it came to smashing lances, piercing shields,   2210
Vanquishing and thwarting arrogant men,
Or helping and counselling worthy men,
Or vanquishing and thwarting villains,
There is no finer knight than you in the world.'

164

When Count Roland sees his peers are dead,   2215
And Oliver, whom he loved so dearly,
His heart melted, and he begins to cry.
The blood drained entirely from his face:
So great was his sorrow, he could not stay upright:
Like it or not, he falls to the ground in a faint.   2220
Said the archbishop: 'What a sorry day for you, brave knight!'

165

When the archbishop saw Roland in a faint,
He felt a greater sorrow than he had ever known.
He reached out his hand and seized the oliphant.
There is a river running through Rencesvals.   2225
He tries to reach it to get some water for Roland.
Taking tiny steps, he stumbles towards it,
But is so weak that he can barely move forward.
He has bled so much that all his strength deserts him.
Sooner than it would take to cover just one acre,   2230
His heart gives out, and he has slumped forward:
His own death is now closing in on him.

166

Count Roland comes round from his faint.
He gets to his feet, but is in intense pain.
2235　He looks downhill and then he looks uphill:
On the green grass, beyond his companions,
He can see the illustrious baron lying there.
The archbishop, God's chosen representative,
Is proclaiming his mea culpa, and looking upwards;
2240　With his hands together, raised towards the sky,
He prays to God to let him enter paradise.
Archbishop Turpin is dead, Charles's warrior.
With mighty battles and most moving sermons
He dedicated his life to fighting against pagans.
2245　May God give him His holy blessing!　　　　　　AOI

167

Count Roland sees the archbishop on the ground;
He can see his bowels spilling out of his body.
His brains are running down his forehead.
Over his chest, squarely in the middle,
2250　He has now crossed his fair white hands.*
He intones a heartfelt lament, as is the custom in his land:
'Alas, noble lord, most highly born knight,
Today I commend you to Almighty God:
No man will ever serve Him more willingly.
2255　Since the Apostles, there has never been a better preacher,
For upholding the faith and attracting converts.
May your soul endure no pain or hardship,
May the gates of paradise stand wide open for it.'

168

Roland realizes now that his death is at hand:
2260　His brains are spilling out through his ears.
He prays first that God will call his peers to Him,

Then he prays for himself, to Archangel Gabriel.
So as to be beyond reproach, he grasped the oliphant,
And in his other hand, his sword Durendal.
Further than a crossbow can fire a bolt,   2265
He walks towards Spain, towards some fallow land.
On a low mound, in the shade of a fine tree,
There are four slabs cut from marble.
On the green grass he has fallen on his back,
Fainting on the spot, because his death is at hand.   2270

169

The hills are high and the trees very tall.
There are four slabs of gleaming marble.
On the green grass, Count Roland has fallen in a faint.
All the while, a Saracen is observing him
And lying among the others, he is playing dead;   2275
His body and his face are smeared with blood.
He has risen to his feet and quickly runs over.
He was handsome, strong, and very bold.
His pride impels him now to fatal impetuosity:
He grabs Roland's body and his weapons,   2280
Saying these words: 'Charles's nephew is defeated!
I will carry this sword off to the land of Araby.'
As he draws it, the count starts to come round.

170

Roland realizes that his sword is being taken.
He opened his eyes and says to the Saracen: 2285
'You do not look to me like one of ours!'
He hangs on to the oliphant, for he will never let it go,
And strikes him on his helmet with its gems set in gold.
He shatters the metal, his skull, and other bones.
He's sent both eyes flying from their sockets,   2290
And he has knocked him down dead at his feet.
After this he says: 'You swine! How dare you

Lay your hands on me, whether provoked or not?
When people hear of this, they will think you a fool.
2295 Now the wide end of my oliphant is cracked,
The crystal and gold decoration have fallen off.'

171

Roland realizes that his sight has failed.
He got to his feet, gathers his strength as best he can.
All the colour has drained from his face.
2300 He sees one of the slabs of stone before him.
He strikes it ten times, in sorrow and frustration:
Steel grates on stone, but it neither cracks nor splinters.
'Alas,' said the count, 'Blessed Mary, help me!
Alas, fair Durendal, this is a dark day for you!
2305 Since I am dying, I have no further need of you.
With you I have won so many battles in the field
And have conquered so many vast lands,
That Charles of the snowy white beard now holds.
No man who flees before another should own you!
2310 A very fine knight has wielded you for a long time.
There will never be another like him in blessed France.'

172

Roland struck a blow on the slab of sardonyx.
Steel grates on stone, but it neither breaks nor cracks.
When he saw that he was unable to destroy it,
2315 He begins to lament privately for his sword:
'Alas, Durendal! How bright and shiny you are!
You gleam and shine so brightly in the sunlight!
When Charles was in the valleys of Maurienne,
God in heaven sent him an angel as a messenger
2320 To tell him to give you to a count and captain.
So the noble and great king girded me with it.
With this sword I conquered for him Anjou and Brittany,
And with it I conquered for him Poitou and Maine,
And with it I conquered for him Normandy the free.

With it I conquered Provence and Aquitaine   2325
And Lombardy and the whole region of Romagna.
With it I conquered for him Bavaria and all of Flanders,
And Burgundy and the whole of Apulia,
Constantinople, where he received an oath of homage,
And Saxony where he can do exactly as he pleases.   2330
With it I conquered for him Scotland and Ireland
And England, while he himself stayed at home.
With it I have conquered so many lands and countries
Over which white-bearded Charles continues to rule.
I feel anguish and sorrow for this sword.   2335
I would rather die than leave it among pagans.
God, Our Father, save France from this humiliation!'

173

Roland struck down on a piece of dark rock,
With greater force than I can possibly describe.
Sword grates on stone, but it neither shatters nor breaks,   2340
It rebounds back up, rather, silhouetted against the sky.
When the count sees that he cannot destroy it,
He laments his sword softly to himself:
'Alas, Durendal! How fair and holy you are!
There are many relics in your golden pommel: 2345
One of Saint Peter's teeth and a drop of Saint Basil's blood,
A lock of hair from my lord Saint Denis,
As well as a piece of Blessed Mary's clothing.
It is not right that pagans should own you:
By rights you should be served by Christians.   2350
No man capable of cowardice should have you!
I shall have conquered with you many vast lands,
Which Charles with his hoary beard now rules.
As a result, the emperor is mighty and powerful!'

174

Roland realizes that death has him in its grasp,   2355
First his head, then moving down towards his heart.

He ran over to the shade of a pine tree,
Where he lay face down on the green grass,
Placing underneath him his sword and oliphant.
2360 He turned his head so it was facing the pagans.
He has done this because he fervently wants
Charles and all his retinue to be able to say
That the noble count died a conquering hero.
Over and over he proclaimed his mea culpa,
2365 And in penance offered up his glove to God.   AOI

175

Roland realizes that he has no time left.
He is lying atop a steep hill facing Spain.
With one hand he has been beating his breast:
'Almighty God, to you I proclaim my mea culpa:
2370 On account of my sins, both great and small,
All those I have committed since the day I was born
To this very day, as I lie here mortally wounded!'
He has held out his right-hand glove to God:
Angels descend from heaven to meet him.   AOI

176

2375 Count Roland lay down in the shade of a pine.
He has turned his face towards Spain.
He began to reminisce about various things:
About the many lands he had valiantly conquered,
About France the fair, and about his kinsmen,
2380 About Charlemagne, his lord, who raised him.
He cannot help but weep and sigh,
But he does not wish to neglect his own salvation.
He proclaims his mea culpa, begs God's mercy:
'Father most true, who never let us down,
2385 You raised Saint Lazarus from the dead,
And you kept Daniel safe in the lions' den,
I beg you, safeguard my soul from all the perils

Caused by the sins I have committed in my life!'
He offered up his right-hand glove to God;
The angel Gabriel took it from his hand.   2390
Roland let his head fall over his arm,
With his hands together, he went to meet his Maker.
God sent down His angel Cherubin to him,
And Saint Michael of the Peril,
The angel Gabriel himself came to join them;   2395
They carried the count's soul off to heaven.

177

Count Roland is dead, his soul is with God in heaven.
The emperor now arrives in Rencesvals,
Where there is no pathway or track,
No waste ground, no square foot or yard of land,   2400
That is not covered with Frenchmen or pagans.
Charles cries out: 'Where are you, fair nephew?
Where is the archbishop and Count Oliver?
Where is Gerin and his companion Gerer?
Where is Oton and Count Berenger,   2405
Ivon and Ivoire, whom I held so dear?
What has become of Engeler the Gascon,
Duke Samson, and Anseïs the fierce?
Where is old Gerard of Roussillon,
And the twelve peers that I had left behind?'   2410
What good was all this, when no reply came?
'God!' said the king. 'I am livid with rage
That I was not here when the battle started!'
In his great distress, he pulls at his beard.
Tears stream from the eyes of his brave knights: 2415
Twenty thousand of them faint on the ground,
And Duke Naimon is overcome with pity!

178

There is not a single knight or baron
Who does not weep uncontrollably from pity.

2420 They weep for their sons, brothers, and nephews,
And for their friends and their liege lords.
Most of them fall into a faint on the ground.
Yet Duke Naimon's response was worthy,
Being the first to say to the emperor:

2425 'Look over there, just two leagues from here,
You can see clouds of dust rising from the roads.
There must be huge numbers of pagans there.
Pray ride out! Go and take revenge for this sorrow!'
'Ah, God!' said Charles. 'They are already so far away!

2430 I beseech you, grant me just reparation and honour:
They have taken from me the flower of fair France.'
The king gives orders to Gebuïn and Oton,
To Tedbald of Rheims and to Count Miles;
'Guard the battlefield, and these valleys and hills!

2435 Leave the dead exactly as they are lying:
Make sure no beast or lion touches them,
Nor should any squire, or servant touch them.
I forbid any of you to touch them either
Until God allows our return to this battlefield.'

2440 They reply with great affection and loyalty:
'Just emperor, dear lord, we shall do this!'
They keep a thousand of their men with them.   AOI

179

The emperor orders his bugles to be sounded,
Then the brave man rides out with his great host.

2445 They have made those of Spain turn tail and flee,
They pursue them with one common purpose.
When the king sees that the sun is going down,
He dismounts onto the green grass of a meadow,
Then he prostrates himself, praying to God

2450 That for his sake He stop the sun in its tracks
In order to delay nightfall and extend daylight.
And now here comes an angel, who often speaks with him,
Rapidly he gives him the following orders:
'Charles, ride out, for you will not lack daylight!

God knows that you have lost the flower of France.   2455
You can exact revenge on this criminal race.'
On hearing this, the emperor got back on his horse.   AOI

180

God performed a great miracle for Charlemagne,
For he has stopped the sun in its tracks.
The pagans flee, but the Franks are in hot pursuit.   2460
In the Val-Tenebros they catch up with them.
They are driving them back towards Saragossa.
They are killing them with their mighty blows,
Cutting off all the main roads and their escape routes.
The river Ebro now stretches out before them: 2465
It is very deep, dangerous, and fast-flowing.
There are no barges, ferries, or lighters.
The pagans appeal to one of their gods, Tervagant,
Then they jump in, but there is no one to protect them.
Those wearing armour are the heaviest: 2470
Some sink to the bottom immediately,
Others are carried downstream by the current.
Even the luckiest ones swallow so much water
That they all drown and suffer terrible agony.
The French cry out: 'Rue the day you met Roland!'   AOI 2475

181

When Charles sees that all the pagans are dead,
Some of them slain but the majority of them drowned,
His knights are allowed great quantities of booty.
The noble king now dismounts from his horse,
And prostrates himself giving thanks to God.   2480
When he gets back to his feet, the sun sets.
The emperor said: 'It is time to pitch camp.
It is too late to return now to Rencesvals.
Our horses are weary and exhausted:
Unsaddle them and take off their bridles,   2485

Let them cool down in these meadows.'
The Franks reply: 'My lord, you speak wisely.'   AOI

182

The emperor has pitched his camp.
The French dismount in open countryside,
2490   They have taken the saddles off their horses
And remove the golden bridles from their heads,
Turning them loose on the meadows' young grass.
They have provided for them as best they can.
The most weary now sleep directly on the ground.
2495   That night they post no sentinels to keep watch.

183

The emperor has lain down in a meadow:
The warrior places his mighty spear by his head.
That night he did not want to take off his armour.
He was still wearing his gleaming, golden hauberk,
2500   Still had his helmet fastened with its gems set in gold,
And still had Joiuse girded, his peerless sword,
Which reflects light in thirty different ways every day.
We have lots of stories to relate about the lance
With which Our Lord was wounded on the cross.*
2505   By the grace of God, Charles owns the metal tip,
And has had it mounted in the golden pommel.
Because of this honour and divine favour,
The name Joiuse was bestowed upon the sword.
French warriors must always remember this.
2510   For this is why their war cry is 'Monjoie!',
And why no race can hold out against them.

184

The night is clear and the moon shines brightly.
Charles is lying down, but he grieves for Roland,

And feels intense sorrow on account of Oliver
And of the twelve peers, and all the Frenchmen   2515
Whom he'd left at Rencesvals, dead and bloody.
He cannot help but weep and lament.
And he prays to God to save their souls.
The king is weary, for his sorrow is so great:
Finally he fell asleep, he could not stay awake.   2520
The meadows are now covered with sleeping Franks.
Not a single horse can remain on its feet:
The ones needing to graze do so lying down.
A man learns a good deal from intense suffering.

185

Charles sleeps the sleep of a troubled man.   2525
God has sent the angel Gabriel to him.
He commands him to watch over the emperor.
The angel spends the whole night by his head.
Announcing to him, through a dream,*
That a battle was to be fought against him,   2530
The meaning he conveyed was deeply ominous.
Charles looked up towards the heavens,
He sees thunderstorms, gales, and hail,
Torrential rain, cataclysmic tempests,
With flames and conflagrations all around,   2535
Which rain down upon his entire army.
Their ash and applewood lances burst into flames,
As do their shields as far as their pure gold bosses.
The shafts of all the sharp lances shatter.
The hauberks and steel helmets grate.   2540
He sees his men suffering great torment.
Bears and leopards then want to devour them,
Serpents and vipers, dragons and demons,
With more than thirty thousand griffins.
Each one of them sets upon the French,   2545
And the French cry out: 'Charlemagne, help us!'
The king is racked with sorrow and pity.
He wants to go to them, but there is an obstacle.

A huge lion is coming towards him from a wood:
2550　It was terrifying, proud, and extremely ferocious.
It goes to attack him and pounces upon him.
They grapple with each other in close combat.
But he cannot tell which will win and which will lose.
The emperor is still sleeping soundly.

186

2555　After this, he has yet another dream.
He was in France, at Aix, beside a marble slab,
To which a bear cub was attached with two chains.
He saw thirty bears approaching from the Ardennes,*
Each one speaking as if he were human.
2560　They were saying: 'My lord, give him back to us!
It is not right that he remain any longer with you.
It is our duty to come to the aid of our kin.'
A hound now comes running out of his palace.
It attacks the biggest bear from among them,
2565　On the green grass beyond the other bears.
There the king watches this mighty combat,
But he cannot tell which has the upper hand.
This is what God's angel shows the warrior.
Charles sleeps on until daybreak next morning.

187

2570　King Marsilie is fleeing towards Saragossa.
He has dismounted in the shade of an olive tree,
Where his sword, helmet, and byrnie are removed.
He lies down on the grass in an undignified manner.
He has completely lost his right hand,
2575　Fainting and in agony because of the loss of blood.
His wife Bramimunde stands before him,
Weeping and crying out; her grief is intense.
With her there are more than twenty thousand men,
All of whom are cursing Charles and fair France.

They run over to a statue of Apollo in a crypt,   2580
Where they rail against him, hurling ugly insults.
'Alas, you wicked god, why have you shamed us?
Why did you allow this king of ours to be defeated?
You reward badly those who serve you loyally.'
Then they snatch from him his sceptre and his crown,   2585
And they hang him by his hands from a column.
Then they knock him to the ground at their feet,
And smash him to smithereens with great clubs.
And they rip out Tervagant's carbuncle
And they kick Mohammed into a ditch,   2590
To be mauled and trampled by pigs and dogs.

188

Marsilie has now regained consciousness.
He has himself carried into his vaulted chamber,
Decorated with colourful painting and writing.
And Bramimunde, his queen, weeps for him.   2595
She tears out her hair, and bewails her lot,
Continuing in this vein at the top of her voice:
'Alas, Saragossa, how deprived you are today
Of the noble king who ruled over you!
Our gods have committed a heinous crime,   2600
Since this morning they failed him in battle.
The emir will indeed be guilty of cowardice
If he does not do battle with this bold race of men,
Who are so fierce that they care not for their lives.
Their emperor with his hoary beard   2605
Is valiant and reckless in his great courage:
If there is a battle, he will never flee.
What a great shame we have no one to kill him!'

189

The mighty emperor in his great majesty
Has been a full seven years in Spain,   2610

Taking castles and quite a few cities.
King Marsilie has taken the necessary steps:
From the outset he had letters written and sealed,
And then sent to Baligant in Babylon—
2615 This is the emir, a survivor from ancient times,
Who is older even than Virgil and Homer—
Asking the warrior to come to his aid in Saragossa.
If he does not come, he will abandon his gods
And all the idols he habitually worships,
2620 And he will convert to holy Christianity,
And will aim to make peace with Charlemagne.
The emir is far away, and has taken his time.
He summons his people from forty lands.
He has had his great galleys made ready,
2625 His warships, barges, boats, and ships.
There is a port on the coast by Alexandria
Where he has had his great fleet assembled.
This is in May, on the first day of summer:
He has launched all his forces out to sea.

190

2630 The forces of this evil race are immense,
They sail swiftly, row and steer their ships.
Atop their masts and on the lofty prows
There is many a carbuncle and lantern:
They cast such a bright light from above
2635 That throughout the night the sea is resplendent.
And as they arrive in the land of Spain,
The entire country is lit up and illuminated.
News of their arrival even reaches Marsilie.   AOI

191

These pagan peoples do not want to tarry.
2640 They leave the sea and sail up the river,
Past Marbrise and then past Marbrose.
All their ships wind their way up the Ebro.

There is many a carbuncle and lantern:
So all night long their way was brightly lit.
The very next day they arrive in Saragossa. AOI 2645

192

The day is fine and the sun is shining.
The emir disembarks from his river barge:
Espaneliz emerges with him, on his right.
They are followed by seventeen kings,
And lots of dukes and counts, I know not how many. 2650
Under a laurel tree in the middle of a field,
They spread a white brocaded cloth on the grass,
Upon which they place an ivory throne.
The pagan Baligant sits down upon it.
All the rest of them remain standing. 2655
Their overlord was the first to speak.
'Listen to me, my bold and brave knights!
King Charles, the emperor of the Franks,
Should not so much as eat without my say-so.
All over Spain he has waged a bitter war on me: 2660
I will pursue him as far as France the fair,
And will not give up for as long as I live
Until he is either dead or admits defeat.'
He strikes his knee with his right glove.

193

Having said this, he resolved before all 2665
That all the world's gold would not stop him
From going to Aix, where Charles holds court.*
His men approve of this and recommend it.
Then he summoned two of his knights,
One was called Clarifan, the other Clariën: 2670
'You are the sons of King Maltraïen,
Who often willingly carried messages for me.
I command you now to go to Saragossa,
And to inform Marsilie on my behalf

2675 That I have come to help him against the French.
If I have the chance, there will be a mighty battle.
Pray give him this folded glove decorated with gold,
And make sure he puts it on his right hand.
Please give him also this staff of pure gold,
2680 And tell him to come pay homage for his fief.
I shall go to France to wage war on Charles:
If he does not prostrate himself at my feet
And abandon the Christian religion,
I shall forcibly remove the crown from his head.'
2685 The pagans reply: 'Sire, you speak well!'

194

Said Baligant: 'Now ride out, my lords!
One of you take the glove, the other the staff!'
And they reply: 'Noble lord, we will do this.'
They ride until they come to Saragossa.
2690 They go through ten gates, cross over four bridges,
Along all the streets where the townsfolk live.
From the citadel above, as they approach
The palace, they heard a good deal of noise.
There are to be found many of the pagan race:
2695 They are weeping and crying in great sorrow,
Complaining to their gods, Tervagant, Mohammed,
And Apollo, who have done them no good at all.
They say to one another: 'What's to become of us?
We miserable wretches have met a sorry fate!
2700 We have lost our king, Marsilie:
Count Roland cut off his right hand yesterday.
We no longer have Jurfaleu the Blond.
They will now control the whole of Spain.'
The two messengers dismount at the block.

195

2705 They leave their horses under an olive tree:
Two Saracens took hold of their reins.

And the messengers held each other by their cloaks,
Then they climbed up to the lofty palace.
As they entered the vaulted bedchamber,
Despite good intentions they greeted him clumsily: 2710
'May Mohammed, who has us all in his sway,
And Tervagant, and our lord Apollo,
Save the king and watch over the queen.'
Said Bramimunde: 'Now I have heard it all!
These gods of ours are impotent cowards: 2715
They showed their weakness in Rencesvals.
They allowed all our knights to be killed,
And they let my lord down badly in battle.
He has lost his right hand, severed completely.
Indeed, mighty Count Roland sliced it off.   2720
Charles will now be master of all Spain.
Reduced to misery, what is to become of me?
Alas, if only someone would kill me.'   AOI

196

Said Clarïen: 'My lady, do not speak thus!
We bring a message from the pagan Baligant: 2725
He says that he will act as Marsilie's protector.
As proof he sends him his glove and his staff.
We have, out on the Ebro, four thousand boats,
Warships, barges, and swift lighters.
There are galleys aplenty, I can't say how many.   2730
The emir is powerful and mighty,
He will pursue Charlemagne into France,
He intends either to kill or defeat him!'
Said Bramimunde: 'He doesn't need to go so far!
You can find the Franks much closer to home: 2735
He's been in this land already seven full years.
The emperor is a ferocious warrior,
Who would rather die than ever flee the field.
He treats all mortal kings as if they were children:
Charles is not frightened of any man alive.'   2740

197

'Stop this now!' said King Marsilie.
'Speak to me, my lords!' he said to the messengers.
'Can you not see that I am near death?
I have neither son, nor daughter, nor heir:
2745　I did have a son: he was killed last night.
Tell my lord that he should come to see me.
The emir is the rightful ruler of Spain:
I cede it freely to him, if he wishes to take it,
So that he might defend it against the French.
2750　I'll give him good advice regarding Charlemagne:
He will have defeated him within a month from now.
You may take him the keys of Saragossa:
Tell him not to leave if he is willing to trust me.'
And they reply: 'My lord, you speak the truth.'　　　　AOI

198

2755　Marsilie spoke thus: 'Charles the emperor
Has killed my men and laid my lands to waste,
He has taken by force and destroyed my towns.
He slept last night on the banks of the Ebro,
Not seven leagues from here by my reckoning.
2760　Tell the emir to march his army forward.
I ask him through you to join battle with them.'
He has given them the keys to Saragossa.
Both messengers bowed down before him,
Take their leave and with these words went away.

199

2765　The two messengers have mounted their horses.
Swiftly they ride forth from out of the city.
Greatly perturbed, they come to the emir.
They present him with the keys of Saragossa.
Said Baligant: 'What did you find there?

Where is Marsilie, whom I had sent for?'   2770
Said Clarïen: 'He is mortally wounded.
Yesterday, the emperor was riding through the pass,
Intending to go home to France the fair.
He selected a most illustrious rearguard:
Count Roland, his nephew, stayed behind,   2775
And Oliver and all of the twelve peers,
With twenty thousand armed Frenchmen.
Bold King Marsilie attacked them.
He and Roland faced each other on the battlefield:
He struck him such a blow with Durendal   2780
That he cut his right hand clean off his arm.
He killed his son, whom he loved so much,
And the brave men he had brought with him.
He fled away, for he could hold out no longer.
The emperor pursued him a good distance.   2785
The king asks you to come to his aid:
He freely cedes to you the kingdom of Spain.'
Baligant then falls into deepest thought:
He almost goes out of his mind with sorrow.   AOI

200

'My lord emir,' said Clarïen to him,   2790
'There was a battle yesterday in Rencesvals:
Roland was killed, and Count Oliver,
With the twelve peers, so cherished by Charles.
Twenty thousand Frenchmen with them died.
King Marsilie lost his right hand in this battle.   2795
And the emperor pursued him a good distance.
Not a single knight from this land is left,
Who hasn't been killed or drowned in the Ebro.
The French are camped on the river bank.
They have advanced so far into our lands,   2800
That if you want, you can make their return hazardous.'
And a fierce gleam comes into Baligant's eye:
His heart is joyful and full of glee.
He stands up tall from his chair of state,
Then cries out: 'My lords, do not tarry!   2805

Leave your ships, mount your horses and ride!
If old Charlemagne does not flee straight away,
Today King Marsilie will be avenged:
In exchange for his right hand I'll give him Charles's head!'

201

2810 The pagans of Araby have poured out of their ships,
Then they have mounted their horses and mules.
They rode out: what else were they to do?
The emir, who had mustered them all,
Summoned Gemalfin, one of his favourites:
2815 'I put you in command of all my armies.'
Then he mounted one of his brown warhorses.
He was accompanied by four dukes
And rode until he reached Saragossa,
Where he dismounted at the marble block,
2820 While four counts held his stirrups.
He climbs up the steps to the palace,
And Bramimunde comes running to meet him.
At once she says to him: 'Alas, I am a wretched woman!
I have lost my husband in great ignominy.'
2825 She falls at his feet, but the emir caught her.
Full of sorrow, they have gone up to the bedchamber.   AOI

202

As soon as King Marsilie sees Baligant
He called out to two Spanish Saracens:
'Come, support my arms and help me to sit up!'
2830 With his left hand he takes one of his gloves.
Marsilie spoke thus: 'Emir, royal lord,
I hereby hand over to you the whole of Spain,
And Saragossa and all dependent territory.
I am done for and so are all my people.'
2835 To which came the reply: 'My distress is such
That I cannot spend long here talking to you.

I am well aware Charles is not waiting around for me,
And yet I do accept the gift of your glove.'
He went away weeping from his distress.   AOI

203

He went back down the palace steps,   2840
Mounts his horse, rushes to join his army.
He rode right to the head of his troops,
As he goes along he cries out repeatedly:
'Pagans, follow me for the Franks are getting away!'   AOI

204

In the early morning, as dawn begins to break,   2845
The emperor Charles is wide awake.
The angel Gabriel, his divine guardian,
Raises his hand and makes the sign of the cross.
The king gets up and has his armour removed.
The rest of the army also disarms itself.   2850
Then they mount their horses and ride hard
Back along the long tracks and the wide roads,
They come to contemplate their dreadful losses
In Rencesvals, where the battle took place.   AOI

205

Charles has returned to Rencesvals.   2855
Because of the dead he finds, he begins to weep.
He said to the French: 'My lords, ride slowly,
For it is fitting that I myself should lead the way:
I should like to be the one to find my nephew.
I was once in Aix, at a Christmas celebration,   2860
When my valiant knights were boasting
Of great deeds and mighty pitched battles.
It was then that I heard Roland say
That he would never die in a foreign land,

2865 Unless he was out in front of his men and peers,
With his head turned towards the enemy's land.
He said he would die a conquering hero.'
A greater distance than one can throw a stick,
He went ahead of the others to climb a hill.

206

2870 When the emperor goes seeking his nephew,
He found in the meadow so many flowering plants
That are stained crimson from the blood of our men.
Overcome with pity, he cannot help but weep.
Charles has arrived beneath two trees.
2875 He saw Roland's marks on three slabs of stone.
He notices his nephew lying on the green grass.
It is no wonder that Charles is distressed.
He gets off his horse and has rushed over to him.
He then takes the count up in both his arms;
2880 He is so distraught, he faints on top of him.

207

The emperor comes round from his faint.
Duke Naimon and Count Acelin,
Geoffrey of Anjou and his brother Thierry
Help the king to stand up under a pine tree.
2885 He looks down, sees his nephew lying there,
And began so softly to lament his loss:
'Roland, dear friend, may God have mercy on you!
There has never been such a fine knight,
For starting battles and emerging victorious.
2890 My majesty has begun its decline now.'
Charles falls in a faint: he cannot prevent himself.   AOI

208

King Charles came round from his faint.
Four of his barons are holding him up.

He looks down, sees his nephew lying there.
His body seems strong, but is drained of colour,   2895
His eyes are turned upwards and very clouded.
Charles mourns him out of loyalty and love:
'Roland, dear friend, may God place your soul
On a bed of flowers, in paradise, with the glorious.
What a wretched lord brought you with him to Spain!   2900
Not a day will pass that I shall not grieve for you.
How my strength and happiness will drain away.
I will have no one to uphold my majesty.
I feel as if I don't have a friend left in the world.
I have other kinsmen, but none as worthy as you.'   2905
He starts to pull out great handfuls of his hair.
A hundred thousand Franks are so distraught,
That every single one of them is in floods of tears.   AOI

209

'Roland, dear friend, I shall now leave for France:
When I am back in Laon, in my own hall,   2910
Men from many foreign lands will come.
They will ask: "Where is the count, your captain?"
I shall tell them that he has died in Spain.
I shall rule my lands henceforth full of grief:
Not a day will pass without tears and sorrow.'   2915

210

'Roland, dear friend, worthy flower of youth,
When I am back at Aix, in my chapel,
My vassals will come to ask me for news.
What I shall have to say is dreadful and cruel.
"My nephew, who won so much land for me, is dead."   2920
The Saxons will rise up in rebellion against me,
The Hungarians, Bulgarians, and other infidels,
The Romans, Apulians, and all the men of Palermo,
And the Africans and the people of Califerne.

2925 Then my woes and suffering will just be beginning.
      Who will lead my armies with such authority
      When the man who has always led us is dead?
      Alas, fair France, how bereft you are now!
      I am so grief-stricken, I no longer wish to live.'
2930 He begins to tear out his white beard,
      And with both hands, the hair on his head.
      A hundred thousand Franks fall in a faint on the ground.

                              211

      'Roland, dear friend, may the Lord have mercy on you!
      May your soul find its place in paradise!
2935 The man who killed you has ruined France.
      I am so grief-stricken, I no longer wish to live,
      Because so many of my household have died for me.
      May God, the son of Blessed Mary, grant that today,
      Before I reach the highest pass of Cize,
2940 My soul should part ways from my body,
      And that it be lodged and placed among theirs,
      So that my body might be buried beside them.'
      His tears well up, he pulls on his white beard.
      And Duke Naimon said: 'Charles's sorrow is deep!'   AOI

                              212

2945 'My lord emperor,' thus spoke Geoffrey of Anjou,
      'Do not carry on lamenting so grievously!
      Have the whole battlefield searched for our men,
      Who were killed by the Spanish in this battle.
      Order your men to bear them to a common grave!'
2950 The king spoke thus: 'So blow your horn now!'   AOI

                              213

      Geoffrey of Anjou has sounded his bugle.
      The French dismount, as Charles has ordered.

All their dead comrades that they could find
They at once carried to a common grave.
There are many bishops and abbots present,   2955
Monks, canons, and tonsured priests:
They absolved them and made the sign of the cross.
They had myrrh and incense burnt there.
They perfumed them abundantly with incense,
Then they buried them with great solemnity.   2960
They then left them there. What else could they do?   AOI

214

The emperor has Roland's body prepared,
And Oliver's and Archbishop Turpin's.
He has them opened up before him,
And all three hearts wrapped in a silk brocade,   2965
Then placed in a white marble sarcophagus.
The bodies of the barons were then taken,
And these lords were wrapped in deerskins.
They are carefully washed with spices and wine.
The king gives orders to Tedbald and Gebuïn,   2970
To Count Miles and the marquis Oton:
'Accompany them in three separate carriages!'
They are carefully covered in silk from Galatia.   AOI

215

Emperor Charles is about to set off,
When the pagans' advance party suddenly appears.   2975
Two messengers came forth from the front line,
To announce the emir's imminent attack:
'Arrogant king, there is no question of your leaving.
Behold Baligant, who is riding up behind you!
He brings great armies with him from Araby.   2980
This very day, we shall see how brave you are!'   AOI

216

King Charles has begun to stroke his beard.
He is remembering his grief and all he has lost.
He gazes upon his army with a fierce glint in his eye.
2985 Then he cries out in a strong and clear voice:
'Frenchmen, barons, mount your horses, to arms!'   AOI

217

The emperor is the first to take up his arms.
He has quickly put on his byrnie,
Fastened his helmet, and girded on Joiuse,
2990 Whose brightness is not dimmed by the sun;
He hangs a shield from Viterbo around his neck,
Takes up his lance, and brandishes its shaft.
He then mounts Tencendur, his fine warhorse,
Which he captured at the ford below Marsonne,
2995 When he unseated and killed Malpalin of Narbonne.
He spurs his horse often, gives him free rein,
And gallops out before a hundred thousand men,   AOI
Calling upon God and upon the pope in Rome.

218

Throughout the battlefield the French dismount;
3000 More than a hundred thousand arm themselves as one;
They have equipment exactly to their liking:
Horses swift of foot and very fine armour.
Then they remount, confident in their expertise.
If they get the chance, they intend to join battle.
3005 Their pennons hang down over their helmets.
When Charles sees such fine expressions,
He summoned Jozeran of Provence,
Duke Naimon, and Antelme of Mayence:
'In such vassals one can place one's trust!
3010 One would be a fool to lament in their presence.

Unless the Arabs think twice about coming back,
I intend to make them pay dearly for Roland's death.'
Duke Naimon replies: 'May it be God's will!'   AOI

219

Charles summons Rabel and Guinemant.
The king spoke thus: 'My lords, I command you   3015
To take the place of Oliver and Roland.
Let one of you have the sword, the other the oliphant,
And ride at the very head of our troops,
Accompanied by fifteen thousand Franks,
Made up of young fighters and our bravest men.   3020
Behind these forces there will be just as many,
Whose leaders will be Gebuïn and Lorain.'
Duke Naimon along with Count Jozeran
Expertly go about arranging the men into divisions.
If they get the chance, there will be a great battle.   AOI 3025

220

The first two divisions are made up of Frenchmen.
After these two, they draw up the third:
Vassals from Bavaria are assigned to the latter,
Which they judged to contain twenty thousand knights;
These men will never be the ones to abandon a fight.   3030
There are no people on earth that Charles holds more dear,
Except for the French, conquerors of so many lands.
Count Ogier of Denmark, the famous warrior,
Will lead them, for they are a fierce band of men.   AOI

221

The emperor Charles now has three divisions.   3035
Duke Naimon then drew up the fourth,
Consisting of brave knights with courageous hearts:

These are Germans and they come from Germany;
There are twenty thousand of them, so all the others say,
3040 Very well equipped with horses and armour;
They would rather die than give up the fight.
They will be led by Herman, the Duke of Thrace,
He would rather die there than commit a cowardly act.　　　AOI

222

Duke Naimon along with Count Jozeran
3045 Have drawn up the fifth division from Normans:
There are twenty thousand of them, so all the Franks say.
They have excellent armour and fine, swift-footed steeds.
These men would rather die than give up the fight:
There are no soldiers on earth more effective in the field.
3050 Richard the Old will be their battle leader,
He will deal many a blow with his razor-sharp spear.　　　AOI

223

They have made up the sixth division with Bretons,
Bringing thirty thousand knights with them.
These men ride their horses like true warriors,
3055 Holding their lances upright, with their pennons attached.
The lord of these men is called Eudon.
The latter gives orders to Count Nevelon,
Tedbald of Rheims and Oton the marquis:
'Lead my troops; I am handing them over to you.'　　　AOI

224

3060 The emperor now has six divisions ready.
Duke Naimon then made up the seventh
From Poitevins and brave men from Auvergne:
These knights could well number forty thousand.
They have swift-footed steeds and excellent armour.
3065 They muster by themselves in a valley beneath a hill,

And Charles blessed them with his right hand.
They will be led by Jozeran and Godselme.   AOI

225

Naimon has now drawn up the eighth division,
Comprising Flemish men and barons from Frisia,
Who bring with them more than forty thousand knights;   3070
These men will never be the ones to abandon a fight.
The king spoke thus: 'These men will serve me well.
Rembalt together with Hamon of Galicia
Will lead them with consummate chivalry.'   AOI

226

Naimon along with Count Jozeran   3075
Have formed the ninth division of worthy fighters:
Of men of Lorraine and of the Burgundians;
They number fifty thousand knights in total.
With their helmets fastened and their byrnies donned
They have sturdy spears with compact shafts.   3080
If the Arabs do not delay in coming,
And risk fighting them, these men will strike them hard.
They will be led by Thierry, the Duke of Argonne.   AOI

227

The tenth division consists of brave men from France:
In it are a hundred thousand of our best captains.   3085
Their bodies are robust and their expressions fierce,
Their hair is hoary and their beards are white.
Clad in hauberks and double-thickness byrnies
They have girded on their swords from France and Spain.
Their fine shields bear many distinctive devices.   3090
Then they mount their steeds, eager for battle,
And cry out 'Monjoie!'; with them is Charlemagne.
Geoffrey of Anjou is carrying the oriflamme:

It once belonged to Saint Peter and was called 'Romaine',
3095 But in this very battle it took the name 'Monjoie'. AOI

228

The emperor dismounts from his horse,
He has prostrated himself, face down in the green grass;
Then he turns his face towards the rising sun,
And prays to God from the bottom of his heart:
3100 'Father most true, pray protect me today,
You, who, without a lie, saved the life of Jonah
From the whale who had swallowed him up.
You, who also spared the King of Nineveh
And Daniel from the dreadful suffering
3105 Which threatened him in the lions' den,
And the three children from the burning blaze,
May your love be vouchsafed me on this day!
By Your Grace, if it pleases You, pray allow me
To avenge the death of my nephew Roland.'

229

3110 Once his prayer is finished, he rises to his feet,
Blessing himself with the powerful sign of the cross.
The king mounts his swift-footed steed—
The stirrups were held for him by Naimon and Jozeran—
Then he takes up his shield and his razor-sharp spear.
3115 He is a fine figure of a man, robust and handsome,
With a bright, open face and a noble bearing;
Then he rides off with the utmost resolve.
They blow their bugles in the rear and front ranks,
The sound of the oliphant dominating all the rest.
3120 The French are weeping out of pity for Roland.

230

Like a true nobleman the emperor rides forth,
He has arranged his beard to flow over his byrnie;

Out of love for him the others follow suit:
A hundred thousand Franks are similarly recognizable.
They pass by those hills and those rocky peaks,   3125
Those deep valleys and those treacherous defiles;
They leave behind the passes and the barren land.
Now they are entering the Spanish marches;
Stopping on a plain, they have taken up position.
Baligant's advance party returns to their lord;   3130
A Syrian delivers his message to him:
'We have caught sight of arrogant King Charles;
His men are fierce and have no desire to fail him.
Don your armour, you'll soon have a fight on your hands!'
Said Baligant: 'I am hearing talk of great courage.   3135
Sound your bugles, so that my pagans can be warned.'

231

Throughout the army they have their drums beaten;
Their trumpets and their bugles clearly sound.
The pagans dismount in order to put on their armour.
The emir has no intention of delaying: 3140
He puts on a byrnie, whose skirts are burnished metal,
Fastens on his helmet with jewels set in gold,
Then at his left side he girds on his sword.
In his arrogance he has invented a name for it,
Having heard that Charles's sword had a name.   3145
And so he called his 'Precious'.
This was also his war cry on the battlefield;
He ordered his knights to shout it out loud.
He hangs from his neck his large, broad shield:
Its boss is of gold and has crystal round the rim;   3150
Its strap is of fine silk with roundel patterns.
He takes up his spear, which he calls Maltet,
The shaft of which is as thick as a wooden club;
Its iron head alone would be a full load for a mule.
Baligant has climbed onto his warhorse;   3155
The stirrup was held for him by Marcule from Outremer.
This brave warrior's thighs are widely spaced apart,

His hips are slim and his ribcage broad,
He has a large chest, beautifully defined,
3160   Broad shoulders and a bright, open face.
His expression is fierce and his hair falls in curls,
It was quite as white as a flower in the summer;
On many an occasion he has proved his great courage.
Heavens! What a great warrior, if only he were a Christian!
3165   He spurs on his horse, drawing bright, clear blood,
He gallops out in front, leaping over a ditch,
Which measures at least fifty feet across.
The pagans cry out: 'Here's a man to defend our borders!
There is no Frenchman, if he faces him in combat,
3170   Who would not lose his life, whether he likes it or not.
Charles is a fool for not leaving this place.'   AOI

232

The emir looked every bit a warrior;
His beard is white, just like a flower,
And he is very knowledgeable about his religion,
3175   And he is fierce and impetuous in battle.
His son Malpramis is an excellent knight;
He is tall and strong, and takes after his ancestors;
He said to his father: 'My lord, let us ride to the attack!
I shall be very surprised if we ever get to see Charles.'
3180   Baligant said: 'Oh yes, you will, for he is most brave.
Accounts in many annals redound to his honour.
He no longer has his nephew Roland with him,
And so will lack the strength to resist our attack.'   AOI

233

'Fair son Malpramis,' thus spoke Baligant,
3185   'The great knight Roland was killed yesterday,
Along with Oliver, the valiant and the brave,
The twelve peers, whom Charles loved so much,
And twenty thousand soldiers from France;
I would not give a fig for all the other men.'

234

'The emperor is returning, that's for sure,   3190
My messenger, the Syrian, told me so,
And they have formed ten huge divisions.
The man who is blowing the oliphant is very brave,
His companion is responding with a clear bugle call
And they are both riding at the very head of the army,   3195
And with them there are fifteen thousand Franks,
Young fighters whom Charles calls his children.
Coming after these are just as many again;
They will all strike mighty, vicious blows.'
Malpramis said: 'Pray, grant me the first blow.'   AOI 3200

235

'Fair son Malpramis,' Baligant said to him,
'I grant you everything you have just asked of me:
Go, rain blows on the French immediately,
And you will take Torleu, the Persian king, with you,
And Dapamort, another Lycian king too.   3205
If you are able to put a stop to their great arrogance,
I shall reward you with a portion of my land
Stretching from Cheriant to the Val-Marchis.'
And his son replies: 'My lord, many thanks.'
He steps forward and accepted the gift—   3210
Being part of the land that belonged to King Flurit—
From that time onwards he never saw it again,
Nor was it granted to him or given as a fief.

236

The emir is riding around amongst his troops,
His son, who is large of stature, is following him.   3215
King Torleu along with King Dapamort
Quickly draw up some thirty divisions;
In each they have amazing numbers of knights:

Even the smallest contained fifty thousand men.
3220   The first is made up of men from Butentrot,*
And the next of Milceni with their enormous heads;
On their spines, which run the length of their backs,
These men sprout bristles just as pigs do.   AOI

237

The third division is made up of Nubles and Blos,
3225   And the fourth consists of Bruns and Slavs,
While the fifth contains Sorbres and Sors,
And the sixth comprises Armenians and Moors,
And the seventh is made up of men from Jericho,
The eighth contains Nigres, the ninth Gros,
3230   And the tenth men from Balide-la-Forte:
This is a people always intent on evil.   AOI

238

The emir swears an oath to the best of his ability,
On the power and body of Mohammed, saying:
'Charles of France is mad to be riding against us;
3235   There will be a fight if he does not turn back,
Never will he wear a golden crown on his head.'

239

Then they draw up ten more divisions:
The first consists of the ugly race of Canaanites;
They have cut across country from Val-Fuït.
3240   The second is made up of Turks, and the third of Persians,
While the fourth comprises cruel Petchenegs,
And the fifth contains Soltras and Avars,
Then the sixth consists of Ormaleis and Ugleci,*
And the seventh is made up of the people of Samuel,
3245   The eighth those from Bruise and the ninth of Clavers,
The tenth is formed of men from Occian by the desert:

This is a people who refuses to serve Our Lord,
And you will never hear of a more treacherous race.
Their hides are rock hard, just like iron,
Because of this they spurn helmets and hauberks;   3250
In battle they are treacherous and bloodthirsty.   AOI

240

The emir then puts together ten more divisions:
The first is made up of the giants from Malprose,
The second of Huns and the third of Hungarians,
And the fourth of men from Baldise-la-Longue,   3255
And the fifth contains soldiers from Val-Peneuse,
And the sixth is made up of *those from* Marose,
And the seventh has Lechs and men from Strymonis,
And the eighth troops from Argoille, the ninth from Clarbonne,
And the tenth consists of the bearded men of Fronde: 3260
This is a race that never once loved Our Lord God.
The Frankish annals report a total of thirty divisions.
Throughout this huge army trumpet calls sound.
Like true warriors, the pagans ride out to battle.   AOI

241

The emir is a very powerful man indeed,   3265
He has his dragon standard carried before him,
And his banner with Tervagant and Mohammed,
And a statue of Apollo, that most treacherous god.
Ten Canaanites form an escort around them,
Shouting at the top of their voices this exhortation: 3270
'Whoever wishes to be protected by our gods
Must pray to them and serve them with great humility.'
The pagans then bow their heads and chins,
Lowering their shiny helmets in deep obeisance.
The French say: 'You are about to die, scoundrels!   3275
Today may you suffer crushing humiliation!
May you, Our Lord God, offer protection to Charles.
Let this battle be dedicated to His name.'   AOI

242

The emir is an exceptionally skilled leader.
3280 Thus he addresses his son and the two kings:
'My lords, barons, you shall ride out in front of us,
And together you will lead all of my divisions,
Except that I wish to retain three of the best:
One will be made up of Turks, and the second of Ormaleis,
3285 And the third will consist of the giants from Malprose.
The men of Occian will be with me too,
And will join battle with Charles and with the French.
If the emperor engages me in single combat,
He is destined to lose his head from his trunk.
3290 Let him be assured that he will deserve nothing else.'   AOI

243

The two armies are huge and the divisions impressive.
Separating them there is neither hill, valley, nor mound,
Wood nor forest—indeed, nowhere to hide;
They can see each other clearly on the open plain.
3295 Thus spoke Baligant: 'My army of unbelievers,
Spur your horses on and ride into battle.'
Amborre of Oluferne carries their standard.
The pagans cry out, invoking Precious.*
The French say: 'May your losses be great today!'
3300 Then they renew even louder their cry of 'Monjoie!'
The emperor has his men sound their bugles,
And the oliphant, which lifts all their spirits.
The pagans say: 'Charles's forces are impressive.
Our battle is going to be harsh and merciless.'   AOI

244

3305 The plain is vast and the countryside extensive;
Their helmets shine with their jewels set in gold,
And their shields and their shiny byrnies

And their lances, with their standards attached.
Their bugles sound, which ring out crystal clear,
The blasts of the oliphant resounding above the rest. 3310
On hearing this, the emir summons his brother,
He is called Canabeus and is the king of Floredee,
He held all the land as far as Val-Sevree,
Saying as he shows him Charles's ten divisions:
'Just look at the arrogance of France, the renowned! 3315
The emperor is riding out most proudly.
He is at the back with his bearded men;
On top of their byrnies they have placed their beards,
Which are just as white as snow on ice.
These men will strike with lances and with swords. 3320
This battle is going to be both cruel and harsh;
Never before has anyone seen such a battle joined!'
Further than one can throw a whittled stick
Baligant has overtaken his companies,
Then he addressed them, speaking these words: 3325
'Follow me, pagans, for I am launching the attack!'
He has brandished the shaft of his spear,
And has turned its point in Charles's direction. AOI

245

When Charles the Great caught sight of the emir,
With his dragon standard, pennon, and banner—
The forces of Araby are so very great indeed, 3330
Occupying the countryside in all directions
Apart from the area held by the emperor—
The King of France shouts at the top of his voice:
'French barons, you are excellent vassals,
You have fought so many great battles in the field. 3335
Just look at the pagans: they are treacherous cowards!
All their beliefs will not be worth a penny to them,
Even if they have a mighty army, who cares, my lords?
If anyone would rather not come with me, he can leave!' 3340
He then drives on his horse with his spurs,
And Tencendur leaps forward four times.

The French say: 'This king is a valiant warrior!
Ride on, brave lord, not one of us shall fail you.'

246

3345 The day was clear and the sun shone brightly;
The armies are impressive and the companies huge.
The divisions in front have now engaged in battle:
Count Rabel along with Count Guinemant
Allow their fleet-footed steeds free rein.
3350 They spur on their horses; then the Franks charge,
And go to strike with their razor-sharp lances.   AOI

247

Count Rabel is a courageous knight:
He urges on his horse with his spurs of pure gold,
And goes to strike Torleu, the Persian king;
3355 Neither shield nor byrnie could withstand his blow:
He has driven his golden lance right into his body,
Thus knocking him down dead onto a small bush.
The French say: 'May Our Lord God protect us!
Charles is in the right and we must not fail him.'   AOI

248

3360 And Guinemant joins combat with a Lycian king;
He completely smashes his shield decorated with flowers,
Then he destroyed the byrnie he was wearing,
Plunging the whole pennon right into his body,
Thus knocking him down dead, willy-nilly.
3365 In response to this blow the French cry out:
'Strike, my lords, do not hold back!
Charles is in the right against this *pagan* race.
God has appointed us to exact His supreme justice.'   AOI

249

Malpramis is riding on a pure white horse
And makes his way into the thick of the Franks.
He goes around repeatedly inflicting great blows   3370
And finishing men off, one after another.
Baligant is the first to cry out, saying:
'My barons, I have nurtured you a long time,
Look at my son, who is out to get Charles,   3375
Fully armed and challenging so many knights;
I could never wish for a better vassal.
Come to his aid with your razor-sharp spears.'
On hearing this, the pagans surge forward,
They inflict heavy blows, the fighting is intense.   3380
The battle rages on, taking a dreadful toll.
Never has one so terrible been fought before or since.   AOI

250

The armies are huge and the troops fierce.
All of the divisions are now engaged in fighting
And the pagans are striking amazing blows.   3385
Oh God, there are so many lances broken in two,
Shields smashed and byrnies ripped to shreds.
You would have seen the ground completely strewn with them.
The grass of the battlefield, which is green and tender,
Has been *stained crimson by the blood they have shed.*   3390
The emir calls out to his household troops:
'Inflict blows, my barons, on these Christian people!'
The battle rages on, harsh and unrelenting,
Never has one so terrible been joined before or since.
It will not end until they are all dead.   AOI 3395

251

The emir calls upon his men, saying:
'Strike, pagans, since you aren't here for any other reason.

I shall give you in return noble and beautiful wives,
And I shall give you fiefs, domains, and lands.'
3400 The pagans reply: 'It is our clear duty to do this.'
While inflicting great blows they break their lances,
More than a hundred thousand swords are then drawn.
See how the fighting is agonizing and cruel!
Anyone wishing to be there would have seen a real battle.   AOI

252

3405 The emperor addresses his Frenchmen:
'My lords, barons, I love you and believe in you.
You have fought so many battles on my behalf,
Conquered kingdoms and brought down kings!
I acknowledge completely that I owe you a reward
3410 Paid with my life, my land, and my possessions.
Avenge your sons, your brothers, and your heirs
Who were killed the other evening at Rencesvals.
As you well know, I am in the right against the pagans.'
The Franks reply: 'My lord, your words are true.'
3415 He has twenty thousand of them with him;
Acting as one, they promise loyalty to him:
They will not fail him, even if it means death and suffering.
Every one of them makes good use of his lance
And they immediately strike with their swords;
3420 The battle rages on with dreadful ferocity.   AOI

253

Then Malpramis rides across the battlefield
Inflicting huge losses on the men of France.
Duke Naimon looks at him ferociously,
And goes to strike him like a powerful man,
3425 And smashes the very top of his shield.
He rips off his hauberk's two metallic skirts,
And plunges his yellow pennon right into his body,
So that he knocks him dead among seven hundred others.

254

King Canabeus, the brother of the emir,
Drove his horse forward with his spurs.   3430
He has drawn his sword with its crystal pommel
And strikes Naimon on his magnificent helmet;
He breaks off half of it from one side,
And with his sword blade cuts off five of its laces.
His hauberk's hood is not worth a penny to him;   3435
He slices through the coif right down to his scalp,
And lops off a piece, which falls to the ground.
The blow was mighty; the duke was stunned by it
And would have fallen straight away, had God not helped him.
He held on tightly to the neck of his warhorse;   3440
If the pagan had managed to attack him once more,
The noble vassal would have died on the spot.
Yet Charles of France arrived in time to save him.   AOI

255

Duke Naimon is in such great distress,
And the pagan cannot wait to strike him again.   3445
Charles said: 'Scoundrel, you'll regret laying hands on him.'
Showing great courage he goes to strike him,
Smashing his shield, which breaks against his chest.
He tears the ventail clean off his hauberk,
Thus he knocks him dead; his saddle is left empty.   3450

256

King Charlemagne is full of anguish
When he sees Naimon wounded before him,
His bright blood falling onto the green grass.
The emperor gives him this piece of advice:
'Fair lord Naimon, pray ride by my side!   3455
The villain, who was pressing you hard, is dead;
With one thrust I have plunged my lance into his body.'

The duke replies: 'My lord, I can well believe this.
If I live a little longer, you will be well rewarded.'
3460 Then they ride together, bound by love and loyalty.
With them are twenty thousand Frenchmen;
Not one of them fails to strike and inflict blows.   AOI

257

The emir is riding across the battlefield,
And goes to strike Count Guinemant;
3465 He smashes his white shield against his chest,
And rips the skirts off his hauberk;
He severs both ribs from his waist,
Thus knocking him, dead, from his swift mount.
Then he dispatched Gebuïn and Lorain,
3470 And Richard the Old, lord of the Normans.
The pagans cry out: 'Precious is mighty.
Strike, barons, we are under its protection.'   AOI

258

If only you had seen the knights from Araby,
Those from Occian, Argoille, and Bascle!
3475 With their lances, they strike and inflict great blows,
While the French have no desire to flee.
On both sides the death toll is very high.
They fight tooth and nail right until nightfall.
The Frankish barons suffer tremendous losses:
3480 There will be anguish before the fighting stops.   AOI

259

The French and the Arabs inflict mighty blows;
They shatter their spears and polished lances.
You should have seen those shields so battered,
And heard those shiny hauberks ring out,

And those swords grating against helmets. 3485
If only you had seen those knights cut down,
And men howling, falling dead to the ground,
Then you would have known what true suffering is.
This battle is most terrible to experience.
The emir calls upon his god Apollo, 3490
And also Tervagant and Mohammed, saying:
'My lord gods, I have served you well;
I shall make all of your statues out of pure gold. AOI
It is your duty to protect me against Charles.'
One of his favourites, Gemalfin, appears before him. 3495
He brings with him bad news and says:
'Baligant, my lord, you are suffering badly today:
You have lost Malpramis your son
And your brother, Canabeus, has also been killed.
Things turned out well for two Frenchmen: 3500
In my view the emperor is one of them.
He is large of stature and looks like a true warrior.
His beard is as white as blossom in April.'
At this the emir bows his helmeted head
And as a result he then lowers his face. 3505
His anguish is so great he thought he was going to die;
And he then summoned Jangleu from Outremer.

260

The emir said: 'Jangleu, pray come closer!
You are brave and your expertise is great:
I have always followed your advice in every matter. 3510
What is your opinion on the Arabs versus the Franks?
Are we going to be victorious on the battlefield?'
And he replies: 'You are a dead man walking, Baligant;
Your gods will never be able to protect you.
Charles is fierce and his soldiers are brave. 3515
I have never before seen such warlike people.
But call together the knights from Occian,
Turks and Enfruns, Arabs and Giants.
Do not postpone whatever fate has in store.'

261

3520 The emir has made his beard clearly visible—
It is as white as hawthorn blossom—
Whatever happens, he will not hide away.
He places a clear-sounding trumpet to his lips,
And blows it so loudly that his pagans heard it.
3525 His companies rally throughout the battlefield.
The men from Occian bray and neigh
And those from Argoille yelp just like dogs;
They attack the Franks with such great audacity,
They breach and part their most tightly closed ranks.
3530 In this onslaught they kill seven thousand men.

262

Count Ogier was never guilty of cowardice;
No better vassal than he ever wore a byrnie.
When he saw the French divisions being breached,
He called upon Thierry, the Duke of Argonne,
3535 Geoffrey of Anjou and Count Jozeran,
Then addressed Charles in a very aggressive way:
'Look at how the pagans are killing your men!
May God never allow you to wear a crown on your head,
Unless you fight here to avenge your shame!'
3540 Not one of them utters a single word in reply.
They eagerly spur on their horses, giving them free rein.
They go to strike them wherever they encounter them.

263

Charlemagne the king deals many mighty blows,   AOI
And so do Duke Naimon, Ogier the Dane,
3545 And Geoffrey of Anjou, who was bearing the standard.
Lord Ogier the Dane is extremely courageous.
He spurs on his horse, letting it gallop at top speed
And goes to strike the pagan carrying the dragon;
Thus Amborre crashes to the ground in front of him,

Along with the dragon banner and the royal standard.   3550
Baligant sees his banner fall to the ground
And Mohammed's standard brought so low.
At this point the emir begins to realize
That he is wrong and Charlemagne is in the right.
The pagans from Araby do not utter a word.   3555
The emperor calls upon his closest kin:
'My lords, in God's name, shall I have your support?'
The Franks reply: 'You should not need to ask us.
A traitor he must be who does not strike with all his might.'   AOI

264

The day draws to a close, turning into evening.   3560
The French and the pagans inflict many a sword blow;
Those who came together in battle are real heroes,
And they have not forgotten their war cries.
The emir has been shouting 'Precious!',
While Charles shouts his famous war cry 'Monjoie!'   3565
Each man recognizes the other from his clear loud voice:
In the middle of the field the two men came together.
Then they attack each other, exchanging mighty blows
From their lances on their shields with roundel patterns.
They have broken them beneath their wide bosses.   3570
They sliced off the skirts of their hauberks
Yet did not reach as far as their flesh.
They break their girths, upturning their saddles;
The kings take a tumble, falling to the ground.
They quickly jumped back up on their feet,   3575
Drawing their swords most courageously.
Their combat cannot be put off any longer;
Until one of them is dead, it cannot be resolved.   AOI

265

Charles of fair France is a mighty warrior,
Yet the emir does not fear or dread him.   3580

They present to each other their naked swords,
They inflict mighty blows on each other's shields,
Slicing through the leather and double thickness of wood.
The rivets fall to the ground as they shatter the bosses;
3585   Then, unprotected, they strike each other's byrnie;
Flashing sparks fly out from their bright helmets.
In no way can this combat ever be resolved
Until one of them admits he is in the wrong.   AOI

266

Said the emir: 'Charles, think carefully about this:
3590   You would be well advised to repent of your ways.
I am aware of the fact that you have killed my son;
Your attempt to wrest my country from me is most unjust.
Become my vassal and I shall return it to you as a fief;
Come and serve me from here to the Orient.'
3595   Charles replies: 'This seems hugely shameful to me:
One should not grant a pagan peace or friendship.
Adopt the religion that God has revealed to us,
Christianity, and I shall immediately be your friend;
Then serve and believe in the Almighty Lord!'
3600   Said Baligant: 'You are preaching evil.'
Then they go to strike with the swords they had girded on.   AOI

267

The emir is exceptionally powerful and strong;
He strikes Charlemagne on his helmet of burnished steel
And has broken and split it right down to his head.
3605   His sword reaches Charles's thick curly hair,
Removing a huge handful of flesh and more.
In this spot his bone is completely exposed.
Charles falters, he has very nearly fallen,
Yet God does not wish him to die or be vanquished.
3610   The angel Gabriel is once more at his side
And asks him: 'Great king, what are you doing?'

268

When Charles heard the angel's sacred voice
He was no longer afraid nor did he fear death.
His strength and consciousness return to him.
He strikes the emir with the sword of France,   3615
Smashing his helmet with its glittering gems.
He slices through his head, spilling his brains,
And through his face right down to his white beard.
Thus he kills him once and for all.
He shouts 'Monjoie!' to gain recognition for his act. 3620
On hearing this, Duke Naimon rides up.
He grabs Tencendur and the great king has remounted.
The pagans flee, God does not wish them to remain.
Now, the French have what they have so desired.

269

The pagans flee, according to Our Lord God's plan;   3625
The Franks, accompanied by the emperor, pursue them.
Thus spoke the king: 'My lords, avenge your anguish,
And lighten your spirits and your hearts,
For this morning I saw tears stream from your eyes.'
The Franks reply: 'My lord, this we must indeed do.'   3630
Then each of them deals the mightiest blows possible.
Few of the pagans there present manage to escape.

270

The heat is intense and the air is full of dust.
The pagans flee while the French bear down on them.
The pursuit continues from there to Saragossa.   3635
Bramimunde has climbed up to the top of her tower,
Accompanied by her clerks and her canons,
Whose beliefs were false and hated by God.
They do not belong to orders, nor are their heads
    tonsured.

3640 When she saw that the Arabs had been so routed,
     She cries out at the top of her voice: 'Help us, Mohammed!
     Oh, noble king, now our troops have been defeated
     And the emir has been so shamefully slain.'
     On hearing this, Marsilie turns his face to the wall;
3645 Tears fall from his eyes and he bows his head.
     He has died of grief and is weighed down by sin.
     He gives up his soul to the devils incarnate.   AOI

271

     The pagans are dead, some have taken to flight,
     And Charles is the victor of this battle.
3650 He has battered down the gates of Saragossa;
     Now he is certain it can no longer be defended.
     He takes the city and his army have burst in,
     That night they slept there victorious.
     The king with the hoary beard is very fierce
3655 And Bramimunde has surrendered her towers to him;
     Ten of them are lofty, the other fifty shorter.
     Men supported by Our Lord God always fare very well.

272

     The day draws to a close and night has fallen.
     The moon is bright and the stars glow in the sky.
3660 The emperor has captured Saragossa;
     A thousand Frenchmen thoroughly search the town,
     Including its synagogues and its mosques.
     With iron hammers and wielding hatchets
     They smash the statues and all their idols.
3665 No magic spell nor false belief will survive there.
     The king believes in God, and wishes to serve Him
     And his bishops bless the holy water,
     Then they take the pagans into the baptistery.
     If any of them dares to oppose Charles,
3670 He has them hanged or burnt or slain.

They have baptized a good hundred thousand
True Christians, all except for the queen;
She will be taken as prisoner to fair France:
It is the king's aim to convert her through love.

273

The night draws to a close and daylight appears.   3675
Charles placed garrisons in the towers of Saragossa,
Leaving there a thousand fighting men.
They guard the town on behalf of the emperor.
The king mounts his horse and so do all his men
Plus Bramimunde, whom he takes to his prison;   3680
Yet he has no desire to harm her in the least.
They have returned joyful and jubilant.
Powerfully they force their way through Narbonne.
He arrived at Bordeaux, the *famous* city;
On the altar dedicated to noble Saint Seurin   3685
He places the oliphant filled with gold and mangons;*
The pilgrims who travel there can see it now.
He crosses the Gironde on huge ships moored there,
As far as Blaye he has taken his nephew
And with him Oliver, his noble companion,   3690
And the archbishop, who was wise and brave;
He orders these lords to be placed in white coffins.
These great warriors lie in the church of Saint Romain.
The Franks commend them to God under all His names.*
Charles rides through the valleys and over the hills,   3695
Not wishing to pause until he arrives in Aix.
He rode for so long until he dismounted at the steps.
Once he is inside his lofty palace,
He sends his messengers to summon his judges:
Bavarians and Saxons, men from Lorraine and Frisia;   3700
He summons the Germans and summons the
   Burgundians,
And the Poitevins and Normans, and Bretons,
And from amongst the French the wisest of all.
Now begins the trial of Ganelon.

274

3705 The emperor has returned from Spain
And arrives in Aix, the principal seat of France;
He goes up into the palace and enters the hall.
See how Aude, a beautiful young woman, greets him,
Saying to the king: 'Where is Roland, our captain,
3710 Who vowed to take me as his wedded wife?'
At this Charles is full of grief and anguish,
Tears fall from his eyes, he tugs at his white beard:
'Sister, dear friend, you are asking after a dead man.
I shall give you an even better replacement:
3715 I mean Louis, I can say nothing better,
He is my son and will rule over my kingdom.'*
Aude replies: 'I am amazed by these words.
May it not please God, his saints, or his angels
That I remain alive after the death of Roland!'
3720 The colour drains from her face, she falls at Charlemagne's feet;
She dies on the spot, may God have mercy on her soul!
The French barons weep and lament her passing.

275

Beautiful Aude has gone to her Maker.
The king thinks that she has simply fainted;
3725 Full of pity the emperor weeps for her,
Takes her by the hands and has raised her up;
Yet her head is drooping onto her shoulders.
When Charles realizes that she is already dead,
He immediately summons four countesses.
3730 She is carried into a convent church,
The nuns watch over her all night until daybreak.
They buried her with due ceremony beside an altar.
The king has endowed the convent magnificently.   AOI

276

The emperor has returned home to Aix.
3735 Treacherous Ganelon in iron chains

Has been brought into the city in front of the palace.
The common people have tied him to a stake
Binding his hands with deerskin straps.
They thrash him soundly with clubs and cudgels.
He gets exactly what he deserves; 3740
Standing there in great pain he awaits proceedings.

277

It is written in the ancient annals
That Charles summons his men from many countries;
They all assemble in the chapel at Aix.
It was on a holy day, a very important festival, 3745
Some say it was dedicated to noble Saint Sylvester.
Now begin the prosecution and defence
Of Ganelon, who committed the act of treachery.
The emperor had him dragged before him. AOI

278

'My lords, barons,' said King Charlemagne, 3750
'Pray, decide on the justice of Ganelon's case.
He came with me in my army all the way to Spain,
And robbed me of twenty thousand of my Frenchmen
And of my nephew, whom you will never see again,
And of valiant Oliver, such an excellent courtier; 3755
He betrayed the twelve peers in return for money.'
Said Ganelon: 'A curse on me if I hide the facts!
Roland wronged me in matters of gold and money;
For this reason, I sought his death and destruction;
But I do not concede that I am a traitor.' 3760
The Franks reply: 'Now let us consider the matter.'

279

Ganelon stood there before the king.
He has a sturdy frame and a good complexion;

If only he were loyal, he would be a great hero.
3765 He looks at the men of France and all his judges,
And his thirty relatives who are with him.
Then he cried out in a loud voice:
'For the love of God, hear me out, brave knights.
My lords, I was with the emperor, in his army,
3770 I served him loyally and faithfully.
Roland, his nephew, conceived a grudge against me,
And nominated me for death and suffering.
I was sent as a messenger to King Marsilie,
Managing to survive thanks to my wits;
3775 I issued a challenge to battle-hardy Roland
And to Oliver and all of their companions.
Charles heard it and so did his noble barons;
I took my revenge, but this was not treachery.'
The Franks reply: 'Let us consider the matter.'

280

3780 Ganelon, seeing that serious proceedings have begun,
Was accompanied by thirty of his relatives;
There is one of them to whom the others listen:
This is Pinabel of Castel de Sorence;
He is an eloquent speaker, offering clear reasoning,
3785 An excellent vassal and victor in the field.   AOI

281

Thus spoke Ganelon: 'In you *I place my trust*.
Release me today from death and these charges.'
Said Pinabel: 'You will be saved forthwith.
No Frenchman here will condemn you to hang,
3790 Without the emperor arranging a single combat
In which my steel blade will prove him wrong.'
In gratitude Ganelon fell at his feet.*

282

Bavarians and Saxons have gone off to deliberate,
Along with Poitevins, Normans, and Frenchmen;
With them are lots of Germans and Teutons,   3795
The men from Auvergne are the most skilled in law;
Because of Pinabel they dare not speak out,
Saying to one another: 'It's best to let things be.
Let's dismiss the charge and beg the king
To let Ganelon off scot-free on this occasion   3800
So that he can serve him loyally and faithfully.
Roland is dead and you will never see him again;
Neither gold nor money will bring him back:
A man would be a real fool to fight over this.'
Every one of them agrees and approves this plan,   3805
Except for Thierry, the brother of Lord Geoffrey.

283

All of his barons return to Charlemagne;
They say to the king: 'My lord, we beg you
To let Count Ganelon get off scot-free,
So that he can serve you loyally and in friendship.   3810
Let him live, for he is a man of very noble birth.
Even if he dies, our brave knight will not be seen again,
And no amount of money will bring him back.'
Thus spoke the king: 'You too are betraying me.'   AOI

284

When Charles sees that everyone has let him down,   3815
His expression is sad and his demeanour darkens.
In his grief he calls himself a miserable wretch.
Then before him comes a knight, Thierry,
Brother to Geoffrey, an Angevin duke.
He was lean in build, slender and slim,   3820
His hair was black and his complexion olive,

He is not too tall, but nor is he too small.
He addressed the emperor in a skilful manner:
'Fair Majesty, do not lament in this way.
3825 You already know that I have served you well.
By hereditary right I must uphold the accusation.
Whatever Roland might have done to wrong Ganelon,
The service he owed to you should have protected him.
Ganelon is guilty because he betrayed him,*
3830 Thereby violating and breaking his oath of fealty to you.
For this reason I recommend death by hanging
And his body *shall be destroyed painfully*
As befits a traitor, who has committed treason.
If he now has a relative who wishes to prove me wrong,
3835 With this sword that I have girded on here
I shall immediately defend my judgement.'
The Franks reply: 'You have spoken very well.'

285

Now Pinabel has come before the king.
He is tall and strong, brave and agile;
3840 A man cannot survive a blow struck by him.
He said to the king: 'My lord, you are in charge of proceedings,
So order everyone to stop this noisy arguing.
Here I see Thierry, who has passed judgement;
I declare it false and shall fight him over it.'
3845 He places his right deerskin glove in Charles's hand.
Said the emperor: 'I require some noble hostages.'
Thirty kinsmen stood surety for Ganelon.
Thus spoke the king: 'And I'll place him in your custody.'
He has those men guarded until justice has been done.   AOI

286

3850 When Thierry sees that combat is now imminent,
He hands over his right-hand glove to Charles.
In exchange for hostages, the emperor sets him free.

Then he has four benches brought to them there;
Those involved in the combat go to sit on them.
Supervised by the others appropriate terms were set, 3855
And negotiated through Ogier of Denmark;
Then they ask for their horses and their arms.

287

Now that combat between them has been agreed AOI
They confess fully, and are absolved and blessed.
They hear mass and have received communion, 3860
Making generous offerings to the churches.
Then they return to stand before Charles;
They have buckled their spurs onto their feet
And put on their shiny hauberks, strong yet light.
They have fastened their bright helmets onto their heads, 3865
Girded on their swords with their pure gold hilts;
From their necks they hang their quartered shields
And hold in their right hands their razor-sharp lances.
Then they mount their fleet-footed steeds.
At this, a hundred thousand knights weep 3870
From pity for Thierry and on account of Roland.
God knows full well what the outcome will be.

288

Beneath Aix there is an extensive meadow;
The combat between the two knights has begun.
They are both brave men and display great courage 3875
And their horses are speedy and swift;
They spur them on, allowing them free rein.
With all their might they go to strike each other,
Completely shattering and smashing their shields.
They pierce their hauberks and snap their girths, 3880
The side-bars swivel, the saddles fall to the ground.
The hundred thousand men watching them now weep.

289

Both of the knights are now on the ground,   AOI
Rapidly they both leap to their feet.
3885 Pinabel is strong, fleet of foot and agile,
Each attacks the other, no longer on their horses.
With swords boasting hilts of pure gold
They land blow after blow on their steel helmets;
These blows are so great that they slash the helmets to bits.
3890 The French knights lament grievously.
'Oh, God,' said Charles, 'make clear whose cause is just!'

290

Said Pinabel: 'Thierry, why don't you concede defeat?
I shall become your vassal and a loyal ally,
I shall give you as much of my wealth as you desire.
3895 But you must reconcile Ganelon with the king.'
Thierry replies: 'Never shall I countenance this.
Let me be cursed if I agree to it at all.
May God's justice decide between us on this day.'   AOI

291

Thus spoke Thierry: 'Pinabel, you are very brave,
3900 You are tall, strong, and a fine figure of a man.
Your peers acknowledge you as a courageous vassal.
Why don't you just drop this single combat?
I shall have you reconciled with Charlemagne;
Ganelon will be punished in such a way
3905 That people will never stop talking about it.'
Said Pinabel: 'May it never please Our Lord God!
I want to support the whole of my family,
No man alive will make me concede defeat.
I would rather die than be criticized for this.'
3910 They begin to hack away with their swords,
Striking their helmets with jewels set in gold;
Bright sparks fly out towards the heavens.

It is not possible for anyone to pull them apart,
Until one of them is dead, it cannot be resolved.   AOI

292

Pinabel de Sorence is very courageous indeed;   3915
He strikes Thierry on his helmet from Provence,
Sparks leap from it, setting fire to the grass.
He turns the point of his steel blade towards him,
Driving it down onto his forehead,*
Driving it down right across his face.   3920
His right cheek is all covered in blood,
And his hauberk is ripped open down to his waist.
God saved him from being killed outright.   AOI

293

Thierry is aware that he is wounded in the face;
From it falls his bright blood onto the grassy meadow.   3925
He strikes Pinabel on his burnished steel helmet,
Cleaving and splitting it right down to the nosepiece
And spilling Pinabel's brains from his head.
Brandishing his sword, Thierry has struck him dead.
With this mighty blow the combat is won.   3930
The Franks cry out: 'God has performed a miracle.
It is right and proper that Ganelon should be hanged
And his relatives who have pleaded for him.'   AOI

294

Once Thierry has won the single combat
Charles the emperor comes up to greet him,   3935
Accompanied by forty of his barons,
Including Duke Naimon, Ogier of Denmark,
Geoffrey of Anjou, and William of Blaye.
The king has taken Thierry in his arms;

3940 He wipes his face with his great marten fur cloak,
Discards it and then they put another on him.
They disarm the knight very gently.
He is mounted on an Arabian mule;
He returns joyfully and with knightly pomp.
3945 They enter Aix and dismount in the square.
Now begins the execution of the others.

295

Charles says to his counts and his dukes,
'What do you advise me to do with the hostages?
They came to the trial to support Ganelon,
3950 Serving as sureties for Pinabel.'
The Franks reply: 'Not one of them shall live.'
The king commands one of his officers, Basbrun:
'Go and hang them all from the gallows tree!
By this my beard with its hoary strands,
3955 If one man escapes, you will be dead and done for.'
Basbrun replies: 'What more could I possibly do?'
With a hundred sergeants he forcibly drags them away.
There are thirty of these men who are hanged.
Traitors bring death on themselves and others.*   AOI

296

3960 Then the Bavarians and Germans went away,
And the Poitevins, the Bretons, and the Normans.
Above all the others it was the Franks who agreed
That Ganelon's execution should be extraordinarily painful.
They have four warhorses brought forward,
3965 Then they tie his hands and feet to them.
The horses are high-spirited and swift,
Four sergeants catch hold of them in front.
Near a stream in the middle of a field
Ganelon is sent to eternal damnation:
3970 All his ligaments are stretched to their limit

And his entire body is torn limb from limb;
His bright blood spills onto the green grass.
Ganelon has died like an evil traitor.
Traitors must not live to boast about their deeds.

297

Now that the emperor has carried out his revenge 3975
He addressed his bishops from France,
Those from Bavaria and those from Germany:
'In my house there is a noble prisoner;
Having listened to many a sermon and moral tale
She wishes to believe in God and become a Christian. 3980
Pray, baptize her so that God may save her soul!'
They reply: 'Let it be done and let godmothers be found:
Some highly trustworthy ladies of noble birth.'
At the baths in Aix huge crowds have gathered;
There they baptize the Queen of Spain, 3985
Choosing the name Juliana for her.
Acknowledging the true faith she is now a Christian.

298

Now the emperor has dispensed his justice
And has assuaged his sorrowful anger;
He has converted Bramimunde to Christianity. 3990
The day draws to a close and night has fallen;
The king has gone to bed in his vaulted chamber.
The angel Gabriel, representing God, came to him,
Saying: 'Charles, summon the troops of your empire!
By force you shall enter the land of Bire, 3995
And you shall come to the aid of King Vivian in Imphe,
In the city the pagans are besieging;
The Christians there are crying out for your help.'
The emperor did not wish to go at all.
'Oh God,' said the king, 'my life is full of toil!' 4000
Tears fall from his eyes and he tugs at his white beard.
Here ends the ancient tale that Turoldus relates.*

DAUREL AND BETON

I

Would you all like to hear a noble song?
Pay attention, please, and listen to the story
Of a powerful French duke and of Count Guy,
Of the minstrel, Daurel, and the boy, Beton,*
Who suffered so greatly during his childhood.   5
Duke Bovis of Antona was sitting on a terrace,
Surrounded by all his bravest Frenchmen.
Count Guy, may the Lord God damn him, was there:
This man held no town and had no property
Other than a single castle, called Aspremont.   10
The duke took his hand and began to speak to him:
'Sir, though of noble birth you are my poor subject:
I know truly that you are my most loyal vassal.'
'My lord,' said Guy, 'this is most undoubtedly true.'
'I will share all I have with you, let my men be my witness,   15
And you will be lord in my house, equal to me.
Swear to be my companion for as long as I live.
Then if I take a wife and yet have no children,
If I should die first, companion, I give her to you.
My castles and my cities, my land and my house,   20
I share and place at your disposition, dear companion.'
'My lord,' said Count Guy, 'this is a most generous gift,
And I accept it, with your permission, with this proviso:
That I will lead your armies and be at your disposal,
Wherever you want and wherever it pleases you.'   25
Count Bovis replies thus: 'We will swear an oath.'
He had a book brought that contains the Gospels:
They swear companionship, kiss each other on the cheek.
Once both the companions had taken the oath,
One loved loyally, and the other treacherously.   30

2

Bovis, the Duke of Antona, has sworn the oath
In his palace at Antona, with five hundred witnesses.
One is a faithful friend and the other untrustworthy.
For ten full years they lived together peacefully
35 And they shared their land as well as their troops,
Until one day God sent Bovis a significant boon.
He was in his palace with the most worthy of his men,
Judging a legal case, when a messenger from Charles
Came galloping up; and he dismounted on a block,
40 After which he came forward and greeted the assembly.
And he took the duke by the hand and started to speak.
'Charles, the King of France, has sent me to you,
In order to summon you and your entourage to him,
For he seeks a pact with you that will make us all prosper.'
45 Duke Bovis replies thus: 'I will certainly go there,
And I will bring along Guy, my worthy companion.'
The duke trusts him completely; but this ended badly for him.
'My dear friend,' he says, 'I will give you a present:
My valuable palfrey and my swiftest of warhorses,
50 Take them with you to the king, may God protect him,
And tell him that I will come before the month is out.'
'My lord,' says the messenger, 'I will obey your command
With the greatest of pleasure, and I thank you warmly
For the gift you have given me and for the welcome.'

3

55 Charles's messenger got ready for his return journey.
Duke Bovis of Antona summoned a runner:
'Go for me to Aspremont, and pray do not tarry;
To my companion Guy, tell him to come and speak with me.'
'My lord,' said the messenger, 'I will do this willingly.'
60 And he arrived in Aspremont, where under an olive tree,
He came upon Guy, the slanderer and traitor,
Who was playing backgammon; then he saw the messenger.
'My lord,' said the messenger, 'I want to speak with you.

The duke sends me here, for you have business with him.'
Count Guy sent for Bertran, his squire: 65
'Go and put the saddle on my warhorse for me.
Let's go to see what the duke wants and needs.'
So then all of them willingly made ready to leave,
And they came to Antona, to the vast palace.
And when Bovis saw him, he went to embrace him: 70
'May God save you, my friend and dear companion!
Charlemagne sends for me to go and speak with him:
I will take you, as my companion, to the court in Paris.'
'My lord,' says the count, 'it will be as you wish.'
Duke Bovis made his preparations for going to court, 75
And he was accompanied by two thousand knights.
The mighty duke rejoiced, for he goes to speak with the king.
But then, look, here comes a minstrel before him,
And he played his viol pleasantly, gaily and true.
Though he was impoverished, he knew how to entertain. 80
The mighty Duke of Antona began questioning him:
'What is your name, my friend? Please be frank with me.'
Daurel, who had a way with words, replies:
'My lord, Daurel is my name, and I am skilled with my harp,
And playing the viol, and I am a gifted composer of poetry. 85
And I am, my lord, your subject, from a mighty castle,
Which goes by the name of Monclar.'
'My friend,' thus spoke the duke, 'I like you all the more now!
I should like to take you with me to the king's court.'
'My lord,' said Daurel, 'I am afraid I cannot go there, 90
For I need to take care of my wife and two sons:
I have neither gold nor silver to leave them.'
Duke Bovis then sent for his valet Ademar:
'My friend,' thus spoke the duke, 'for my sake,
Look after his wife for him, keep her well clothed, 95
And please take good care of these two children.
For my sake, give them everything they might need,
If money can buy it and if it is available anywhere!'
'My lord,' said Ademar, 'may God speed your return!
They will want for nothing as long as we can help them.' 100
'Daurel,' thus spoke the duke, 'you can have as a mount
This white palfrey, for he will bear you very well.'

Daurel was so full of joy, he was unable to speak.
He bowed down low to kiss the duke's feet.
105 The duke raised him up and equipped him for the trip.
'My lord,' thus speaks Guy, 'we are losing too much time.
My good friend and companion, let's spur on our horses!'
They give their horses free rein and set off at once.
And they arrived in Paris on a Saturday evening.

4

110 On Sunday morning, as the day was dawning,
Duke Bovis and Guy begin to get dressed.
Each one puts on a fine silk tunic from Tyre.
Duke Bovis of Antona had Daurel summoned
To go with him to court to play his viol and entertain.
115 When the Emperor of France saw the duke coming,
He gets up from his throne and goes to greet him,
And he took him by the hand, and has him sit beside him.
He put his arm around him, and then began to say:
'Count, you have no idea why I have summoned you,
120 But you will know very soon, before I dismiss you;
Before you go away from here, I intend to enrich you.'
'My lord,' thus speaks the duke, 'I should thank you warmly,
Feel free to enrich me, but only if this is your pleasure.'
Guy heard this and says to himself under his breath:
125 'Companion, you will die because of this gift.'*

5

The French court, up in the lofty palace, was huge,
Presided over by Duke Bovis of Antona and the emperor.
Many dukes, counts, and worthy men were there,
Bishops, archbishops, and the flower of chivalry.
130 Duke Roland, who is exceptionally worthy, was there,
And also the twelve peers, who are so very strong.
Then Charlemagne said: 'Listen to me, my lords.
Bring my noble sister: I'll give her as a token of my love
In marriage to the mighty Duke Bovis, with your approval,
135 And I will give him Poitiers, the living quarters and fortress.

I also want to make him the lord of Bordeaux.'
And Guy said softly like the felon and traitor he was:
'He will die a painful death because of this bride!'

6

Then Charlemagne, the Bavarian, calls out:*
'Get to your feet now, Count Oliver, my lord,   140
Pray bring my fair-faced sister here to me.'
He brings her out to him in a jubilant mood:
She was as fresh as an unplucked rose,
Her delicate complexion a feast for the eyes.
The king stands up and addresses Bovis: 145
'Well-born duke, son of my dear friend Ogier,
Get to your feet now, and take as your wife
My noble sister, for I wish to give her to you.'
The count said: 'It would be churlish to refuse.'
The king takes her and has her kiss him three times: 150
And Charles has the archbishop give her to him.
They celebrate the wedding up in the main palace:
You should have seen their joyful gathering.
Sir Guy, the treacherous slanderer, spoke thus:
'Companion, this lady will be your downfall!'   155
'Ah! My lord duke,' said handsome Charles,
'I bestow on you the office of standard-bearer,
And the leader and captain of my army.'
The mighty duke goes to kiss his hand
And takes his glove to bear as a token.   160
The duke stayed there a whole month,
Then he goes to Charles with his companion:
'King and emperor, concerning Guy I beseech you
To love him and hold him dear for my sake.'
The king says this: 'I will make him one of my council: 165
For your sake, I intend to love him dearly.'
The mighty duke goes at once to embrace him
And to take his leave, before setting off with his wife.
And Daurel is playing a merry tune on his fiddle
Because the King of France has given him a warhorse.   170
Now Bovis sets off in a jubilant mood,

Yet the traitor Guy, may Jesus forsake him,
Has begun to covet the lady Ermenjart, his wife.

7

In a jubilant mood, mighty Duke Bovis
175 Makes his way to Poitiers, and very joyfully too,
With Lady Ermenjart, who is all smiles.
She is riding upon a swift palfrey
With an ivory saddle and a silver breastplate,
And with them are two thousand worthy knights.
180 And the traitor Guy spoke charmingly to the duke:
'Companion,' he says, 'here is what I think.
My lady is beautiful and has a comely body.
Will you give me a share in her, as you promised?'
The worthy duke laughed as he replied,
185 For he saw no treacherous intention in Guy's words:
'Companion, you should pray to Almighty God
To end my life sooner rather than later and quickly,
Then you will have her, since she pleases you.'
The traitor Guy replies under his breath:
190 'I will kill you with my gleaming spear.'
They rode until they saw before them
The lofty towers of the fine citadel,
And the townsfolk come out to greet them,
Five thousand of them, all smartly dressed.
195 Celebrating joyfully, they enter the palace,
Giving over both the town and the lofty fortress.*
And the powerful duke takes command of the garrison,
Giving the income from it to the wicked traitor,
And all the land as far as the eye can see,
200 Including Bordeaux, with all its dependencies,
As far as Agen, and the territories it commands.

8

The mighty duke summons his court.
Then along comes the minstrel's wife,
And Daurel is fiddling as she does acrobatics,

Moving over to perform before the noble lady.   205
The duke is delighted to see them all so happy.
He says to the lady: 'These are good people.'
'Daurel,' he said, 'I want to give you
A mighty castle that is called Monclar.
It is close at hand, by the seashore,   210
And you can make money from the port.
Let everyone there be under your command.
Pray go to live there with your wife,
I want you to have it for your lifetime,
And for you to leave it to whomsoever you like.'   215
And he has the castle put in his name
And handed over. Now the minstrel is well rewarded!
And Count Guy, may God confound him,
Is thinking about how to amass gold and silver.
But Duke Bovis cannot bear to wait any longer   220
To be the bearer of the emperor's standard:
When the king wants to ride somewhere
He sends for him and he goes to help him.
One day the duke had gone hawking,
And Count Guy wanted to talk to him.   225
He did not find him, but passing close by
Was Lady Ermenjart, who greets him courteously.
She knows the duke loves him and wants to honour him.
He takes her by the hand and they sit down
Upon a bench in order to talk with each other.
'Lady,' he says, 'I can no longer conceal from you,   230
I have fallen in love with you and beg you for mercy,
So that I may be yours and you might deign to love me.
Take me to bed with you: don't keep me waiting.'
'You pig,' said the lady, 'how dare you think like this?   235
The duke loves you and holds you very dear,
While you only think about how to deceive him!
No mortal man can put his trust in you
Since you wish to betray Duke Bovis.'
'Lady,' said Guy, 'you can love him all you like,   240
But by the Lord who was raised up on the cross,
Before two months are out, I will make you suffer,
For I will kill him, and he has no way of escaping me.'

'You pig,' said the lady, 'may you be despised by God!
245 Just for saying this, I shall have you shamed!'
Now Guy goes off, for he does not wish to tarry;
And the noble duke returns from his leisure;
He goes to leave his falcon on its perch.
And when he came back he was ready to eat,
250 So he washes his hands and goes to take a seat.
The noble lady burst into floods of tears.
The duke sees this and stops eating,
He is so upset he fears he may go out of his mind.
'Lady,' he said, 'I see you are distraught!
255 Who has upset and distressed you thus?
Or are you in this state because you have left
Your homeland, and are no longer in France?*
Sweet lady, do you wish to return there?'
The lady spoke thus: 'This never crossed my mind,
260 But I'll tell you about it after the table is cleared.'
When they had eaten, she went to embrace him.
'Alas! My lord duke, I have to inform you
That disloyal Guy, may Jesus confound him,
Came here a while ago, and finding no one else,
265 He began to speak with me in a shameful manner.
When I rebuffed him, he began to threaten me,
Saying he would kill you, that you'll have no escape,
That he intends to put an end to our love.'
'My lady,' he said, 'don't get upset about this.
270 He only said this in order to put you to the test,
To see if any man could cause you to err.
I could not love any man more than him!'
Oh God, how can the noble duke trust him so?
For it was Guy who killed him as they hunted.

9

275 God gave a son to mighty Duke Bovis.
Nobles and peasants alike rejoiced.
He sent him to Roland, the Count Palatine,
To be baptized amid great celebrations.
This he did willingly, for he was his kinsman.

In his wisdom he chose a fine name for him: 280
He was called Beton, yet he was to suffer many trials.
He sends him back to the duke in a silver cot
And a thousand worthy knights accompanied him.
They were welcomed back most joyfully.
The duke was very happy and offered thanks to God.   285
The child was raised in peace for just one year,
Then a terrible thing happened to his father
When he went to hunt in the great Ardennes forest.
Mighty Duke Bovis was sitting on a bench,
With worthy and virtuous Lady Ermenjart,   290
When a messenger comes running up.
'Sire,' he says, 'listen to what I have to say.
In the Ardennes there is a boar that is so huge,
He is hunted everywhere, notably among the oaks.
The likes of this beast have not been seen before!'   295
The duke spoke thus: 'I will definitely go there.
The beast will be killed and we will offer it
As tribute to our lady, and to our son Beton.
I will take Guy with me, my worthy companion.'
When the lady hears this, she is so dismayed   300
That she rips her gloves in two with her bare hands.
'Alas, my lord duke, why do you trust him so?
He has never loved you, nor will he ever love you.
He will kill you, and you will have no protection.'
'My lady,' he said, 'you can say what you like.   305
I will not be harmed nor suffer in any way
As long as I live if he can do anything about it.'
'Ah God,' said the lady, 'just listen to this folly!
I can't help thinking this will break my heart.'
The mighty duke summons a runner: 310
'Go and fetch Guy for me from Aspremont castle.
Go at once and as swiftly as you can.'

                              10

The traitor Guy has arrived hastily
By the causeway, plotting his treachery,
For he will kill the duke as they hunt together.   315

He at once went into Beton's quarters.
Bovis saw him and started to speak with him.
'My lord, fair companion, we will go hunting a boar,
For it is huge and strong, and we will catch it.'
320 Guy replies thus: 'My lord, I should like this very much:
It cannot be so strong that we cannot catch it.
We will bring it here and will give it to Beton.'
From the chamber where the mighty lady was,
She heard what Guy had to say.
325 She grinds her teeth and tears at her clothes.
She summons the duke and kisses him on the cheek.
'My sweet and fair friend, may Jesus protect you.
I implore you, do not believe this traitor Guy.
I rue the day he became your companion.
330 You believe this faithless felon at your peril.
He will kill you, and you will have no protection.'
'My lady,' he said, 'what you say is madness.
You and I are going to argue over this.'
'My lord,' she said, 'since you think this a good idea,
335 Go with him, and may God bless you!'

11

Guy said to him: 'My lord duke, let's go.
Have the hounds and hunting dogs put on a leash,
And let's go with only a few companions,
Taking no more than four skilled huntsmen;
340 And we will be mounted on the swiftest of warhorses.
You and I alone will strike down the boar, my lord,
And it will indeed fall: it is not so very strong!'
The lady realizes that this speech augurs ill:
She goes to her chamber, rips the buttons off her dress.
345 Her eyes brim with tears and she tears at her clothes.
The duke's swiftest of warhorses is brought to him.

12

And just as the duke went to mount his warhorse,
Up came Daurel, the worthy minstrel.

'Good my lord and duke, I have a lot to be joyful for.
I have a small son and I want to beg you,   350
If you would be so kind as to come and baptize him.'
The duke spoke thus: 'Go and bring him to me.'
Daurel goes off, for he wants this to happen at once.
He has brought him and presents him to the duke,
Who gave him the name Daurelet of Monclar.   355
Then he mounts his horse ready to go hunting.
The noble lady goes to kiss the duke,
And this was the last kiss she was ever to give him.
'My lord,' she said, 'may God speed your return!'
The worthy duke goes to call the dogs: 360
They found the boar in the dark Brunas Vals,
And on account of the dogs it did not deign to stir.
The worthy duke unleashes the dogs,
He has the huntsmen blow their horns,
And the boar does then stir, and disperses them,   365
He has wounded three of them with his sharp tusks.
He leaves the cover of one wood, but enters another.
This is the Ardennes forest, which cannot be avoided.*
They need now to leave the huntsmen behind.
And the duke says to Guy: 'Let's follow him.'   370
'My lord,' he replied, 'we can bring him down.'
The worthy duke spurs his horse into a gallop,
He goes to strike the boar with his spear such a blow
Along his spine that the blade passes clean through
And his guts spill out all over the place.   375
'Companion,' he said, 'come to help me,
For this boar will never be able to right itself.'
Guy spurs his horse over as fast as he can,
And strikes the duke beneath his spaulder,*
Impaling him completely with his spear.   380
He knocks him down right beside the boar.
The duke makes a supreme effort to get up,
But the blade remains fast and he cannot stand up.
He began to speak, still on his knees:
'My Lady Ermenjart, I can hardly blame you.   385
If I had believed you, I could not have gone wrong.
You tried to warn me, my lady, with such nobility,

That I should desist from loving Guy here!
Alas, dear lady, I can see that you spoke the truth!
390 Alas, deceitful companion, what a fine friend you are!
You have killed me rather than the boar.
Alas, deceitful companion, how could you plot
Such treachery, and why did you do this?'

13

And the noble duke, who was severely wounded,
395 Said to disloyal Guy: 'Listen to me a moment.
Be sure not to pull the spear from my body
Until I have told you, companion, what to do.
I realize you will be accused of my death.
But I will tell you, my friend, what to do.
400 Embed the boar's tusks in my sides,
Then thrust your spear into the boar.
Everyone will say that I was injured by the boar.
No one will contradict or challenge you.
You were my sworn and avowed companion:
405 You have killed me, companion, I know full well,
Because of my wife, whom you coveted so much.
May God help me and pardon my sins,
If you had told me how much you wanted her,
I'd have given her to you, with her great inheritance.
410 I would have gone overseas on crusade.
I beg you, in God's name, bear her no ill will.
Ask good King Charles for her hand.
He'll give her to you, for he is worthy and honourable.
I beseech you too: take care of little Beton.
415 Please, count, take him to your court.
He is Charles's nephew, this will not dishonour you.
I want you to have half of everything he owns.'
Guy looks right at him like a chained lion,
And the duke returns his gaze like a wingèd angel.
420 Disloyal Guy said: 'You are talking rubbish!
By the Lord who was raised up on the cross,
He will not live more than fifteen days.

If only he would fall into my hands,
Neither town nor citadel will offer him any protection.
I have killed you; I haven't finished with him!'   425
And the noble duke had turned to look at him
And places his hands together: 'Companion, please,
Give me holy communion using leaves.'*
'Oh God,' says Guy, 'you are talking rubbish!
Can't you die quickly? Why are you taking so long?   430
I'll slice your heart in two in your breast!'
'Companion,' says Bovis, 'you are talking rubbish!
You will be avenged of any wrong I have done you:
Take my heart, my lord, and eat some of it!*
Lord Jesus Christ who was raised up on the cross,   435
And who deigned to be born for our sins,
And Holy Mother Mary, I beg you, please,
Keep my son Beton from falling into his hands,
And I beseech you to forgive my sins.'
And disloyal Guy has drawn close to him: 440
He pulls out the spear and the duke passes away.
The duke is dead, and will never come round again.
And the traitor Guy has thrust the spear into the boar,
And embedded the boar's tusks in the duke's side.
He takes his knife and has made small cuts   445
To make it look as if the boar has eaten him.
And then disloyal Guy has sounded the horn,
And the huntsmen come rushing up
And they see the duke, dead and struck down,
His face and sides covered with blood.   450
I am not surprised that they were so distraught!
They began to speak at once to the traitor:
'Tell us, Count Guy, who did this to the duke?'
'My lords,' he said, 'I have gained nothing from this,
For in my considered opinion I have lost   455
My dear lord as well as my sworn companion.
When I arrived, the boar had knocked him over,
Already cut him to shreds, and finished him off.
When I saw him, my heart was distraught:
I struck the boar and wounded it as you see,   460
Since I have impaled his body with my spear.

I have killed the boar and avenged the good duke.'
'You felon,' one of them said, 'it was wicked of you
To kill the duke, and a grave, mortal sin,
465 Of which the rest of us will be accused.
That wound on his side was not made by a boar,
For we can clearly see that it is the width of a hand.'
'My friend,' he said, 'you can say what you like,
I would not dream of doing so, even for great riches.
470 Just look at all the marks made by the boar,
And see its tusks embedded in his side.'
And the huntsmen did not tarry any more:
They have placed their lord on a stretcher.
And Count Guy, the treacherous renegade,
475 Laughs in his heart, while weeping for joy!

14

The traitor Guy at once runs ahead of the others
And arrives first on his prancing warhorse.
The noble lady was in the lofty palace.
She has heard the noise being made outside
480 And she runs out and was at once struck with fear.
She finds Guy and she looks at him, terrified.
'Tell me, Count Guy, how is my husband?'
'My lady,' said Guy, 'he died in the great forest.
The boar killed him, my heart grieves for him sorely.'
485 'You are lying, you double-crossing swine.
Rather you have killed your rightful lord.
Alas, I am the wretched captive of a renegade traitor
Who has taken my love completely from me!'
She sighs deeply and is very agitated,
490 Fainting from grief, distress, and weeping.

15

The others soon arrive with Duke Bovis's body.
Many others rush up: you should have heard their cries,

And how they tear at their faces and pull their hair out.
You would have seen many knights faint,
Many townsfolk ripping their clothes to shreds,   495
Many worthy ladies with faces bloody from scratching:
Such grief has never before been seen by mortal man.
Lady Ermenjart came round from her faint
And she saw Guy standing close by her side.
She looks at him for a moment, then she sighed.   500
The noble lady cannot stand it any longer:
She goes to grab the knife of a townsman,
Intending to strike him, but she doesn't make it.
For they hold her back, not wanting to let her act.
'My lords,' she said, 'will you listen to me?   505
The other day this man came to me, and threatened
He would deprive me of my husband and peer.
Now I see him dead, I want to stab myself in the heart.
Yet Beton is alive: he will know how to take revenge!'
She runs over to the duke and draws back the shroud.   510

16

'My lords,' she says, 'look and see what you think:
This wound was never made by wild boar,
Rather, in the name of God, it's the work of a spear.'
Having said this, she was overcome with distress:
She actually rips chunks from her delicate flesh.   515
They all look at her and they begin to weep.
More than ten thousand men are heard lamenting:
'Alas, my lord duke, why didn't you want to bring
Your retinue, for they would have protected you?'
At this moment, along came Daurel, the good minstrel,   520
He practically falls off his fine dark grey warhorse,
Threw himself on the ground, unable to stay upright,
And when he came round, he began to speak,
Reproaching bitterly Our Lord for what had happened:
'Alas, Lord God, how is it that you can allow   525
Such a noble duke to depart from this world?
For he bestowed upon me the castle of Monclar:

I was a poor man, he made me into a rich one!'
His grief was such that I am unable to describe it to you.
530 They keep the body for three days before burying it
In Saint Hilary's church, at the corner of the altar.*
May God save his soul! But now let's leave him be:
Let's talk about Guy, whom God should by rights hate!

17

And when disloyal Guy saw the duke was buried,
535 He at once made his way to Aspremont:
Without delay he summoned his best men:
'My lords,' he said, 'bring me my treasure.'
They reply: 'My lord, we will do as you ask.'
They bring forward fifteen packhorses, fully laden.
540 'Barons,' he says, 'pack all this up for me now
And also put on your very best armour.'
There were three hundred of them, with fine mounts,
All bearing swords and burnished hauberks.
Guy, the renegade traitor, rides out in front,
545 Not pausing until they get to Paris.
He rode all the way up to Charles's palace:
The king saw him and has got to his feet.
Then he asked him what brought him there:
'How is the duke, my dearest companion?'
550 Guy, the renegade traitor, replies thus:
'My lord,' he says, 'he is not well at all.
The duke, my sworn companion, is dead.
A ferocious boar, a curse on the creature,
Gored his stomach and then all his ribs.'
555 On hearing this, the king goes out of his mind:
He punches the air, considers himself to be cursed.
A wave of sorrow has spread throughout the court,
And Duke Roland has rent his clothes entirely.
Guy says to the king: 'My lord, enough of this grief.
560 If grief could bring him back, know this truly,
We would already have grieved enough to do the trick.
Come over here to speak with me a little.'

They sat themselves down on a bench.
'My lord, king and emperor, listen to me a little.
I have heard that your treasury is depleted,   565
That you have had to pay your mercenary soldiers:
My lord, I want to replenish it, if you so wish,
Outside you can see fifteen packhorses for you laden
With gold and silver that is pure and most refined.'
The traitor says this: 'I have in my possession the wealth   570
Left behind by the duke, who has gone to a better place.
My lord king, if you so wish, grant it to me:
All the gold and silver will be brought to you.
Give me the lady, I will be your brother-in-law.
I shall love you more than any man born of woman.   575
I am a powerful man: you will be greatly honoured.
I shall take the place of the duke, who has passed away.'
The king says this: 'You have brought me a fine present.
Let's go and see once we have eaten dinner.'
When the king hears about the vast amount of money,   580
Grief for the duke is forgotten pretty quickly!
The gold and silver is quickly stashed away.
And the king cries out: 'Knights, saddle your horses!'
No more than a hundred have gone with him,
And they do not tarry until they reach Poitiers.   585
One of the knights has now entered the palace:
'My lady,' he says, 'why do you remain inside?
Your brother is here: you should go out to meet him.'
When she heard this, her heart leapt with joy:
'By God,' said the lady, 'now I know for certain   590
That the renegade traitor will die at once,
And I think that the worthy duke will be avenged!'
The lady Ermenjart goes down the staircase.
She approached King Charles and kissed him warmly.
It was just then that the traitor Guy dismounted.   595
When the lady saw him, she at once cried out:
'My lord,' she said, 'you cannot love me much,
If you bring this traitor as part of your court
Since he killed the duke as he hunted with him,
Plunging his spear deep into his ribcage.'   600
'My lord,' said Guy, 'do not believe a word she says.

She is a woman and she says exactly what she likes.
If a man were to say this to me, I would be ready
To justify myself as soon as I had put on my armour.
605　He was my pledged and sworn companion,
　　　Not for sixty cities would I think of doing this.'
　　　'My king and emperor, what I say is the truth,
　　　For he did kill him and this can be proved:
　　　Have a fire prepared out there on the square:
610　I will pass through it, in full view of all your men.
　　　If even a single hair on my head is singed,
　　　Then let me burn, have no mercy upon me!
　　　But if God and truth offer me salvation,
　　　Tie this traitor to horses to be dragged in the dust.'*
615　The king said this: 'Enough of this arguing!
　　　None of this will bring the duke back to life:
　　　You will be given Guy who will take the duke's place.'
　　　When the lady heard this, she at once cried out:
　　　'My lord king, alas, your decision is too hasty
620　If you give me a traitor instead of the mighty duke!
　　　I suppose you have been given a good deal of money.
　　　It's a mighty king, destined for greatness from birth,
　　　Who is prepared to trade his own sister for money!*
　　　If Beton, who is so little now, lives long enough,
625　The wrong I am done will be paid for dearly.
　　　His father is dead and you use force to coerce me.
　　　With lawful coercion you give him to me as husband,
　　　But may God never show you any mercy!'
　　　'Brother,' she went on, 'just give me a knight,
630　So that my son might not be called a traitor,
　　　And you will bring great comfort to my heart.'*
　　　The king said this: 'Don't speak so foolishly.
　　　A count is worth more than an ordinary knight.*
　　　I am giving you Guy: I am asking you to take him.'
635　Then he turned to him: 'Count, will you marry her?'
　　　'My lord,' said Guy, 'most willingly, if you so wish.'
　　　The king himself has now got to his feet.
　　　He takes her by the hand, and has her kiss him.
　　　'Brother,' she says, 'you are coercing me into this.
640　May God, who was raised up on the cross, confound you!

May lightning strike you before I see you here again!'
And she takes the ring with which she's just been
    married
And in full view of everyone, has cast it into the fire.

18

Everyone is watching her, lesser men and the mighty:
Not a single one of them has a dry eye, such is their grief,   645
For all are moved with the exception of the emperor.
They dare say nothing, since they are afraid of him.
Guy marries the lady, joyfully and with delight;
Yet she marries him, tearfully and with sorrow.
The wedding celebrations take place in the lofty palace.   650
Then along came Daurel, the worthy minstrel.
'My lady,' he said, 'entrust me with my lord,
The child Beton, for I am afraid that the traitor
Will kill him just as he did my master.
I have Monclar, and can keep him in the tower.   655
I will bring him up joyfully and with delight,
Until such a time as he is strapping and sturdy.
As long as he is there, he need have no fear
That any count or emperor might take him away.'
The noble lady was frightened for her son.   660
She said to Daurel, softly and fearfully:
'I have sent him away to one of my sisters,
Who'll bring him up until he's strong enough to fight.'

19

The noble lady has risen from the dinner table,
And she's gone to her chamber with three countesses.   665
She has punched and beaten her face so much,
Rung her hands and lamented her sorry fate,
That blood pours from her swollen mouth.
'Alas, I am wretched, destined for misery from birth!*
I had a husband with whom I was very happy: 670

The man to whom I am now given murdered him!
Blessed Mary, who was crowned queen of heaven,
Tell me what to do, so that a stop may be put to this!'
And one of her ladies in waiting gives her this reply:
675 'I will tell you what to do, if you listen to me:
Have your little son brought up in hiding,
So that no one might know he remains in this land.
When grown up, he will come with a retinue of knights,
And then quickly he will take the land back.
680 He will take revenge for you on the man who coerced you:
He'll capture the traitor, whether in the hills or on the plain.'
Ermenjart said: 'You have counselled me very well.
I consider myself well advised with this counsel.'
She leaves her chamber sorrowfully and distraught.
685 The king embraces her and takes his leave of her.

20

The king heads off, the traitor Guy goes with him,
Conversing with him until the evening comes.*
The noble lady sent for a man from the town,
Who had been a friend of the noble and mighty duke.
690 And he came at once, for he had never failed him.
'Sir,' she said, 'I beg for your pity and mercy.
Come to my aid, for I am greatly in need of it.
The worthy duke, who is now dead, loved you dearly:
You should now take pity on his little son.
695 There he is, wrapped in a Greek silk cloth.
You know full well that he is your lord:
Help him, and pray have no hesitation in this.
If the traitor finds him here, he is done for:
He will kill him, and he will not get away.'
700 He replies to her: 'Lady, by your leave,
I will have him brought up out at sea on an island:*
Neither storm nor cold weather will reach it,
Nor wind, nor frost, nor any bad thing.
We will give him a wet nurse, a good creature,
705 One of my daughters, whose husband has died,

And also her own son, before she ever nursed him.
She will care for him, for she has no child of her own.
My oldest son, who is worthy and courtly,
Will bring them everything they need, and supplies:
Nothing bad at all will happen to him there.'   710
The noble lady thanks him most warmly:
'Take him then and take very good care of him.'
And the wealthy townsman does indeed take him
From the chamber, as if he were kidnapping him.
He takes him at once to the island out at sea: 715
Lady Aicelineta, who is very happy on account of this,
Nursed the child for no more than two months.

21

They made for the duke's son such a house
That inside there is no latticework or roof tiles.
Instead it's out at sea, in the midst of huge waves,   720
On a rock where an elephant seal used to live.*
The walls were lined with beech, as used for doors,*
To keep the water and stormy weather out.
Lady Aicelineta, may Jesus Christ bless her,
Kisses him gently when the time is right,   725
Then wraps him in a fine oriental silk cloth
Before putting him in an ermine cloak,
After which she sings him a beautiful melody,
Kissing him on the eyelids and all over his face.
And she prays to God to give him a long life.   730
Thus the child was brought up in secret,
But the townsman and the men of his household
Bring bread and wine aplenty for Aicelineta,
Who lays the child down in sheets from France.
Let's leave him be for a while with God's blessing,   735
And let's speak instead of the traitor Guy.
'Lady Ermenjart, you have a most perfidious heart,
For on my account you've arranged Beton's flight.
I love him as I do you, may Jesus Christ save me!
Have him brought here and we'll bring him up nobly,   740

Then I will restore to him all his estates.
The duke treated me well, I will pay him back in kind.'
The lady stood still and said neither yes nor no.
In her heart she could see treachery in this.

745 Then she replies: 'Since you ask me this,
     It is quite right that you should now know:
     It's still no more than a full week ago
     That I found Beton lying dead by my side.
     The child is buried in the church of Saint Hilary,
750 So if you want him, ask for him inside the church.'
     'Lady,' he said, 'your behaviour is outrageous,
     When you show no shame at telling such lies.'
     'Disloyal count,' she says, 'why are you arguing?
     You peddled a much greater lie to me,
755 When I know full well, whatever you say,
     That you killed the duke, whom you claimed to love.
     I want you to know that never will you have in me
     A true wife, and this for as long as you may live,
     For a traitor is not at all worthy of being loved.'
760 Guy was furious and has risen to his feet.
     He is wearing spurs of pure gold on his boots:
     He grabs her by the hair and kicks her repeatedly,
     So that her body is streaming with her crimson blood.
     'Felon,' says the lady, 'kill me, I beseech you.
765 Beton is alive, you should know this truly.
     The child is being brought up deep in France.
     When he returns, your fate will be sealed:
     Your body will be cut up into tiny pieces!'
     The renegade traitor leaves the chamber.
770 He summons two heralds to speak to him.
     'Go forth,' he said, 'announce throughout the land
     That if Beton is anywhere to be found round here
     Then he must be brought to me without delay.
     Whosoever brings him to me will not be sorry:
775 We will pay him a reward of one thousand silver marks.'

So they announce this news in the towns and cities,
As if Beton were a notorious robber.
A day came when quite by unhappy chance
A fisherman set sail out upon the sea.
This renegade traitor was called Ebram   780
And he made his way directly to Beton's refuge.
He knocks on the door and went in at once.
The lady Aicelina was cradling the child in her arms:
The child was laughing, for he was a cheerful soul.
'My lady, may God save you, for you do a good deed,   785
And you nurse him as if he were your own child.'
She greets him, but nonetheless lowers her eyes.
'My lord, friend, turn your gaze towards God.
For the love of God keep this small child's secret,
Pray have mercy and take pity upon him,   790
For he is your lord, worthy of your loyalty,
Since he is an orphan and very much to be pitied.
Just see what a fine-looking child he is.
It would be a great tragedy if he were betrayed.
See his comely mouth and his fair complexion!   795
He was the duke's son, we know this truly.
Alas, my lord, if you take him to the traitor,
He will kill him, for he is his sworn enemy.
But if he lives to grow old, you will be richly rewarded,
For I will tell him how he was found by you.   800
It is up to you whether he dies or is kept safe.'
'My lady,' he said, 'don't speak such nonsense.
He is my lord and I would never betray him.
Keep well, my lady, and look after him carefully.
Drink well now, my lady, and be of good cheer,   805
For I will bring you everything you could wish for.'
And Lady Aicelina takes the child in her arms.
'Ebram,' she said, 'touch this child now:
This will do you good for as long as you live.'
As she lifts the blanket, the child laughs out loud.   810
And the lady said: 'Ebram, just take a look!
As soon as he sees you, he is happy as can be.'
The traitor replies: 'He will be dearly loved by me.'
But under his breath the wicked churl says:

815 'Today I've found a thousand silver marks out at sea!'
He takes leave of them, and has rushed away.

23

The disloyal fisherman—may Jesus forsake him—
Goes directly to Guy without stopping at all.
When he arrived, Guy is on the point of eating:
820 He is looking straight ahead and saw Ebram come in.
'My lord,' said Ebram, 'I would like to speak with you.
How much will you give me in exchange for Beton?'
Guy is so happy to hear this, he can hardly speak.
'A thousand silver marks, just as I had announced.'
825 'My lord,' says Ebram, 'have them prepared for me.'
'My friend,' says Guy, 'I shall do so with great pleasure.'
'Daurel,' Guy continued, 'am I able to trust you?'
'Come now, my good lord, how can you ask this?
I love no man on earth more dearly than you.'
830 'Will you prepare for this man on my behalf
A thousand silver marks, before nightfall,
If he can tell me where Betonet is to be found?'
Daurel speaks thus: 'I will have him paid.'
Ebram said to him: 'I am ready to do this.
835 You should follow me to the seashore,
For I found him when I went out fishing.
He is hidden, but I know where to find him.'
And worthy Daurel goes to saddle his horse.
He goes directly to the sea without stopping;
840 He came to the shore, but could go no further.
'Lord Jesus Christ, you who gave me life,
Give me the means now to go out to sea
So that I might save my lord from death.'
The young man who brings them food
845 Approached the shore in his ship just then.
Daurel saw him and called out:
'My friend,' he said, 'come and talk with me,
If you give me passage, you can travel on horseback,
For I will let you have this grey horse,

Since Guy intends to murder the duke's son.'
The young man began to weep profusely.   850
'My lord,' he said, 'let's go as quickly as we can.'
On hearing this, Daurel got into the boat.

24

They made their passage as quickly as they could
And Lady Aicelina addressed Daurel thus: 855
'My lord,' she said, 'you seem completely terrified.
Dear brother, why have you brought him here?'
'My dear sister, lady, you shall be told everything.'
Daurel speaks thus: 'I'll tell you the truth of the matter.
Guy has discovered that the duke's son is here: 860
The fisherman Ebram has betrayed him for money.
I have prepared a thousand silver marks for him,
On Guy's behalf and according to his wishes.
From that moment on, I have prayed to God
With His divine grace, to help me find him;   865
Lady, I am overwhelmed with joy to find him.
Entrust him to me, for I have tarried here too long.'
'My lord,' she said, 'don't speak such nonsense,
I will die by his side, for this is my destiny.'
All three are transfixed as they look at the child,   870
But then Daurel stepped forward and snatched him.
He flees with him as if he had kidnapped him.
The two men make the crossing in great haste.
The lady stays behind: it was wrong to leave her.
She was tired; after she had wept for a while   875
She fell asleep, for she had been awake all night.
And Daurel mounts his horse, spurring it so much
That its flanks are covered in blood.
The child cried and Daurel sought to calm him:
'There, there, my little lord, I sought you near and far.   880
I think God has brought you to a safe haven.'
He didn't draw in his reigns until he reached Monclar.
His noble wife then spoke to him thus:
'Daurel, my lord, alas: you seem so exhausted!'

885 'My lady,' he said, 'fortune smiles upon you:
I have brought the duke's son for you,
For I found him on an island, out at sea.
Here he is,' and he placed him in her arms.
When she held him, she let out a sigh:

890 She looks up to heaven, and praised God.
The lady speaks thus: 'This is our destiny.
Our lord is dead, but we have this one instead.
He will be cared for assiduously and willingly.'
She takes him indoors and made him comfortable.

895 Daurel's children are delighted by this,
More so than if they'd found all the gold in the world.
They are all thrilled and completely content.
But they were wrong to forget the wet nurse,
For she was, alas, unjustly in dire straits.

25

900 The traitor Guy soon got up from eating:
'Ebram,' said Guy, 'now it is time for us to go.'
'My lord,' he said, 'there is no reason to tarry.'
'Let's saddle up,' they cry, and so they get ready.
Four hundred of them go to hunt the duke's son,

905 But many of them were coerced into going.
They do not stop until they reach the sea,
Where they find the boat and take passage.
They quickly come to where the child used to be,
And the traitor Guy goes to embrace the lady.

910 'My good lady, why do you weep in this way?
Hand Beton over: do not try to hide him.'
'My lord,' she said, 'give me a chance to speak:
By the Lord in heaven, I cannot give him to you,
For some sailors dropped anchor here

915 And they snatched him from me, taking him out to sea:
This is why I am so upset, as you can see.'
The churl said this: 'You will be made to talk!'
He has many large switches of hawthorn brought
And he at once has Ebram sharpen them further.

He starts to beat her on the breasts with them 920
Until a hundred spines are embedded in her flesh:
Blood and milk are running together down her body.
The noble creature started to shout out:
'Ah, my lord Guy, do not kill me, I beg you!
Daurel took him away: I can tell you no more.' 925
The traitor says this: 'This seems likely to be true.
For I did not see him at the lunch table today.'
'Barons,' he said, 'let's look for somewhere to stay.
It is almost dark, we should get something to eat.
First thing in the morning, we'll go to Monclar. 930
And if the child is there, I will be able to find him.
No man on earth can escape my clutches.
By the time evening comes, we'll be in Aspremont.'
And Lady Aicelina, may Jesus save her,
Was beaten until she was entirely helpless. 935
Her brother arrived as vespers were sounded.
He loves her dearly and takes her away with him.
And when the townsman saw his daughter
In such a sorry state, he could only weep.
'Lord Jesus Christ, I pray and beseech you 940
To deign to protect Beton from death.'

26

The traitor Guy got up first thing in the morning:
He chose one hundred of his best knights.
'Barons,' he says, 'make yourself ready at once.'
They reply to him: 'My lord, as you wish.' 945
Their well-rested horses are brought to the square
And they mount using their golden stirrups.
Guy, the renegade, rode at their head.
Just after midday they arrived at Monclar,
Coming to a halt beneath Daurel's battlements, 950
Which are crenelated with towers inset.
Three of these turrets are massively fortified:
Never will they be taken or stormed by anyone.
The gate is closed: Guy called out to those inside.

955 And they hear him and were upset by this.
Daurel's sons say to him: 'Father, go and confront him:
Do not, for anything in this world, give him this child.
We already have plenty of gold and silver.'
'Ah! My bold sons, how very bravely you speak!
960 I will go out to him: you close the gates behind me.
Whatever horror you see him subject me to,
Do not agree to give him my dear lord.
If he kills me, let me tell you what to do.
Do not move from here until it is dark.
965 Once night has fallen, find some ropes,
Then scale the cliffs in order to take to the sea.
Take my lord away from here in a little boat,
And you will be blown, my dear sons, where God wills.'
Daurel went out of the gate, which they closed after him.

970 Guy said to him: 'Would you like us to be friends?
Give me Beton, whom you've been sheltering in there,
Then I will give you one of my cities.
I will bring him up: he will be dearly loved by me.'
'My lord,' he said, 'you should know full well
975 That I will not give him to you, not for any amount,
And even if you were to cut me to pieces.
He is my lord, and I will bring him up safely.'
So disloyal Guy shouted out in short measure:
'Knights, burn the castle to the ground for me!'

980 The knights begin to carry out his orders,
They take up torches, but Daurel said: 'Wait!
I will go in and bring him to you at once.'
And Guy replies: 'This is a wise decision.'
Worthy Daurel has gone into the castle,
985 While disloyal Guy waits outside, furious.
Daurel has sat down upon a bench,
He is weeping and tearing his hair out.
He has beaten his chest and his ribs so much
That blood is gushing from his mouth.

990 He spoke thus: 'Alas, wretch that I am.
I rue the day that I came to live here.
If I give him the child, he'll soon be cut to pieces,
And if I don't, he will be burned alive in here.'

His sons are weeping, on the point of fainting.
His wife weeps too and comes to his side.   995
'My friend,' she said, 'you are very upset.'
'Indeed I am, my lady, for I was born unlucky.
I can see now that I am entirely undone.
My dearest love, what do you advise me to do?'
Beatrice said: 'My sons, all of you, listen,   1000
And I will tell you what you should all do.'
They all reply: 'My lady, what is your plan?
Whatever you have to say, we are ready.
We will do whatever you command us.'
'Can you see the child lying over there?   1005
He is your brother and my very own son.
Both boys were born on the same night:
It was the late duke who had him baptized.
Wrap him in the silk cloth that belongs to Beton,
Then lay little Beton down in my son's cot.   1010
Take our son and give him to the traitor,
So that he might do as he wants with him.
My son will die, but my lord will be saved!'
All three of them reply: 'Praise be to God!
This plan could not be more to our liking.'   1015
Daurel went out of the gate, his son in his arms.
He was a fine boy, for he had been nursed well.
Daurel said to Guy: 'Assure me that the child
Will come to no harm at all in your keeping.'
The traitor said this: 'I can assure you truly   1020
That I will not harm him, that he will be kept safe.'
Daurel hands him over and the other grabs him.
He uncovers his head and looks at his face.
'Beton,' said Guy, 'you got away from me once,
But shortly you will be taken care of for good.'*   1025

27

'Daurel,' said Guy, 'henceforth we are sworn foes.*
You were seeking to conceal my enemy from me.'
'My lord,' he said, 'justice made me do this

For a vassal should always love his overlord.'
1030 The traitor said: 'Just watch what I will do with him.'
He takes the child by the feet, slams him against a pillar
So that both eyes fly right out of their sockets
And his brains are smashed completely to pieces.
'Beton,' said Guy, 'I can rest easy now
1035 That I never again need to be wary of you.'
All those present can hardly stand what they see:
They cover their faces and begin to weep.
And Guy goes off, and has now left Monclar.
They say to one another: 'What are we to think?
1040 Jesus Christ, Our Lord, why do you stand for this?'
And Daurel goes over to pick up his son's body.
He has him wrapped in a fine silk cloth.
I simply can't tell you how distraught he was.
He does not tarry now until he gets to Poitiers.
1045 Lady Ermenjart is being told about how her son
Was murdered by Guy, and she starts to grieve.
But just at this moment along came Daurel.
He carries the child and lays him down in the square.
Everyone looks at him and begins to weep.
1050 Lady Ermenjart was on the point of fainting,
But worthy Daurel goes over to comfort her.
He takes her to one side and begs her forgiveness.
'My lady,' he says, 'pray do not be upset.
For I swear on my life that this is my child.
1055 This is my son, and I switched him for yours.
My son is dead; I am having yours nursed.
Take command of the castle at Monclar,
For I will take myself off overseas with your son.
I do not expect you will see me back here
1060 Until he is old enough to carry arms.'
The noble lady goes to kiss him three times.
'My dear lord, may God safeguard and protect you!
For you've done what no man should have to do,
In sacrificing your son in order to save your lord.'
1065 The lady goes over to look at her godson.*
She recognizes him and her grief melts away.
I have never seen such grief for a minstrel's son.

She has the child buried beside the duke.
He died for him, so it is right he be so honoured.
And worthy Daurel returns to Monclar,   1070
To have ships made ready as fast as possible.
He has food and water stowed away on board,
And weapons, so as to ensure their protection,
As well as a harp and a viol for entertainment.
He takes a wet nurse to nurse the child,   1075
His palfrey, and also his grey warhorse.
And he does not want to forget his shield!
His two other sons are beginning to weep.
The sails are hoisted and they set off.
And Daurel's wife climbs up into the tower: 1080
She watches them until they disappear from view.
Then she begins a most desperate lament.
'Alas, woe is me, what am I to do now?
My son is dead and I can never get him back.
Now I see my little lord going away from me too   1085
Along with my husband, who should protect me.'
She falls from the tower, never to get up again,*
Until her sons come to try to help her,
But she dies anyway, may God save her soul!
Let's leave Daurel and little Beton for a while,   1090
And talk instead about Sir Ademar, the seneschal.

28

The lady Ermenjart calls her servant to her:
'Go and bring Sir Ademar here to speak with me.'
Along came Ademar as quickly as he could,
And he wept as he came, his eyes brimming with tears.   1095
'My lady,' he said, 'my heart is full of sorrow
On account of the passing of your little Beton,
Whom the miscreant traitor has murdered.'
'My friend,' she said, 'pray don't be upset,
For, God willing, he is in fact alive and kicking.   1100
Happily, Daurel has taken him off overseas.
He substituted his own little son for Beton.

I am entrusting Monclar to your keeping.
His other sons, who are in dire straits, are there.
1105 Here is gold and silver aplenty for you.
Strengthen the tower and the rest of the castle,
Make sure you have stocks of oat, rye, and wheat,
And meat and wine, waffles and peppers.
Put in store supplies sufficient for fifteen years,
1110 For within twelve, you'll be more than a hundred.
Make sure there are plenty of weapons and armour.
Stay in the castle day and night, my friend,
And whosoever attacks, give as good as you get.
Do not surrender the castle, no matter what.
1115 For it is my belief that before twelve years are up,
Beton will return, accompanied by Daurel,
With many knights and many other soldiers,
And that he will kill the miscreant traitor
And then make you a rich and powerful man.'
1120 'My lady,' he said, 'rest assured your orders will be
Followed by me, every day and without fail.
My only desire is to be in your service.
I will defend this castle to the best of my abilities.
My heart is overjoyed and thrilled with this news
1125 Of Little Beton, whom I now know to be alive.'

29

And Sir Ademar, who is worthy and expeditious,
Fills all the storerooms with good-quality grain:
There's plenty, bushels and barrels full,
Hay and oats for the swiftest of warhorses.
1130 Four thousand fine hams are put in store,
Plenty of good wine, as much as they will need.
He gathers thirty archers and twenty crossbowmen
In the castle, and forty carefully chosen knights.
These men, together with their wives, will nobly
1135 Rear goshawks and sparrowhawks in the castle,
And hunting dogs and the swiftest of warhorses.

They play draughts and chess, and gamble.
They have a merry old time within the castle.
Henceforth the lying traitor has a war on his hands.

30

When disloyal Guy heard the story of how   1140
Worthy Daurel had taken off with Beton,
And when he saw that Monclar was impregnable,
Then he tears at his beard and rips his garments,
For he knows that he will have to go on fighting.
He goes to find his wife and takes her to task.   1145
He has placed her under guard in a tower.
He imprisoned her a whole year: no one could help.
He sent for his men: more than a thousand knights
Do not delay until they have reached Monclar.
He looked at the towers and rides around the castle.   1150
Those in the citadel could not care less about him.
Daurel's sons are extremely courtly and brave:
They can take care of themselves like true knights.
In unison they shout at the top of their voices:
'We have nothing but contempt for the traitor Guy   1155
Who murdered the duke and wanted to kill Beton.'
And Sir Ademar began the following speech:
'Disloyal traitor Guy, you'll find no forgiveness.
Why do you not now flee to another country?
Our lord is alive and you will not escape him.   1160
For you surreptitiously murdered your lord.'
'By God,' said Guy, 'churl, you're wrong to mock me!
By the Lord who is enthroned in heaven,
I shall hang you all high from the rafters.'
Bertran, who was one of Daurel's sons, replies: 1165
'What you say couldn't be further from the truth!
We know full well how to avoid your treachery.'
'Antona!' they shout with great enthusiasm.
And when Guy sees that nothing can help him,
He turns away with treachery in his heart.   1170

Let's leave Monclar and the traitor Guy be,
And let's talk about Daurel and the boy, Beton.

31

Daurel sets sail joyfully and cheerfully,
Heading straight out to open sea at full speed.
1175 He knows nothing of the fate of his noble wife,
Who jumped from the top of the tall tower,
So that she died up there in the lofty palace.
When he discovers this, his grief will be immense.
When the child cries, Daurel is dismayed,
1180 So he takes up his viol and plays him a love song;
'Alas,' he said, 'my poor noble, little lord,
You are being taken far from your great lands.
Our flight from them is the result of dishonour.*
I gave up my youngest little son for you,
1185 And I rescued you from the traitor's clutches.
You are a duke's son and an emperor's nephew,
And yet we flee as if we were bandits!
You have neither brother nor sister
Who can avenge you of this dishonour.'
1190 Having said this, he can't help but weep,
He kisses the child, joyfully and tenderly.
'Lord Jesus Christ, I pray that in your kindness
You may guide us to a safe and secure haven,
And protect us from evil and from harm.'

32

1195 Daurel has arrived in the land of Babylon
Where there is a major port, praise be to God.*
He came to the palace where the emir resided
And his squire carries the child in his arms.
The emir has just risen from the dinner table,
1200 Along with some fifty worthy knights.
Daurel stepped forward to greet the assembly.
'God save the king, who is both duke and emir,

And the queen, and all the knights here present.'
They reply: 'Minstrel, come forward now;
We are very happy to welcome you here!'   1205
Daurel approaches, and performs for them
Several different tricks, for he knows a fair few.
Then he takes up his harp to play a couple of lays,
And he also delights them all with his viol.
He leaps and somersaults: they are all thrilled.   1210
The king himself is very pleased to see this.
Daurel speaks thus: 'My lord, listen to me now.
I've made my way here all the way from France,
For in Charles's court the barons sing your praises.
You are the greatest king there has ever been,*   1215
And I spurn all other kings and counts for you.
My love for you has brought me here,
And I will remain with you as long as you live.'
The king was sitting, but now he gets up.
'My good man,' he said, 'tell me your name.'   1220
'I am called Daurel, my lord, if you please.'
'Daurel,' he said, 'I want you to stay here with me
And I will bestow upon you one of my castles.
You shall also have gold and silver aplenty.'
'My lord,' he said, 'you give me great wealth,   1225
But I don't need all this, and am amply rewarded
If you just have this child brought up for me.
He is my son, and I love him most dearly.
My wife is dead, which is a source of great sorrow.'
He thinks he is lying, but in fact this is true.   1230
The king speaks thus: 'Let me see the child.'
Daurel holds him out and he takes him at once.
He parts the silk and the child opens his eyes,
And gives a smile that melts the king's heart.
'Well,' he said, 'what a bonny child you are!   1235
In all my life I've never seen such a happy child!
I'd like you to be looked after most comfortably.
My lady, my queen, will you keep watch over him?
Take good care of him, for the sake of our love.'
'My lord,' she said, 'just place him in my arms.   1240
By the Lord who made all living creatures,

He will be very well cared for and nursed,
As if I had carried him in my very own womb.'
The lady takes him and lays him down snugly.

1245 He was cared for thus until he was just over three,
In the queen's chambers and well looked after.
Then he was brought out and was much admired.
Everyone gazed at him because he was so fair.
He had a noble shock of attractive blond hair.

1250 His eyes were as bright as those of a moulted falcon.
The skin of his neck was as delicate as a summer rose,
As white as snow, and he had striking good looks.
The king spoke thus: 'My lords, knights, listen to me.
This child cannot possibly be the son of Daurel.

1255 He doesn't look a bit like him.' Daurel drew near.
'My lord king, methinks you have no regard for me
When you cast such aspersions concerning my son.'
The king spoke thus: 'Daurel, don't get so upset.
I don't say this unkindly, for goodness' sake.'

1260 By the time he was four, Beton was loved by all.
One day he went to stand by the king's side.
He grabbed his gloves and snatched them from him:
They were made of fine cloth with a gold border.
He takes them from the king and went at once

1265 To the queen in order to offer them to her.
She takes them from him and kisses his eyelids.
The king laughs about this and said: 'Listen all:
I would willingly give up thirteen of my cities
If I myself could have a son born in wedlock

1270 Like this boy, for he would then become emir.
It would be more fitting if he were an emir's son
Than the son of a minstrel with little to give him.'
By the time Beton was past his fifth birthday,
He had grown strong, and was worthy and clever.

1275 He rode on horseback and knew how to use his spurs.
He was well spoken and had a good logical mind.
He plays draughts and chess, and rolls dice,
And he was much loved by the entire court.
Let's leave Daurel and little Beton be for a while

1280 And go back to those we left earlier.

33

The traitor Guy has gone out hunting fowl.
He has an escort of more than a hundred men,
All fully armed, as they fear being unprotected,
And ten falcons with which to hunt for cranes.
A spy went from watching them to Monclar   1285
To report, and they make ready for a sortie.
They don their hauberks, and their shining helmets,
They sharpen their good blades to strike mighty blows.*
Sir Ademar rides out in front to guide the way,
And Bertran, who was the minstrel's son.   1290
They ride out of the gate, in rank for battle;
Twelve knights remain to guard the castle.
Sir Ademar said: 'My lords, I now beseech you
To ride and seek them out in the dark Brunas Vals,
Where we will find them hunting with falcons.'   1295
Guy is on the lookout and sees them riding up.
He leaves his falcons and rushes to arms.
He shouts out to his men: 'Barons, remember
How you saw me outlaw the men of Monclar.'*
On hearing this, they prepare themselves to fight.   1300
Here comes Bertran mounted on a grey horse,
And he was spurring it to go as swiftly as possible.
He started now to shout at the top of his voice.
'Disloyal traitor Guy, you can't get away from me.
I seek retribution for the death of my brother: 1305
The tiny child you smashed against a pillar!'
The count hears this and gets on to his horse.
He saw where Bertran was and rode towards him.
They crashed into each other, piercing their shields.
Bertran strikes again, hoping to decapitate him,
And the count likewise, knocking him off his horse.   1310
'Enough!' he says. 'You base son of a minstrel!
How dare you ever engage battle with a count?'
His companions rush over in order to help him.
They shout out loudly as they lower their lances.   1315
If you'd been there you'd have seen a great melee,
Splintered spears and smashed shields,

Shredded doublets and hauberks rent asunder.
Now you can see courtly Sir Ademar riding up.
1320 He lowered his standard, gives his horse free rein,
And he strikes Guy, but he fails to unseat him.
'Antona!' he shouts. 'There will soon be a revolt
Led by young Beton, whom you thought you had killed!'
At this, the count thought he'd explode with rage.
1325 He draws his sword and gives his horse free rein;
He strikes the gleaming helmet of a young man,
Thrusting the blade clean through his teeth.
He falls to the ground dead, never to get up again.
Guy strikes out furiously at other men, scattering them.
1330 'Aspremont!' he shouts. 'Come and help me with this.
You'll not see even one of these outlaws leave here!'

34

Bertran hears this and it made him furious.
He spurs his warhorse, which advances friskily.
And Sir Ademar thinks he is about to be defeated:
1335 But fifteen men sporting shields run towards Guy:
They lower their spears and their sharpened pikes.
Three of them strike his hauberk, with its fine mail:
His shield protects him from all the others.
They all strike him, but he handles himself well.
1340 They have not even caused him to lose a stirrup.
He struck out at one who came a little too close,
And he fell dead in the midst of the other men.
Bertran saw this and was absolutely furious.
He spurs his warhorse and draws his shiny sword,
1345 Striking him on his gleaming, pointed helmet
So that it splits in two and the bits fall to the ground.
All around them the battle was raging violently.

35

Then here came Sir Ademar, who is so agile,
And four other knights are just behind him.

Three of them strike his chequered shield,   1350
The blows crushing his pennon right into his flesh.
And Sir Ademar strikes Guy's warhorse.
The horse falls to the ground and Guy with it.
Guy is on the ground, but he has not passed out.
Mighty blows rain down on him from all sides.   1355
He defends himself with his steel sword:
Whomsoever he strikes is knocked to the ground.
So mighty are his blows, they struggle to respond.
Most of them look at him, but don't dare hit him,
Until young Bertran starts to shout out to them: 1360
'Come on, men, what is it with this lying traitor,
That we are unable to knock him off his feet?'
Now they are all eager once again to strike him
With the result that they quickly smash his shield.
Here comes a knight who heard Bertran's words: 1365
He is called Geoffrey and he singles out Riquier.
While his lance remains intact he tries to unseat him.
He grabs hold of the middle of the warhorse's reins.
He strikes indiscriminately in the fray, shouting:
'Count Guy, you need a horse, get on this one!'   1370
Guy jumps on the horse, back in the battle.
Guy's men really can't hold out much longer:
They turn to flee straight along a wide road.
The others go after them to chop off their heads.
They strike often and cut some of them down.   1375
They have killed seven and take twenty prisoner.
And disloyal Guy, when he is able to slip away,
Does not pause once until he gets to Aspremont.
And the men of Monclar make their way home,
Together with the hostages they have just taken.   1380
They make these prisoners swear on holy relics
That they will now side with them in the war,
And that they will be neither false nor disloyal.

36

The traitor Guy was miserable and distraught.
Throughout his lands he summons men to arms.   1385

He had one thousand three hundred knights
And a thousand hand-picked foot soldiers.
They go directly to Monclar without delay,
And they lay siege mercilessly to the inhabitants.
1390 They pitch their tents all around the castle walls
And erect catapults as well as trebuchets.
But whatever they do, they inflict no damage.
Then they swear oaths on relics of holy saints,
That nothing will make them leave the city
1395 Until the inhabitants have all been hanged.
The men inside shout at the top of their voices:
'Ah, Guy! You wicked and miscreant traitor,
These false oaths will make you guilty of perjury.'
Those inside grow cheerful and make merry:
1400 Night and day they have a whale of a time.
They have enough to eat for twelve long years:
Within the walls they have cool, fresh spring water.*
They indeed all stayed in there for twelve years
Until Beton was old enough to bear arms.
1405 Let's leave Monclar for now under siege.
At six years old, Beton was handsome and noble,
With a fair complexion and dazzling, smiling eyes.
The king loves him and cherishes his presence,
As does the queen and their daughter as well.
1410 The young maiden was most charming indeed.
Her name was Erimena and she was most comely.
Worthy Daurel was at that time in good spirits.
He called the boy and spoke to him affectionately:
'My dear son, Beton, you should learn an instrument,
1415 The harp or viol, for they'll give you great pleasure.'
The child, who was extremely well brought up, replies:
'Father, my lord, it shall be as you command,
For as you see I am ready to carry out your wishes.'

37

By the time Beton was seven, he played the viol well,
1420 He strummed the citole, and he was a gifted harpist,

As well as a fine singer and composer of his own lyrics.
One day it so happened that Daurel was out at sea
In a fishing boat, looking to catch dolphins.
And little Beton sees a group of children gambling:
The sons of noblemen who were well-to-do.   1425
He went straight over in order to wager his tunic,
Running up to the gaming table and sitting down.
Several courtiers go to tell the king about this.
The king sees what is happening and starts to watch.
God grants Beton considerable winnings at this table,   1430
For he takes the clothes off the backs of ten boys,
Winning their tunics, and not leaving a single one.
He throws them over his shoulder and goes to leave.
And the king calls a young man over to him.
'My friend,' he said, 'go and see what he wants to do   1435
With all those tunics that he has on his shoulder.'
Beton goes out of the palace and sets off
Into the city, where he went about shouting out:
'Come and get tunics, anyone who wants them.'
He hands out the tunics to various young men.   1440
He then went back into the palace to boast:
'Lads,' he said, 'however well you roll the dice
Believe me, you'll not cut others down to size.'*
And the young man goes to tell the king all this,   1445
Just as he has seen it, holding nothing back.
And the emir summons all the members of his court,
Commanding his loyal subjects to gather round.
He has had more than a hundred thousand people
Summoned, and the queen who is much revered.   1450
The king spoke thus: 'My lords, what do you think
About this child you can all see over there,
My little Beton, whom I love so very much?
I see him undertake so many acts of prowess,
And he won ten tunics at the gaming table,   1455
And as soon as he had them, he gave them away.
By the Lord who endowed us all with speech,
I cannot believe he is the son of a minstrel,
For I see he is a most skilled horseman,
That he dons and removes hauberks dextrously,   1460

And that he holds and handles a shield perfectly.'
The queen said: 'I will offer you proof of this.
Send for him and have him brought to my chambers
So that he might recite poetry to my daughter.

1465   I will have him offered a thousand silver marks.
If he takes the money, then he is a minstrel's son,
If he doesn't accept it, then he really can't be one.'
Everyone agrees that this is an excellent plan.
And so the king has the child sent for,

1470   He came at once and knelt before the king.
'Beton,' he said, 'I would like to ask you
To go to my daughter and to entertain her.
Please perform some of your lays with your viol.
She is feeling rather miserable: go and cheer her up.'

1475   'My lord,' he said, 'I will be glad to do this.'
He goes running off, tuning his viol as he goes.
And the queen goes to explain to her daughter.
'My daughter,' she said, 'I want to speak to you.
I want to leave a hundred silver marks with you.

1480   When young Beton comes to play for you,
Give him the money when he makes to leave.'
The king himself now begins to speak:
'My lords,' he said, 'let's go and listen in,
To hear just how he conducts himself.'

1485   They all go to hide themselves about the room,
So that they can hear everything that goes on.

38

Beton went on up to the queen's chambers,
Wearing a tunic that is edged with fine braids,
And the young maiden has at once got to her feet:

1490   'I am delighted, my friend, that you are here.'
She is young and quite exceptionally beautiful.
She has not yet quite reached her tenth birthday.
She was lovely, and she has in her hand three dice,
Which were made of pure, solid gold right through.

1495   'My lady,' he said, 'I have been sent here to you,

By your father the emir, who asked me to come.
And in this I consider myself very fortunate indeed.
I know beautiful songs, my lady, that I'd like you to hear.'
And he sang his song, while she listened attentively.
The king heard all this, for he had hidden himself 1500
At the side of the chamber, with his queen alongside,
And along with them a hundred worthy knights,
Who are all listening to how he entertained her.
For quite a while he entertained her in this way.
He sings and fiddles, and really enjoys himself. 1505
'Lady,' he said, 'now I'll go, with your permission.
Just send for me, my lady, if you want me again.'
'Beton,' she said, 'just listen to me for a moment.'
She has placed the hundred silver marks before him.
'My friend,' she said, 'I'd like you to take this money 1510
So that you can buy a palfrey that's fit and well.
Pray do not turn your nose up at my first gift to you.'
'My lady,' he said, 'I thank you most sincerely,
But, my lady, I have gold and silver aplenty
Just so long as you look kindly upon me.
Other minstrels will come, from near and far; 1515
Give all this money, my lady, to those minstrels:
They will sing your praises in foreign lands,
And your reputation will be all the greater for it.
I consider myself, my lady, well rewarded by you,
For you already have given me so very much, 1520
Since my lord the emir has brought me up.'
'Beton,' she said, 'if I have your esteem at all,
You can't leave here without something of mine.'
'My lady,' he said, 'why do you berate me thus? 1525
If I do take something, I will feel uncomfortable.
But only because I realize this is what you want,
I will take those dice you are holding in your hand.'
'My friend,' she said, 'you ask me for very little.
Have them then, and have them with my love.' 1530
She held them out and he took them from her.
'My lady,' he said, 'may I take my leave now?'
'Beton,' she said, 'go off with my blessing,
And may God grant you your every desire.'

1535 'My lady,' he said, 'and may God be with you.'
The boy goes out and catches sight of the servants,
Who are about to water the resting warhorses.
When he saw them, he does not hesitate,
He goes off directly with them to the stables,
1540 Where he takes the king's horse, and mounts it,
Taking it off to be watered along with the others.
The king then came out from his hiding place.
He had heard how well Beton had behaved
Then he saw how he has mounted his horse.
1545 'Barons,' he said, 'just take a look over there:
I really cannot believe nor can I credit
That Daurel really is this child's father.'
They all reply: 'No matter what anyone says,
By the Lord who made each and every one of us,
1550 He is the son of a duke, a great lord, or an emir.'
'My lords,' he said, 'why don't you call him over?'
They do just that, and he comes straight away.
The king said this: 'Beton, what made you so bold
As to think it acceptable for you to touch my horse?'
1555 'My lord,' he says, 'he's not yet been watered today:
Your squire has been derelict in his duties.
I will take him to drink, with your permission.'
'Beton,' he said, 'I entrust his care to you.'
'My lord,' he says, 'I will look after him well.'
1560 So he leaves them there, and they all say as one:
'We think this child must have been abducted.'
Beton had been put to the test on that day:
From then on, he was loved a thousand times more.

39

By the time Beton was nine, he was the king's squire.
1565 He was handsome, of noble bearing, and well spoken.
He plays draughts and chess, and gambles,
And he goes hunting with hounds and greyhounds,
And he goes out with the falcons and sparrowhawks.
He can joust and ride a warhorse at full gallop.

The king loves him and the queen adores him,　1570
While her noble daughter holds him most dear.
All the ladies, young men, and knights like him,
And he often served them food at dinner.
He was always extremely attentive to the king,
Anticipating his every wish and his every need.
Then he willingly sings and fiddles for them.　1575
Daurel saw all this and is absolutely delighted.

40

At the age of eleven, he was a good swordsman
And he waited on all the knights personally.
And worthy Daurel was most considerate.
He buys him a horse, arms, and some armour,　1580
Which is fine and light, and so easier to wear.
Then he employs a Saracen instructor,
Who has already trained many young men.
'My friend,' he says, 'listen to my instructions.'
And he had Beton brought before him.　1585
Daurel starts to speak to the Saracen:
'I'd like you to teach my son here to fence.'
'I can see that you wish him to be accomplished.'
He takes the boy off and teaches him to fence.
Also how to jump hedges and ditches on a horse,　1590
How to attack and defend himself with his shield,
How to land mighty blows on his opponents,
How to hold and brandish an upright lance,
And how to train and handle warhorses,
How to strike mighty blows and parry them,　1595
And how to conduct himself in a tournament.
A whole year, he taught him thus uneventfully,
Until Beton knows how to fence and bear arms.

41

At the age of twelve, he was very accomplished:　1600
Daurel saw all this and his heart fills with joy.

Daurel calls him over and he came at once.
'My dear son,' he said, 'pray don your armour,
Take up your best arms, and fetch swift warhorses.
1605 Let you and I ride out, just the two of us.'
'Of course, father, my lord, as you command,
And everything shall be as you have requested.'
Both of them ride off into a beautiful green meadow.
'My dear son,' he said, 'arm yourself fittingly.'
1610 And he put on his armour dextrously, as one should.
Once he has armed himself, he said with a smile:
'So father, my lord, what do you want me to do now?'
'My dear son,' he said, 'I would see how brave you are.
Joust with me, if God allows this, and for real.'
1615 'My lord, my dear father, I will do no such thing!
I would not raise my gleaming blade against you,
Not even for a hundred thousand silver marks.'
'You must do this, for the love of Almighty God!
Do not have any concerns about striking me
1620 For I will strike you back with all my might.'
They move a furlong away from each other,
They lower their lances and strike each other hard,
So hard that the steel penetrates their shields,
Through to the hauberk, which saves their lives.
1625 Daurel attacks Beton as ferociously as he can,
The child likewise, knocking him to the ground.
He rides on by, and then circled round nobly.
Daurel is laughing beneath his gleaming helmet.
'Beton,' he said, 'a young man like you is blessed!'
1630 It seems to me that all is well with the world now.
Ah, Lord God, I offer you my thanks for this.'
The child dismounts, and he is weeping profusely.
He came up to Daurel and takes him by the hand.
'Ah, father, my lord, your request was foolish.
1635 Why on earth did you want to test me in battle?
If I had killed you, I would have killed myself too.'
'My dear son,' he says, 'but now I know truly
That if you live a long life, you will be worthy.'
They put down their arms at the same time
1640 And go to sit down together on the green grass.

42

'Beton, my friend,' said the minstrel Daurel,
'Whose son are you? Can you tell me his name?
'My lord, I am your son, I'd want it no other way.'
'It is not so, dear friend, by God who gave me speech,
Rather you are my lord, but you must keep this secret.   1645
You're grown now, are handsome and can bear arms.
You are a duke and a count, and I will explain everything.
You are the nephew of Charles, whose renown is great,
Of the best king to be found anywhere in the world.
You are his sister's son, but you should not love him,   1650
For it was on his account you had to flee like an outlaw.
Your father, the duke, bestowed upon me Monclar,
A mighty castle that overlooks the ocean.
A traitor count, who goes by the name of Guy,
Killed your dear father when they were out hunting,   1655
Then he bought your mother with much gold and silver.
You were being brought up on an island out at sea,
But this traitor Guy found out where you were:
He tried to kill you, but I went to snatch you away.
Yet I was unable to escape his clutches entirely   1660
Until I had given my own small son up in your stead.
Right in front of me, he struck him against a pillar
So that both his eyes flew out of their sockets.
Once he had killed him, he thought he had killed you.
When I saw this, I thought I could bear it no longer.   1665
I fled here, because I wished only to save you.'
The boy Beton is starting now to weep.
'My lord,' he said, 'how can you have done all this?
How can I ever pay you back for what you have done?'
'My dear lord, I'll tell you exactly how to do this.   1670
As soon as we can, I would like us to go back,
So that we can kill Guy, who will not get away.
All of Poitiers will be yours to command as you will,
Bordeaux, Antona, as far as the castle of Monclar.
I have two sons whom I left on your account   1675
And my wife, all living in the castle of Monclar.
Do not allow your own thinking to dictate your actions,

Rather let me do the thinking, and you can't go wrong.*
Keep your identity a secret, until you are about to leave.'
1680 'My dear father, my lord, it shall be as you wish.'
They pick up their weapons and make their way back.
Beneath the palace walls, they start to fiddle,
Putting on a merry show before the king.
The boy Beton kneels down before the king,
1685 And lays his instrument at his feet as a tribute.

43

At thirteen, Beton was robust and much respected,
Popular at court and honoured by the best of men.
It was then that King Gormon summoned his barons.
There was bad blood between him and the emir,
1690 And they had been at war for the last twenty years.
He moved against him now with great force,
With more than twelve thousand valiant knights,
And a hundred thousand men, leaving no one behind.
Gormon has arrived at the gates of Babylon.
1695 There was great disquiet throughout the city.
Beton was not in the least derelict in his duty.
He went straight away to find the king's warhorse.
He puts on its bridle and places its saddle on its back.
He went to find the king, and came before him:
1700 'My lord,' he said, 'why are you not already mounted?
Your horse is saddled and ready for you to ride.'
'Beton,' he says, 'take him back to the stable.
We will not ride out, for I am not armed and ready.
There are so few of us and so many of them:
1705 It would be very foolish of us to ride out.'
'My lord,' he said, 'it shall be as you wish.'
And he goes away again, but is annoyed by this.
He cannot but think about his noble lineage.
He quickly gets into the king's hauberk
1710 And girds his sword, crossing himself three times,
And he fastens the helmet, which has a golden trim,

Leaping into the saddle directly from the ground.
He is now fully equipped in the king's armour
And he takes up his densely studded shield,
Which also has on it four golden bosses.
He brandishes the lance, with its polished steel,   1715
He's now also carrying the king's weapons.
He urges his horse forward with his golden spurs,
And doesn't stop until he arrives at the gates.
He shouts to the gatekeeper: 'Open the gates,
For the king rides out together with all his barons.'   1720
And he opens the gates, saying: 'God go with you!'
And the king now has come to the window
And he sees Beton who was galloping away.
He recognizes him and is taken aback by this.
'Come here, my lady, and take a look out there.   1725
See how Beton has got himself ready to fight,
And how he is fully equipped with my weapons:
I think I am going to need to change my warhorse!'
'My lord,' she said, 'I hope to God this is not true.   1730
If you have any regard for me, commend him to God.
I can tell you that if he lives to tell the tale,
He will be in a position to come to our aid.
And if he is captured, this will be a great pity.'
Now here are two men chosen from the great army,   1735
Who have moved forward a little from the trenches.
Beton saw them and went to approach them.
Everyone—in the city and the trenches—is watching.
He shouts out to them: 'Barons, do not flee:
One of you should come out here before the other:
I will joust with him, whichever one you want.   1740
He will lose his warhorse or he can win this one.'
One of them said this: 'Companion, joust with me.'
They both spur their horses, their lances lowered,
Landing mighty blows on their striped shields.
The infidel strikes Beton with exceptional force   1745
So that the steel of his lance pierces his hauberk.
But Beton strikes him like a seasoned warrior:
He smashes his shield and slices into his hauberk,
Knocking the pagan to the ground for all to see.   1750

Beton spoke thus: 'It delights me to see you tumble,*
For you just went head to head with a minstrel.'
His companion saw this, was pained and furious,
But also sorely ashamed that his friend had fallen.
1755 He spurs his horse and rode up as fast as he could.
And young Beton is by no means derelict in his duty:
He brandishes his lance, with its polished steel.
They land on each other mighty blows, mercilessly,
Such that their shields are smashed to pieces.
1760 The infidel strikes Beton with exceptional force.
The boy does likewise, sending golden pommels
Flying everywhere, knocking him on to the grass.
'My friend,' he says, 'go and tell Sir Gormon from me,
That a minstrel's son has just tumbled you both.'
1765 The king sees this, together with all his barons.
At once he cries out: 'Knights, listen to me!
By the Lord who is the creator of us all,
If that man lives another year, he will be emir.'
The enemy army saw all this too and three thousand
1770 Or more move forward, but he does not hang around,
Instead he wisely and prudently returns to the city,
Taking with him the two warhorses, still saddled.
Throughout the town the news rapidly circulates,
From house to house: Beton's conduct is noble,
1775 For he has given the horses away to two young men.
In the middle of the square the boy takes off his armour:
Everyone stared at him because he was so handsome.
Then along came Daurel as quickly as he could,
Holding a large stick whittled to have sharp edges:
1780 'Ah!' he says. 'You wicked son of a minstrel,
By the Lord who is the creator of us all,
You were amiss to go out without my say-so.'
The young lad's reply shows great wisdom:
'Ah, my lord father, why are you so angry?
1785 I am delighted that you should reprove me for this.'
Everyone cries out to him: 'Daurel, calm down!
Don't you see how well the young lad is behaving?'
Very quickly the square is teeming with people,
And the king arrives together with all his barons.

44

The king came rushing up at top speed,   1790
Just as fast as his palfrey could carry him.
He approached Daurel, grabbing him by the hair:
'By the Lord who made each and every one of us,
I'll have you thrown in my prison for twelve years:
It's pitch black in there and you can't see a thing.   1795
You won't eat anything at all for two months on end,
You'll not have bread or wine or anything else,
Unless you tell me who this young man really is,
For as God is my witness, he is not your son!'
Daurel, as ever courtly and praiseworthy, replies: 1800
'Ah, my liege, in the name of God, take pity on me.
Have your court summoned now without delay,
Both the knights and the most worthy burghers.
Then I will tell you whose son the young man is.
He is not my son, you can be sure of that,   1805
There is no duke, count, nor king in the world
More highly born than those of his noble lineage.'
And the emir has a page sound a bugle
Summoning his court to gather in the main palace.

45

Everyone arrives for the court, good and bad,   1810
And worthy Daurel climbed on to the stairs.
He made this speech in a booming voice:
'Ah, my liege, my lords, all those who are here present,
By the Lord who made each and every one of us,
Listen to me, and let no one make a sound.
Behold this young boy in the colourful tunic.   1815
He is a count and a duke, I can promise you,
He was the son of the duke everyone called Bovis,
The Lord of Antona, may Jesus Christ rest his soul.
Then he is also the nephew of the emperor Charles,
The best king there is or ever has been.   1820
Charles gave his sister to Bovis in marriage,

And Duke Bovis had a son by her, young Beton.
And the duke, his father, took as a companion,
A count who was his vassal, known as Guy.
1825 This man killed him, most treacherously.
Then he coerced his fair mother into marriage,
Lady Ermenjart, who was most distraught at this.
The child was cared for secretly on an island out at sea.
Guy, with his perfidious heart, wanted to kill him,
1830 And he stayed there until he was discovered.
I snatched him away and took him to my own house.
The traitor followed me: with treacherous intentions
He asked me to give him up, and when I refused
He threatened to set fire to my home, with us all in it.
1835 When I saw that I really couldn't escape his clutches,
I gave him my own son instead of this child.
In front of everyone, he grabbed him by the feet,
Then smashed his head hard against a wall.
I am his vassal, and so I did all this for him.
1840 I then took flight, landing here, in your kingdom.
You've brought him up, for which God will be grateful.
And now it is high time for us to go back there
To take revenge on the disloyal traitor Guy.
And let anyone who harms Beton be damned,
1845 For his youthful prowess is now apparent.'

46

So when the king hears Daurel's story,
That for years he's been raising Charles's nephew,
He goes over to Beton, and takes him in his arms.
He kisses him a hundred times, as does the queen.
1850 All the barons of the court now proclaim aloud:
'My lord, it would be fitting to give him your daughter!'
The king is delighted at this idea, laughs, and says:
'Beton, I should like to give you my daughter's hand.'
The young lad replies, with exquisite manners:
1855 'My lord,' he said, 'I do not in the least refuse this,
As long as my father, who gave me arms, agrees.

I will take her hand in marriage most willingly.'
Daurel cried out, with a good deal of enthusiasm:
'Take her, my lord, this is most fitting indeed,
So long as she comes to an agreement with you   1860
That out of her love for you she will be baptized,
For you need, in truth, to take her with you to Poitiers.'
And the queen has already gone running off
To her chambers, in order to fetch her fair daughter.
In front of everyone, she leads her to the assembly,   1865
Then she asks her, with five hundred witnesses:
'Lady Erimena, do you willingly accept baptism?
Beton wants you to do this, so that you may marry.'
Lady Erimena replies to her mother with dignity:
'Yes I do, my lady, it should be just as he wishes.'   1870
Daurel speaks thus: 'My liege, pray give him some men,
Give him more than three thousand men at arms,
All fully equipped with fine armour and weapons,
So that within two weeks we can actually set off
For Poitiers, and not put this off any longer.   1875
Beton will take his revenge upon the traitor,
Then he will marry the lady, rest assured of that.
You shall give her away amidst great rejoicing.'
The entire court exclaims that this is most fitting
And then they beseech the king, crying out as one: 1880
'My liege, swear to do this before us right now!'
The king speaks thus: 'Beton, prepare to take an oath.'
'My lord,' he says, 'I will refuse you nothing,
But let my father, Daurel, take the oath first.'
They make their oath of allegiance to the king himself.   1885
They both swear their oath upon a sword
And Daurel, in addition, upon a silver crucifix.
Straight away, for neither wishes to delay,
They prepare their ships and their equipment,
And they load up plenty of stores and supplies,   1890
Everything that can be needed on board ship,
And there are ten thousand three hundred of them.
So the young lad goes to take his leave,
After which he sets sail with his mighty army.
They hoist their sails and God sends a fair wind.   1895

Within three months, and without any storms,
They sail across the seas, then they sight land,
Near Monclar, happy and in very good spirits.

47

Daurel looks around and caught sight of Monclar.
1900 They land nearby, intending to enter the castle,
But they saw how all around it is being besieged,
The lines of tents and the smoking campfires.
Daurel saw all this and pointed it out to Beton:
'My lord,' he says, 'God works in our favour.
1905 I think we will not need to go to much trouble.
We can take revenge on our enemies right here.
You can see Guy, right there: he shan't get away
Provided you are willing to follow my advice.
Have your men don their armour and weapons.'
1910 'My lord,' he says, 'everything shall be as you wish.'
They make ready: no one has to be asked twice.
In the castle, they noticed what was going on
And worthy Daurel held his shield up for them.
They recognized it: imagine how pleased they are!
1915 And they all begin exclaiming to each other:
'It's our lord who has returned from overseas!'
In the castle they prepare themselves for a sortie,
Yet wait attentively for the signal from outside.
Beton puts on a gleaming hauberk and arms himself,
1920 And he does not forget to take up his sword.
Daurel does the same, for he has no wish to tarry.
His beard is very long, longer than you can imagine:
For he has not been shaved for seven full years.
And worthy Daurel goes off to gather all the troops,
1925 Giving them their orders in a most noble fashion:
'Do not any of you spur your horses on any account
Until you hear us give the order from over there.
Then come as quickly as you can, without any delay.'
Daurel covers himself in an enormous cloak,
1930 And he has young Beton put on one just like it.

They take up their viols in order to look like minstrels.
And worthy Daurel explains the plan to Beton.
'My lord,' he said, 'this is what I want you to do.
I will sing for them while you stand by listening.
I will tell a tale that is bound to upset him,   1935
And I am quite sure that he will lay hands on me.'
Beton said this: 'And I will rush in to defend you!'
They go as quickly as they can to Guy's tent.
When they arrived, Guy was sitting down to eat.
Guy cries out: 'Minstrels, come and eat with me!'   1940
Daurel spoke thus: 'We would rather entertain you.'
And young Beton starts to play a beautiful lay
And worthy Daurel began to sing it for them.
'If you want to hear a song, I'll begin one now,
It is a tale of treachery, one that needs to be told,   1945
About the disloyal traitor Guy, may Jesus curse him,
Who murdered the duke when they were out hunting!'
Guy was holding a knife, which he aimed at Daurel,
At which point worthy Beton flung his viol to the floor,
And at the same time he threw off his cloak   1950
In order to draw his sword and go to strike Guy,
Whose right arm he slices off so it falls to the floor.
'Antona!' he shouts in a voice clear and strong.
'You are all my vassals: let no man dare deny this!'
Then the men in the castle heard the shouting,   1955
They open the gates and sally forth to the fray.
Then up come the troops from overseas at a gallop,
So that all you can see is the enemy being routed.
Had you been there, you'd have seen heads cut off,
Many barons falling and dropping to the ground,   1960
Many knights unhorsed, put to death on the battlefield,
And many dismembered feet and hands flying around!
And Daurel goes to give more orders to his men,
That they should not harm any of the foot soldiers,
Since they had been conscripted by the traitor Guy,   1965
Whereas all of his knights are to be slain.
Those who have been spared rejoice at this news,
For I think that no one could have expected this.
And young Beton goes to tie Guy up tightly.

1970 Including putting a rope right around his neck.
Daurel's sons come over to kiss their father,
Next they go over to embrace their lord.
Had you been there, you'd have seen such joy!
Worthy Daurel then starts to ask them:
1975 'Where is my wife, whom I love so dearly?'
And they reply: 'We cannot bring her to you,
For she died as soon as she saw you leave.'
Daurel, hearing this, is unable to stay on his feet,
And faints on the spot. His sons comfort him.
1980 When young Beton sees Daurel so distraught,
He is so upset that he starts to weep.
Everyone does their best to comfort Daurel,
So they begin to chide him for his grieving:
'You should nonetheless rejoice to see your sons.'
1985 They all start to . . . together*
Until morning comes, when they . . .
At which point they all make their way to Poitiers.
And worthy *Daurel* . . .
And has him tied to the tail of a sturdy horse.
1990 They have bugles blown all the way to Poitiers,
Where the burghers have the church bells rung,
And go to greet Beton, dressed in their finest.
All the townsfolk begin to offer thanks to God,
For He has returned their rightful lord to them.
1995 Had you been there, you'd have seen such joy,
Such fine carpets thrown down across the streets.
You'd have seen celebrations on every corner!
'Ah, Lord God, we must indeed offer You thanks,
For You have returned our rightful lord to us.'
2000 Lady Ermenjart hears the great tumult resound.
She goes over to look out from the lofty palace
And sees Guy, all bloody and being dragged along.
She rushes on down to ask what is going on
And finds a young man who is able to tell her.
2005 'Lady,' he said, 'you should indeed rejoice,
For here comes your son, returned from overseas.
And he has brought with him the traitor Guy.'
On hearing this, the lady does not hesitate at all,

She rushes to meet her son, kissing him at once,
And it's worthy Daurel who introduces him to her, 2010
While both of them hand over disloyal Guy to her.
Daurel says: 'Lady, keep this traitor under guard.'
The lady says this: 'Have him strung up in the wind!'
Daurel replies: 'I would have him first confess
To the murder of the good duke, whom we must avenge.' 2015
And young Beton has his army shown to quarters,
Before going up to the palace amidst great rejoicing.
He rests for the night until *dawn breaks brightly*,
When worthy Beton has his court *summoned*.
Then he has the wicked fisherman brought to him, 2020
Namely Ebram, who...

48

The people of Poitiers have got their rightful lord back,
And have celebrated all together their good fortune.
First thing in the morning they gathered before him,
Bearing with them many fine gifts to offer in tribute: 2025
One brings a palfrey and another a well-rested horse;
Another brings gold cups, another finely stitched cloth.
They all gather there, greatly rejoicing all the while.
They confirm his right to command the whole region,
And all the towns that owe the duchy allegiance. 2030
He is count and duke, and they acknowledge this.
Here comes the burgher who longed for his return,
The one whom the duke his father had long honoured,
And Lady Aicelina together with her steadfast brother.
At this point, Lady Aicelina addressed Beton: 2035
'Fair son,' she says, 'I have longed for your return.
Don't forget that once I kissed you a hundred times.
I was tortured for this, unjustly *and criminally*:
I was beaten most cruelly by that renegade traitor,
Whom I see standing there before me in chains. 2040
Now I see that you have escaped from danger,
I cannot forget the wrong that was done to me.
Give me Ebram, who found your hiding place.'

'Lady,' he says, 'I give him to you most willingly.'
2045 Then he embraces her and kisses her affectionately.
He knew all about her because Daurel had told him.
Before he leaves her, he makes her a generous gift:
A well-built and powerful castle in a prosperous place.
And the disloyal fisherman is quartered on the spot.
2050 Now men have gathered from all around the region,
And young Beton addresses himself to Guy:
'Tell me, you disloyal count, and let's hear the truth,
How did it go with the duke, whom you murdered?'
'My lord,' he said, 'I will hide nothing from you.
2055 I did indeed kill him in my most perfidious folly.'
And worthy Daurel asked Beton a favour:
'My most noble count, grant him no mercy.
Hand him over to me: I will avenge my son,
Whom he killed, and I will give him his just deserts.'
2060 Beton replies: 'It shall be exactly as you wish.'
In front of everyone there present, he tied Guy
Directly and securely to the tail of a well-rested warhorse,
Which dragged him all around the streets of Poitiers.
And then he had him tossed into the castle moat.
2065 This traitor ended up with little to show for himself,
For the vultures and crows feasted upon his body.

49

All Beton's barons are exuberantly rejoicing,
Because they have got their rightful lord back.
Young Beton now addresses Daurel:
2070 'Ah father, my lord ... completely
I entrust to you the running of all my lands.
I shan't love anyone who does not love you:
And I shall love all those who are willing to love you.'
And to Sir Ademar, who had helped him so willingly,
2075 He gave Aspremont, such an imposing city.
And he made Bertran a knight, giving him
Two castles to command, all by himself,
While the younger brother became his squire.

When things were...
Then they are...completely. 2080
After this he sent for his noble lady wife.
She arrived accompanied by a thousand knights.
He wants her to keep her name and not change it:*
She is known therefore as Lady Erimena.
The count marries her in Saint Hilary's, 2085
And they were to live happily ever after.

50

It was in May, when the blossom on the branches
And in the woods gives out a fragrant perfume.
Count Beton was a most worthy young man,
He went to see his mother and kisses her warmly. 2090
'My lady,' he says, 'it makes me very sad indeed
That I've not taken revenge on the disloyal emperor
Who made it possible for the traitor Guy
To kill my father so painfully and so tragically,
And who sold you for money so dishonourably, 2095
To that disloyal traitor who took you as his wife,
And who murdered Daurel's youngest son.
If I had not fled to the emperor and king
Who gave me his fair-skinned daughter,
He would surely have killed me, without fail. 2100
I have taken revenge on Guy, thanks be to God,
But I would not truly be the son of Bovis the Bold
If I did not within a month lay waste to his lands,
Even if he is my uncle, may God dishonour him!'
'My son,' said the lady, 'may God exalt your honour! 2105
Precisely because the emperor is so very worthy
And because you are related to many of his best men
There should be *no bad blood* between you.
Summon a messenger who can ride a swift horse
And send a message to the king and emperor 2110
Demanding compensation for his dishonourable act,
For he delivered *his very own sister* to Guy.
If he does not...

Then he should not raise his standard for ten years,
2115 And you should rule over them and be king.
A hundred of your best knights should go with you,
And the emir will send you decisive reinforcements.'
The count spoke thus: 'May God honour you,
For no man ever had a better mother;
2120 I want to avenge the mighty duke, her husband.
And so I will, my lady, let there be no mistake.'

51

Count Beton summons Bertran to him.
'My friend,' he says, 'make ready at once,
And take two valiant knights along with you,
2125 One should be Ademar and the other Gauseran.
Go as quickly as you can to the emperor.
Do not greet him or show any signs of courtesy,
Rather announce that I issue him a challenge.
I do not wish to ask him for peace or for a truce,
2130 Since he consented to my disinheritance.
For fifteen packhorses laden with gold and silver
He gave up my mother, selling her on the spot.
I am *safe and sound*, praise be to God,
And I no longer consider him my lord or kinsman.
2135 Just as long as I am able to bear arms
He shall have no peace in my lifetime.
Greet on my behalf Roland, Count Palatine:
As a token of friendship, take my glove to him.
He is my kinsman, and I should not offend him.
2140 ...Charles guarantees
...
Sir Ademar said: 'We shall follow your orders,
We shall never give up on seeking justice for you.'
On this they have saddled their fine warhorses,
2145 And the knights ride off, very courageously.
Each one of them is fully equipped,
With hauberks and lances and sharp swords.
Within three days, and without stopping,
They arrive in Paris, before the lofty palace.

52

Sir Ademar speaks with the gatekeeper: 2150
'My friend,' he said, 'we wish to come in:
We are three messengers from Poitiers.'
They reply: 'In God's name, most willingly,
But your warhorses must remain outside.'
So they walk up into the immense palace   2155
And they all three go to stand before the king.
It was sir Gauseran who spoke first of all
For he is the oldest and they choose him to speak
Because he was wise and eloquent,
As well as an excellent knight-at-arms.   2160
'May God save and protect Roland and Oliver,
And greetings also to all the twelve peers
From Beton, the noble count and warrior.
But he does not greet the fine-looking man
Called Charles, may God cast him down,   2165
For he sold his sister for silver and shiny gold.
Fifteen packhorses came into this very palace,
And he gave her as wife to the traitor Guy,
Who wanted to put to death little Beton.
Instead of him, he smashed against a pillar   2170
A little child who was the son of a minstrel.
But God in heaven allowed him to escape,
And now he asks for justice for that murder.
He has punished Guy: he does not forgive you.
It is no use promising him money or cash,   2175
For, by the Lord who gave us the power of speech,
He will not let another month go by
Without coming here to enrage and attack you.
Just as long as he is able to bear arms
He shall not leave you alone even for four days.'   2180
The emperor just stares at them for a while,
Then he starts to laugh and to shake his head.
'My friend,' he says, 'you are a very brave man,
Coming here to threaten me in this way.'

[*Here the manuscript breaks off*]

CHARLEMAGNE'S JOURNEY TO JERUSALEM AND CONSTANTINOPLE

I

One day Charles was in the abbey church at Saint-Denis;
He has put on his crown again, crossed himself
And has girded on his sword with its hilt of pure gold.
There were dukes with him and vassals, barons and knights.
The emperor looks carefully at the queen, his wife.   5
She was wearing a fine crown in a most elegant manner;
He led her by the hand beneath an olive tree
And began to address her publically:
'My lady, have you ever seen any man on earth
So suited to wearing a sword and a crown on his head?   10
I have still more cities to conquer with my lance.'
She was not very sensible and answered foolishly:
'Emperor,' she said, 'you may think too highly of yourself.
I know of another man who is more impressive
When he wears his crown amongst his knights: 15
When he places it on his head, it becomes him better.'
On hearing this, Charles is extremely angry;
He bows his head in shame, for the French have also heard.
'Well, my lady, where is this king? Come on, tell me.
Together we shall wear our crowns on our heads   20
In the presence of your kinsmen and all your advisers.
I shall call a meeting of the good knights of my court;
If the French agree with you, then I shall accept it as true.
If you have lied to me, you will pay dearly for it.
I shall cut off your head with my sword of steel.'   25
'Emperor,' she said, 'do not work yourself up over this.
He is richer than you in possessions, gold, and money,
But he is nowhere near as brave as you, nor such a good knight
When dealing out blows in battle and pursuing the enemy.'
When the queen realized that Charles was so furious   30
She deeply regrets her words and is ready to fall at his feet.

2

'Emperor,' she said, 'for the love of God, have mercy on me.
I am after all your wife and I was only joking.
I shall immediately exonerate myself if you command it
35   By swearing an oath or enduring an ordeal.
From the tallest tower in the city of Paris
I shall allow myself to be cast down as proof
That this was not said or intended to dishonour you.'
'This will not be necessary,' said Charles, 'but name the king.'
40   'Emperor,' she said, 'I can't for the life of me remember.'
'By my head,' said Charles, 'either tell me immediately
Or I shall have your head cut off on the spot.'

3

Now the queen realizes that she is in a tight spot;
She would willingly let things drop, but dare not change her tune.
45   'Emperor,' she said, 'do not consider me a fool;
I have heard a lot about King Hugo the Strong,
He is the Emperor of Greece and Constantinople.
He rules over the whole of Persia as far as Cappadocia.
There is no more handsome knight from here to Antioch;
50   Apart from you no one equals him in chivalry.'*
'By my head,' said Charles, 'I shall find out for myself.
If you have lied, I promise you, you will die.'

4

'By my faith,' said the king, 'you have made me very angry.
You have totally forfeited my affection and my favour.
55   I believe your head will yet be severed from your trunk.
You should not, my lady, have doubted my power;
I shall never give up until I have laid eyes on him.'

5

The Emperor of France, once he had taken off his crown
And he had made an offering at the main altar,

Returned forthwith to his palace in Paris. 60
He has taken Roland and Oliver with him,
And William of Orange and battle-hardened Naimon,
Ogier of Denmark, Berin and Berenger,
Archbishop Turpin, Ernaut and Aimer,
And Bernard of Brusban and battle-hardened Bertram,* 65
And some thousand knights hailing from France.
'My lords,' said the emperor, 'listen to me a moment.
If it pleases God, you will go to a far-off kingdom
And seek out Jerusalem and the land of Our Lord God.
My plan is to worship the Cross and Sepulchre; 70
I have dreamt of this three times, I must therefore go,
And I shall go to find a king of whom I have heard reports;
You will take seven hundred camels laden with gold and silver
So that we can stay and live in that land for seven years.
Never shall I return home until I have found him.' 75

6

The Emperor of France orders his army to be equipped
And he gave fine equipment to those who accompanied him.
He gave them plenty of pure gold and silver.
They had neither shields nor lances nor razor-sharp swords,
But iron-tipped ash staffs and pendulous pilgrim scrips.* 80
They have their warhorses shod front and back.
Their servants saddle up their mules and their packhorses,
And fill up the trunks with pure gold and silver,
With vessels and coins, and other fine objects;
They carry golden chairs of state and tents of white silk. 85
At Saint-Denis in France the king takes up his scrip.*
Archbishop Turpin blessed him with due ceremony,
And then took up his scrip, and the French did the same.
And they mount their mules, strong and smooth of gait.
They left the city, spurring their mounts on. 90
From now on Charles will proceed according to God's will.
The queen remains behind, weeping and lamenting.
The king rides on until he reached open country.

He turns to one side and calls to Bertram:
95 'See how noble are these companies of wandering pilgrims;*
There are eighty thousand of them in the front ranks alone.
The man who leads and governs them must indeed be powerful!'

7

Now the emperor is riding with his great companies of men:
In the front ranks alone there are eighty thousand of them.
100 They left the Île-de-France and passed through Burgundy,
Crossing Lorraine, Bavaria, and Hungary, and the lands
Of the Turks and the Persians, and of that most hated race;*
They crossed the waters of the great river at Lycia.*
The emperor rides through the middle of the Croiz Partie,*
105 Its woods and its forests, and they have reached Greece.
They saw the hills and mountains of Romania*
And gallop into the land where God was crucified.*
They catch sight of Jerusalem, an ancient city.*
The day was bright and clear, they procured lodgings,
110 And they come to the church, placing their offerings there.
Then these proud companies return to their lodgings.*

8

The gifts Charles offers there are most impressive.
He entered a vaulted church of painted marble.
Inside there is an altar dedicated to the Paternoster;*
115 God sang mass there, and so did His Apostles,
And all twelve of their seats still remain there.
The thirteenth stands in the middle, hidden and enclosed.*
Charles gladly entered, with great joy in his heart.
As soon as he saw the chair, he goes right up to it.
120 The emperor sat down; he rests for a little while.
The twelve peers sat in the others, surrounding him closely.
No man had sat there before, and none has since.

9

Charles was very happy to see such great beauty:
He gazed at the church with its brightly coloured paintings
Depicting martyrs and virgins, and divine majesty,   125
And the phases of the moon and annual feast days,
And baptismal rivers and fish swimming in the sea.*
Charles's expression was proud, and he held his head up high.
A Jew came in, who had been watching him closely.
When he saw Charles, he began to tremble;   130
His face was so proud that he did not dare to look at him.
He almost falls to the ground, turning to flee,
And climbs all the marble steps at top speed.
He finds the patriarch, and begins to address him:
'Go to the church, my lord, to prepare the font;   135
I want to be baptized and converted forthwith.*
I have just seen twelve counts go into the church,
Accompanied by a thirteenth, never have I seen such a man:
In my humble opinion, the man is God Himself;
He and His Twelve Apostles have come to visit you.'   140
On hearing this, the patriarch leaves to make himself ready.
Having summoned throughout the city his priests in their albs,
He has them don their vestments and put on copes.*
In a fine procession he has gone to see the king.
The emperor saw him and has risen to greet him.   145
Uncovering his head, he bows to him deeply.
They embrace each other and exchange pleasantries;
And the patriarch said: 'Where are you from, my lord?
Never before has a man dared to enter this church
Unless it was at my command or request.'   150
'My lord, my name is Charles and I was born in France,
Through strength and bravery I have conquered twelve kings,
I am looking for the thirteenth, of whom I have heard reports.
I came to Jerusalem out of love of God;
I have come to worship the Cross and the Sepulchre.'   155
And the patriarch said: 'My lord, you are very brave.
You have sat in the seat in which God Himself sat.
Henceforth may you be called Charlemagne, king of kings.'*
And the emperor said: 'By God, I thank you five hundred times.

160 Give me, if you please, some of your holy relics,
     Which I shall take to France so it can bathe in their glory.'
     The patriarch replies: 'You shall have them in abundance:
     You shall have at once the arm of Saint Simeon,
     And I shall have the head of Saint Lazarus brought to you,
165 And some of Saint Stephen's blood, one of God's martyrs.'
     In return Charlemagne offers him good wishes and friendship.

10

     Then the patriarch said: 'You have done the right thing
     In coming to seek out God; it will be to your advantage.
     The relics I shall give you cannot be bettered on earth:
170 The part of Jesus's shroud which covered his head,
     When he was placed and laid down in his tomb.
     Although the Jews were guarding him with their steel swords
     He rose again on the third day, just as he had foretold,
     And appeared before his Apostles to raise their spirits.
175 You will have one of the nails that pierced his foot,
     And the Holy Crown that God wore on his head;
     And you will have the chalice that he blessed;
     I shall also happily give you the silver dish,*
     It is inlaid with gold and with precious stones,
180 And you will have the knife that God held when eating,
     Some hairs from Saint Peter's beard and from his head.'
     In return Charlemagne offers him good wishes and friendship.
     His whole body shakes with joy and with pity.

11

     Thus spoke the patriarch: 'Fortune has smiled on you!
185 In my opinion, God has brought you here.
     The relics I shall give you possess great power:
     Some of the Virgin Mary's milk, with which she suckled Jesus
     When he first came down to earth to be among us,
     And some cloth from the holy tunic which she wore.'

In return Charlemagne offers him good wishes and friendship.   190
The patriarch had the relics fetched and the king received them.
The relics are powerful; through them God performs great
    miracles:
A paralytic was lying there, he had not moved for seven years,
His bones suddenly creaked, his tendons stretched out
And he leaps to his feet; never before had he felt so well.
Now the patriarch can see that God has performed a miracle: 195
Quickly he has the bells rung repeatedly throughout the city.
The king orders a reliquary to be made, never to be surpassed;
For it they melted a thousand marks of purest Arabian gold.
And he had it sealed fast and securely,
Binding it tightly with many a strong silver strap.   200
He orders his men to take it to Archbishop Turpin.
Charlemagne was joyful, as were all of his companions.

12

The king remained in the city of Jerusalem for four months.
He and the twelve peers, his dear companions,
Indulge in great display, as befits the emperor's prestige.   205
They begin to build a church dedicated to the Virgin Mary:
The local inhabitants call it the Latin church,*
For people speaking this language attend it from all over town.
There they sell their brocades, their linen, and their silk,
Ginger, cinnamon, pepper, and other fine spices,   210
And many tasty herbs, too numerous for me to list.
God is still in His heaven and will punish this behaviour.

13

The Emperor of France had stayed there so long
That he took the patriarch to one side and said:
'Give me leave to go, if you please, fair lord;   215
I must return now to France, to my kingdom.
It's a while since I was there and I have lingered here long.
And my barons do not know where I have gone.

220 Pray accept a hundred mules laden with gold and silver.'
     And the patriarch said: 'I shall hear none of it,
     Let my great wealth be entirely at your disposal;
     Let the French take as much of it as they want to carry off.
     But beware of Saracens and of the pagan foe,
225 Who wish to destroy us and the sacred Christian faith.'

14

     And the patriarch said: 'Is it clear what I am asking of you?
     To slaughter Saracens, who so despise us.'
     'Willingly,' said Charles, who then gave him his word.

15

     'I shall summon my men, as many as I can muster
230 And I shall go to Spain; there can be no delay.'
     This he later did: he remained true to his word,
     For there died Roland and the twelve peers with him.

16

     The Emperor of France had been there so long
     That he remembers what his wife had said to him.
235 Now the king will seek out the man whom she had praised;
     He will not give up at all until he has found him.
     That night he tells the French in their lodgings;
     When they heard this, they were joyful in their hearts.
     Next morning, at dawn, when they saw the sun rise
240 Their mules and packhorses are already loaded and packed,
     And the barons mount their horses and set off on their way.
     They arrive in Jericho, gathering many palm branches:
     'Onwards with God's help,' they cry loud and clear.
     The patriarch having mounted a well-rested mule
245 Accompanies and escorts Charles while daylight lasts.
     At night the barons were all lodged together;

Whatever they asked for was given to them.
The next morning, at dawn, when they saw the sun rise,
The barons remount their horses and set off on their way.
Then the patriarch called out to Charlemagne:
'Give me leave to go, if you please, fair lord!'   250
'I commend you to our Lord God,' said the emperor.
They go to embrace each other; now they have parted.
The emperor rides on with his doughty barons.
The relics are powerful; through them God performs great
    miracles:
They arrive at no river whose waters do not part before them,   255
Nor do they encounter a blind man whose sight is not restored,
They make the paralysed stand up straight and the dumb speak.

17

The emperor rides on with his great retinue
And they pass by Monteles and the hills of Abilant,*   260
The rock of Guitume and the plains before it.
They caught sight of Constantinople, a splendid city,
With its bell towers, its eagles, and its gleaming cupolas.*
To the right of the city, stretching for a good league,
They find orchards planted with pine trees and white laurels;   265
Roses, viburnum, and wild briar are in flower.*
They found twenty thousand knights seated there,
And they were wearing brocaded silk and white ermine,
And great marten furs sweeping down to their feet.
They are amusing themselves with chess and backgammon   270
And some are holding their falcons or their hawks.
And three thousand maidens glistened with gold thread,
Whose brocaded silk dresses adorn their comely bodies;
Holding their lovers by the hand they parade around.
Here comes Charles riding an ambling mule.   275
He turns to one side and addresses Roland:
'I do not know where their king is, but what noble barons!'
He calls to one of the knights, saying light-heartedly:
'Friend, where is your king? I have sought him far and wide.'
And he replied to him: 'Just ride on a bit and   280
You will see the king sitting under that brocaded awning.'

The emperor rides on immediately, without delay;
He found King Hugo toiling at his plough.
The yokes are made of gleaming pure gold,
285 As are the axles, the wheels, and the ploughshares.
With his goad in his hand, he does not go on foot,
For he has a strong ambling mule on each side.
They support a golden seat suspended between their backs;*
There sat the emperor on a splendid cushion:
290 It is stuffed with oriole feathers and covered in Persian silk.
There is a stool at his feet, inlaid with shiny silver;
He has a hat on his head and his gloves are very fine indeed.
There are four upright supports of pure gold around him,
On top of them has been spread a fine Greek cloth.
295 In his hand the king held a staff of pure gold
And manoeuvred his plough so expertly
That he produces a furrow as straight as a taut string.
Here comes Charles riding an ambling mule.

18

The king was steering his plough to finish his daily stint,
300 And Charlemagne approached him on a well-trodden path.
He saw the outspread cloth and the gleaming gold.
He greeted King Hugo the Strong most eagerly.
King Hugo looks at Charles, noticing his proud expression;
He has muscular, sturdy arms and a slim, slender body.
305 'My lord, God be with you. How do you come to know me?'
The emperor replies: 'I was born in France,
My name is Charlemagne, Roland is my nephew.
I have come from Jerusalem and wish to return home,
But I am keen first to see you and your barons.'
310 And Hugo the Strong said: 'It has been at least seven years
Since I first heard foreign soldiers say
That no king on earth has such noble barons as you.
I shall keep you here for a year if you wish to remain;
I shall give you much gold and silver, and loads of money;
315 Let the French carry away as much of it as they can load up.
Now I shall unyoke my oxen out of friendship for you.'

19

The king unyokes his oxen and abandons his ploughing;
They graze in the meadows and cultivated land higher up.
The king mounts his mule and ambles away.
'My lord,' said King Charles, 'this plough of yours
Contains more pure gold than I can possibly estimate,
Yet you leave it unguarded; I fear it will be stolen.'
And King Hugo said: 'Do not worry about all this;
In the length and breadth of my land there has never been a thief.
It could stay here for seven years without being touched.'
William of Orange exclaimed: 'May Saint Peter save us,
For if I took it to France and Bertram were there,
It would be destroyed with picks and hammers.'
Hugo spurs on his mule and ambles away.
He went up to his palace, where he saw his wife,
Has her prepare herself and she gets changed.
The palace and the hall are festooned with silk hangings.
Now here comes Charles with his great retinue.

20

The emperor dismounts in front of the shiny marble;
He rushes into the palace by the hall steps.
They found seven thousand knights sitting there,
Wearing ermine cloaks and tunics of Persian silk.
They are amusing themselves with chess and backgammon.
Quite a few of them have come running outside;
They took charge of the horses and strong ambling mules,
Leading them to the stables to be well looked after.
Charles gazed at the palace and its rich splendour:
The tables and chairs and benches are of pure gold.
The palace walls had borders of azure, beautifully decorated
With costly paintings of animals and of dragons
And all sorts of creatures and birds in flight.
The vaulted palace was topped with a dome,
Perfectly symmetrical and tightly ribbed.
The central column was inlaid with shiny silver,

320

325

330

335

340

345

350 Encircled by a hundred upright columns of marble;
     The front of each one is inlaid with pure gold.
     There was a statue of two children in copper and metal,
     Each of them holding in their mouth a white ivory horn.
     If a gust blows from the sea, or breeze, or other wind
355 Buffeting the palace from a westerly direction,
     It makes it revolve rapidly and often
     Like a chariot's wheel rolling along the ground.
     Thus these horns sound and bugle and play
     Like drums or thunder or a huge hanging bell.
360 The figures look at each other as if they are smiling,
     Which made you think that they were actually alive.
     Charles gazed at the palace and its rich splendour;
     He did not give a fig for his own fine belongings.*
     He then remembers his wife and his dire threats against her.

21

365 'My lords,' said Charles, 'this is a very fine palace,
     Unrivalled by those of Alexander or ancient Constantine,
     Or by the great monuments of Crescentius of Rome.'*
     And just as the emperor spoke these words
     He witnessed a wind blow in from the coastal port;
370 It blasted against the palace, buffeting it on one side,
     Setting it in motion, softly and smoothly,
     And making it revolve like the shaft of a mill.
     And the figures blow their horns, smiling at each other,
     Which made you think that they were actually alive.
375 One high-pitched, the other clear, both wonderful to hear.
     Anyone who hears them thinks he must be in paradise,
     Where the angels sing softly and sweetly.
     The storm raged mightily, bringing snow and hail,
     And the wind, harsh and strong, howled and roared.
380 The windowpanes are made of fine crystal,
     Carved and fashioned from ultramarine quartz.
     Indoors, all is tranquil, calm, and serene,
     Just as on a sunny summer's day in May.
     The storm was most violent, frightening, and harmful.
385 Charles watched as the palace turned and shook;

He did not know what was happening, nor had he ever seen
   anything like it.
Unable to remain standing, he sat down on the marble floor.
The French have all been toppled; they cannot remain upright,
And they covered their heads whether face down or up.
And each said to the other: 'We are in dire straits: 390
The doors are open, yet we cannot escape from here.'

22

Charles watched the palace continue to turn rapidly;
The French cover their heads, not daring to look at it.
Yet King Hugo the Strong has come forward
And has addressed the French thus: 'Do not be afraid.'   395
'My lord,' said Charlemagne, 'will it ever stop?'
And Hugo the Strong said: 'Just be patient for me.'
As evening approached the storm grew calm.
The French leapt to their feet; supper was now ready.
Charles sat down, together with his doughty barons;   400
Hugo the Strong had his wife by his side
And his blonde-haired daughter, whose face was pretty and bright.
Her flesh was as pale as summer blossom.
Oliver looks at her and fell in love with her:
'Would that it please God, in His glorious, holy majesty,   405
That I could take her with me to France, or to the city of Dun.
For then I would have my way with her.'
He said this under his breath, so that no one could hear him.
Whatever they ask for was given to them:
There is plenty of game: venison and wild boar,   410
And they have cranes, geese, and peppered peacocks.
A never-ending stream of wine and claret is brought,
And their entertainers sing, playing the viol and the rote.
The French enjoy themselves in a most noble fashion.

23

Once they had eaten their fill in the royal palace   415
And the head seneschals have removed the tablecloths,
The squires leap up from all sides, one by one,

And go off to the stables to look after their horses.
King Hugo the Strong summoned Charlemagne
420 And draws him and his twelve peers to one side.
Holding the king by the hand, he led them into his chamber
Vaulted and decorated with painted flowers and crystal gems.
There shone a carbuncle, bright and luminous,
Set into a pillar dating from the time of King Goliath.
425 There stand twelve soft beds, of copper and metal,
With velvet pillows and fine silk bed linen.
The lightest would need twenty oxen and four carts to move it.
The thirteenth in the middle is constructed to perfection,
Its feet are of silver and its headboard enamelled.
430 The bedcover was excellent, worked by Maseus
—A very noble fairy, who gave it to the king—
This embellishment is worth more than all the emir's treasure.
Whoever gave it to him must really love the king,
Serving him so well and equipping him nobly.

24

435 The French have entered the chamber and seen the beds;
Each of the twelve peers has already chosen one for himself.
King Hugo the Strong has wine brought for them.
He was wise, clever, and full of cunning:
In the chamber, under a slab of marble
440 Which was hollow underneath, he has placed a man.
All night long he watches them through a small spyhole.
The carbuncle glows so that one can see clearly,
Just as on a sunny summer's day in May.
King Hugo the Strong went to join his wife,
445 And Charlemagne and the French take their time to prepare for bed.
Then the counts and the marquises began to boast.*
The French were in their chamber and have been drinking wine.

25

And one said to the other: 'Just look at this great splendour!
Just look at how fair the palace is and at this luxury.

Would that it please God, in His glorious, holy majesty   450
That Charlemagne, my lord, had purchased this
Or won it on the field of battle as the spoils of war.'
Charlemagne said: 'I must be the first to boast:
King Hugo the Strong has no young knight
In his household, however strongly he may be built,   455
Even if he has donned two hauberks and fastened on two helmets,
And is mounted on a swift, well-rested warhorse, whom
—As long as the king lends me his sword with its gilded
    pommel—
I would not strike on the most precious parts of the helmets,
Slicing through the hauberks, the helmets set with gems,   460
And the felt lining plus the saddle of the well-rested steed.
I shall plunge the blade into the ground; if I let it drive home
Then no mortal man will ever manage to pull it out
Without digging up a full lance's length of soil.'
'Good lord,' exclaimed the spy, 'you are strong and well built.   465
King Hugo was foolish when he offered you lodging.
If I hear you speak foolishly one more time tonight,
Tomorrow at dawn, I'll have you sent on your way.'

26

Then the emperor said: 'Now for your boast, fair nephew Roland!'
'Willingly, my lord, I am completely at your command.   470
Tell King Hugo to lend me his ivory horn
And then I shall go outside into the open country.
My breath will be so strong and the resulting blast so violent
That in the whole city, which is so huge and vast,
No gate nor postern will remain standing,   475
And all the copper and steel, however strong and heavy,
Will be forced by such a violent blast to clash.
King Hugo will be very strong indeed if he sallies forth
Without whiskers being singed from his beard,
And without his great marten furs whirling round his neck   480
And his ermine cloak turned inside out on his back!'
'Good lord,' exclaimed the spy, 'this is malicious boasting;
King Hugo behaved foolishly in lodging such people.'

27

'Let's hear your boast, Sir Oliver,' said courtly Roland.
485 'Willingly,' says the count, 'with Charlemagne's permission.
Let the king take his daughter, whose hair is so blonde,
And place her in bed with me alone in her chamber.
If she doesn't swear that I had her a hundred times tonight,
Let me lose my head tomorrow; I promise, on my word.'
490 'Good lord,' exclaimed the spy, 'you will give up before that.
Your words are deeply insulting and if the king were to learn of this,
He would be your sworn enemy for the rest of his life.'

28

'My lord archbishop, will you boast with us too?'
'Yes,' said Turpin, 'if this is Charles's command.
495 Let three of the best horses to be found in his city
Be produced by the king tomorrow, and let him arrange a race
Outside in the open country. When they are running at top speed
I shall come from the right, racing with such vigour
That I shall catch up with the third and leave the other two behind;
500 And I shall be holding four very large apples in my hand,
And I shall juggle them and throw them in the air,
Allowing the horses to gallop unrestrained.
If I lose one of the apples or drop one of them,
Let my lord Charlemagne gouge out my eyes from my head.'
505 'Good lord,' exclaimed the spy, 'this boast is fine and noble;
It is not at all insulting towards my lord the king.'

29

Said William of Orange: 'My lords, now it's my turn to boast.
Do you see that huge ball? I have never seen one bigger.
Note how much pure gold and silver it contains.
510 Repeatedly, thirty men have tested themselves against it,
But they were not able to budge it, so heavy was the load.
In the morning I shall lift it up with one hand,
Then I shall hurl it right through the centre of the palace

And shall demolish more than forty yards of wall.'
'Good lord,' exclaimed the spy, 'this is totally unbelievable.   515
A curse on the king if he does not put you to the test;
I shall tell him in the morning, before you are dressed.'

30

Then the emperor said: 'Now it's Ogier's turn to boast,
The Duke of Denmark, whose toilsome feats are legend.'
'Willingly,' said the hero, 'with your full permission.   520
Do you see that pillar which supports the palace,
Which you saw revolving rapidly this morning?
Tomorrow you will see me take it in my powerful grasp,
And however strong the pillar is, it will still shatter,
Thus demolishing the palace, and razing it to the ground.   525
Whoever is trapped there will find no protection.
The king will be a fool if he doesn't go and hide somewhere.'
'Good lord,' exclaimed the spy, 'this man is raving mad.
May God never allow you to carry out this boast,
For the king behaved foolishly when he gave you lodging.'   530

31

Then the emperor said: 'Duke Naimon, let's hear your boast!'
'Willingly,' said the hero, 'even though my hair is all white.
Tell King Hugo to lend me his burnished hauberk.
Tomorrow, when I have donned it and put it on,
You will see me shake it so vigorously and violently   535
That, however strong, whether of white or burnished steel,
The hauberk's links will still fall off, just like bits of straw.'*
'Good lord,' exclaimed the spy, 'you are old and hoary;
You may have white hair, but you have nerves of steel.'

32

Then the emperor said: 'Let's hear your boast, Sir Berenger!'   540
'Willingly,' said the count, 'since this is your command.

Let the king take the swords from all of his knights
And have them buried up to their hilts of pure gold
So that their tips are pointing up, towards the sky.
545   I shall walk up to the top of the highest tower
And then I shall let myself plunge on to the swords.
Then you will see blades shatter and break,
With one piece of steel smashing and cracking another.
Yet you will find not one that has pierced my flesh,
550   Scratched my skin, or inflicted a deep wound!'
'Good lord,' exclaimed the spy, 'this man is raving mad.
If he fulfils this boast, he is made of iron or steel!'

33

Then the emperor said: 'Let's hear your boast, Sir Bernard!'
'Willingly,' said the count, 'since this is your command.
555   Did you see that mighty river roaring past the ford?
Tomorrow I shall divert it completely from its channel,
Causing it to flood the fields in full view of everyone,
And to fill all the cellars which exist in this city,
Soaking and drenching King Hugo's subjects,
560   And making him climb to the top of his highest tower.
He will not come down until I give the order.'
'Good lord,' exclaimed the spy, 'this man is raving mad.
King Hugo behaved very foolishly when he gave you lodging.
Tomorrow, at dawn, you will all receive your marching orders!'

34

565   Then Count Bertram said: 'Now it's my uncle's turn to boast.'
'Willingly, by my faith,' said Ernaut of Gironde.
'Now let King Hugo take four loads of lead
And have them smelted together in cauldrons,
And let him provide a huge, deep vat,
570   Which he will have filled right up to the rim.
Then I shall sit down in it until the hour of None.*
When the lead has completely set and the ripples have subsided,
When it is really solid, then you will see me shake free,

Splitting the lead in two and breaking it off from under me.
What remains won't weigh even as much as a shallot!'   575
'This is an amazing boast,' exclaimed the spy,
'I have never heard tell of such thick skin on a man.
He is made of iron or steel if he fulfils this boast!'

35

Then the emperor said: 'Let's hear your boast, Sir Aimer!'
'Willingly, said the count, 'since this is your command.   580
I have a hat with a border of almandines,*
Made in a distant land from a huge marine fish.
When, having placed it on my head, I am wearing it,
Tomorrow, when King Hugo is seated at his dinner table,
I shall eat his fish and drink his claret.   585
Then I shall come at him from behind and administer such a blow
That I shall knock his head down onto the table;
Then you will see beards tugged at and whiskers plucked.'
'Good lord,' exclaimed the spy, 'this man is raving mad.
King Hugo behaved very foolishly when he gave you lodging.'   590

36

'Let's hear your boast, Sir Bertram,' the emperor said.
'Willingly,' said the count, 'just as you wish.
In the morning lend me three strong, sturdy shields,
Then I shall go outside and climb that ancient pine tree.
There you will see me strike them together so violently   595
That they will fly into the air. And then I shall shout so loudly
That in the countryside, over a radius of four leagues,
No stag or fallow deer will fail to flee the woods,
Nor a single woodland doe, roe deer, or fox.'
'Good lord,' exclaimed the spy, 'this is an evil boast.   600
When King Hugo learns of it, he'll be angry and annoyed.'

37

'Let's hear your boast, Sir Gerin,' said the emperor Charles.
'Willingly,' said the count: 'tomorrow, in full sight of everyone

Have a strong, sturdy spear brought to me outside;
605 Let it be long and heavy, too weighty for a peasant.
Let its shaft be of applewood, and its iron point a yard long.
At the top of that tower, on the marble pillar,
Place two pennies for me, one on top of the other.
Then I shall stand a good league's distance away
610 And you will see me throw, if you pay attention,
And knock one of the pennies down to the foot of the tower,
So gently and smoothly that the other will not stir.
Then I shall be so agile and swift and fast
That I shall come rushing in through the door of the hall
615 And shall catch the spear before it hits the ground.'
'Good lord,' exclaimed the spy, 'this boast is worth three of the others.
In this there is no hint of insult towards my lord.'

38

Once the counts have finished boasting and have fallen asleep,
The spy, who has heard everything, leaves the room.
620 He came to the door of the chamber where King Hugo lay.
He found the door ajar and then he approached the bed.
The emperor saw him, and addressed him eagerly:
'So tell me, what are the French up to, and Charles of the proud face?
Did you hear them talking, and shall we remain on friendly terms?'
625 'By God,' said the spy, 'they spared no thought for that.
Instead tonight they have been mocking and insulting you.'
He repeated all the boasts that he had overheard.
On hearing this, King Hugo was angry and annoyed.

39

'Goodness me,' said the king, 'Charles behaved foolishly
630 When he joked about me in such a reckless manner.
I lodged them last night in my stone-walled chamber;
If they do not fulfil their boasts exactly as uttered,
I shall cut off their heads with my polished sword.'

Then he summons at least a hundred thousand of his men:
He has commanded them to put on their byrnies, 635
And to don their cloaks and gird on their burnished swords.
Having entered the palace they sat down around him.
Charles was returning from church, having heard mass,
And with him the twelve peers, a proud company of men.
The emperor, being the most powerful, precedes them 640
And is carrying in his hand an olive branch.
King Hugo saw him, and upbraids him from afar:
'Charles, why did you joke about me and deride me?
Last night I lodged you in my stone-walled chamber;
You should never have contemplated such recklessness. 645
If you do not now fulfil the boasts you uttered,
I shall cut off your heads with my polished sword.'
On hearing this, the emperor fears for his life,
And he looks at his Frenchmen, a proud company of men.
'Last night we were all drunk on wine and claret. 650
I think that the king had a spy in his chamber.'

40

'My lord,' said Charlemagne, 'last night you gave us lodging.
You supplied us with lots of wine and claret,
And it is our custom in France—in Paris and in Chartres—
That when Frenchmen are abed, they joke and boast. 655
Hence they say all sorts of things, both wise and foolish.
Pray let me now speak to my doughty barons
And I shall gladly respond to you with sureties.'
'Truly,' said the king, 'the insult was too shameful.
By my faith,' Hugo continued, 'and by my white beard, 660
Once you have left me, never will you mock anyone again.'

41

Charlemagne goes away, accompanied by the twelve peers
And under a vaulted roof they assemble to deliberate.
'My lords,' said the emperor, 'things are going badly for us.

665 We had drunk so much wine and claret
That we said things which ought not to have been said.'
Then he had the relics brought before him.
They prostrate themselves in prayer, proclaiming their mea culpa,
And pray to God in heaven, invoking his power
670 To protect them that day from King Hugo the Strong,
Who has become so angry towards them.
Suddenly an angel sent by God appears before them;
He made for Charlemagne and then raised him up:
'Charlemagne, do not despair, Jesus sends you this message:
675 The boasts that you uttered last night were very stupid.
Christ orders you never to mock anyone again.
Go and get on with it; every one of them will be fulfilled.'
On hearing this, the emperor was happy and joyful.

42

Charlemagne of France had risen to his feet
680 And stretching out his hand he crossed himself.
Then he said to the French: 'Do not despair!
Come with me to see King Hugo in his palace.'

43

'My lord,' said Charlemagne, 'I cannot but speak my mind.
Last night you lodged us in your stone-walled chamber;
685 Some of us were drunk on wine and claret;
When you left us you did us great wrong
By leaving your spy with us in the room.
We know of a land where customary law dictates
That had you done so there, it would have been treachery.
690 We shall fulfil our boasts, this cannot be avoided.
Whomsoever you chose will begin first.'
And King Hugo the Strong said — and he chose very well —
'Here stands Oliver, who boasted so outrageously
That he would have my daughter a hundred times in one night.
695 May I be cursed in every court if I do not hand her over to him.
If I do not give her to him, then I have no regard for my honour.
But if he gives up and falters just once,

I shall cut off his head with my polished sword.
He, along with the twelve peers, are destined to die.'
At this Charlemagne laughed, for he trusts in God.   700
And he replied: 'Woe betide you if you let him off.'
All day long they play, amuse, and enjoy themselves;
Whatever they ask for they receive immediately
Until night fell and everything grew dark.
The king had his daughter brought into his chamber;   705
It was all festooned with silk hangings and curtains.
Her flesh was as pale as summer blossom.
Oliver came in and he began to smile;
When the girl saw him she was very afraid,
And yet she was courteous and spoke most nobly: 710
'My lord, did you come from France to kill us women?'
And Oliver replies: 'Do not fear, fair maiden,
If you are willing to trust me, you will suffer no harm.'

44

Oliver lay in the bed next to the king's daughter;
He has turned her towards him and kissed her three times.   715
She was very comely and he spoke to her courteously:
'My lady, you are very beautiful, for you are a king's daughter.
Despite my boasting, do not be in the least afraid;
I do not wish to take advantage of you.'
'My lord,' said the girl, 'pray have mercy on me.   720
I shall never again be happy if you dishonour me.'
'Fair maiden,' said Oliver, 'I am entirely at your command,
Provided you convince the king I've fulfilled my promise.
I shall make you my beloved; never shall I wish to have another.'
She was very courtly and gave him her word.*   725
In the morning, at daybreak, the king came to them,
And he addressed his daughter, saying to her privately:
'Tell me, fair daughter, did he do it to you a hundred times?'
In reply she says to him: 'Yes, my royal lord.'
There is no need to ask if the king was angry,   730
And he came into the palace where Charlemagne was sitting.
'The first has survived; I think he must be a magician.
Now I need to know if the others are telling lies or the truth.'

45

The king was upset that the boast had been fulfilled,
735 And he said to Charlemagne: 'The first has survived,
And I need to know if the others will do the same.'
'My lord,' said the emperor, 'as it pleases you.*
Whomsoever you choose will go next.'
'Here is William, the son of Count Aimeri,
740 Let him lift up the ball that is lying in the chamber.
If he doesn't manage to throw it exactly as he stated last night,
I shall cut off his head with my blade of steel.
He and the twelve peers are facing imminent death.'

46

Now Count William realizes that the joke is on him,
745 So he takes off his cloak of brown beaver fur,
Casting it off into the brocade hangings.*
He rushed into the chamber where the ball was located
And lifting it with one hand, he hurled it vigorously
And with everyone watching he sent it flying
750 So that it demolished more than forty yards of wall.
This was achieved, not through his strength, but through
    God's might,
For the love of Charlemagne, who had brought them all there.
King Hugo was distressed, for his palace had been breached.

47

He said to his men: 'This is no joking matter,
755 By the loyalty I owe to you, this is evil and ignoble.
These people who have come here are magicians;
They intend to possess my land and all my domains.
Now I need to know whether the others will do the same.
But if one of them fails, by Almighty God,
760 Tomorrow I shall have them hanged in the wind from that pine,
Attached to solid gallows, they will have no escape.'

48

'My lord,' said Charlemagne, 'do you want more of the boasts?
Whomsoever you choose will go next.'
And Hugo the Strong said: 'Here is Bernard,
The son of Count Aimeri, whose boast concerned   765
That mighty river, which roars through the valley.
He would divert it completely from its channel,
Causing it to enter the city and flood everywhere,
And making me climb to the highest point in my palace,
Unable to come down until he gives the order.'   770

49

Now Count Bernard knows that it is his turn to act;
He said to Charlemagne: 'Pray for me to Our Lord God.'
He rushes over to the river, crossing himself at the fords.
God in His glorious heaven performed a miracle
By making the huge river completely leave its bed,   775
Thus flooding the fields in full view of everyone,
And entering the city and filling its cellars,
Soaking and drenching King Hugo's subjects.
The king flees on foot to the top of his highest tower.
Charles of the proud countenance is atop an ancient pine*   780
Along with his twelve peers, his valiant knights
And they pray to Our Lord God to take pity on them.

50

Charlemagne is atop an ancient pine
Along with his twelve peers, his noble companions.
He heard King Hugo lamenting from the top of the tower: 785
He will give him his treasure and escort him back to France
And will become his vassal, holding his kingdom from him.
On hearing this, the emperor is overcome with pity
—In the face of humility one should relent—
And he prays to Jesus to make the waters subside.   790

God performed a great miracle for the love of Charlemagne:
The water leaves the city and flows across the plains;
It returns to its channel, filling up to the banks.
Then the king was able to descend from the tower
795 And he comes to Charlemagne in the shade of a fruit tree.
'Truly, rightful emperor, I know that God loves you!
I wish to become your vassal, I shall hold my kingdom from you,
I shall give you my treasure and have it taken to France.'
'My lord,' said Charlemagne, 'do you want any more of the boasts?'
800 And Hugo the Strong replied: 'Not this week!
If they are all fulfilled, I shall regret it for the rest of my days.'

51

'My lord,' said Charlemagne to King Hugo the Strong,
'Now you are my vassal as all your men can testify.
Today, we should hold a lavish celebration and enjoy ourselves.
805 And together we shall wear our golden crowns;
Out of friendship for you I am happy to wear mine.'
'And I am happy to wear mine in your honour,' said Hugo.
'And we shall walk in procession inside that cloister.'
Charlemagne is wearing his great crown of gold;
810 King Hugo is wearing his just a little closer to the ground,
For Charlemagne was a good foot and three inches taller.
As the French behold them, each one of them exclaimed:
'My lady the queen's words were foolish and false;
Charlemagne is an excellent warrior and leader of men:*
815 We shall never enter a country without being victorious.'

52

Within Constantinople Charlemagne is wearing his crown;
King Hugo is wearing his even closer to the ground;
As the French behold them, many of them exclaim:
'My lady the queen's words were extremely foolish
820 When she deemed other barons equal to us in worth.'
So they walk in procession inside the cloister.
King Hugo's wife, who is wearing her crown,
Is leading her blonde-haired daughter by the hand.

When she glimpses Oliver, she is keen to speak to him;
Her expression is friendly, revealing her love;   825
But for her father, she would happily have ventured a kiss.
They enter the church as they come out of the cloister
Archbishop Turpin, who was the highest-ranking priest,
Sang mass for them and the barons make their offerings,
Then they come to the palace in very high spirits.   830

53

The French are in the palace and dinner was ready.
The tables had been set up and they have gone to eat.
They were made to wait for nothing that they asked for.
There is plenty of game: venison and wild boar,
And they have cranes, geese, and peppered peacocks.   835
A never-ending stream of wine and claret is brought,
And their entertainers sing, playing the viol and the rote.
King Hugo the Strong addresses Charlemagne thus:
'Let my great wealth be entirely at your disposal;
Let the French take as much of it as they want to carry off.'   840
And the emperor said: 'I shall hear none of it;
I shall never take from you even a penny coin.
They already have more of my wealth than they could possibly carry!
But now give us leave to go; we must depart.'
And King Hugo the Strong said: 'I daren't refuse you.'   845
The mules were held for them at the marble steps.
Then the emperor said: 'I am at your command.'
They embrace and commend each other to God.

54

Once the French have eaten, they will leave straight away.
The mules and packhorses were held for them at the steps.   850
Now the French have mounted and set off joyfully.
King Hugo's daughter rushes towards them;
When she sees Oliver, she grabs his flapping cloak:
'I have bestowed on you my friendship and my love
So take me to France and I shall leave with you.'   855

'Fair lady,' said Oliver, 'I willingly grant you my love,
But I shall go to France with my lord Charles.'

55

Brave Charlemagne was full of happiness and joy,
Having overcome such a king without fighting in the field.
860 Why should I string out this story any longer?
They travel through countries and foreign kingdoms
And have arrived in Paris, that wonderful city.
Now they go to Saint-Denis and have entered the abbey church.
Brave Charlemagne prostrates himself in prayer;
865 When he has prayed to God, and risen to his feet,
He places the nail and the crown on the altar,
And he distributes the other relics throughout his kingdom.
The queen was there, she has fallen at his feet.
The king's anger subsides as he forgives her
870 For love of the Holy Sepulchre, at which he has worshipped.

EXPLANATORY NOTES

In the notes that follow, each note is keyed to the line number in the text. References to other editions of the texts are to the name of the editor, for example Whitehead, followed by page number: full details for each reference are given in the Select Bibliography.

THE SONG OF ROLAND

9 *AOI*: much scholarly ink has been spilt over the possible significance of this collocation of letters which ends some *laisses* and occasionally occurs at the end of lines within *laisses*, but no firm conclusions have been reached. AOI is probably a lyrical refrain of some kind.

39 *land and goods . . . vassal*: the French reads 'Serez ses hom par honur e par ben', but *honur* and *ben* are ambiguous and could refer in each case to ethical worth or material wealth, land and goods respectively. Cf. line 45.

152 *Michaelmas*: this feast celebrates Saint Michael, patron of the Mont Saint-Michel, dubbed *in periculo maris* (in danger from the sea); cf. lines 1428 and 2394.

190 *marches*: the French *marches* seems here to have the technical meaning of border territory, but see line 275, where it is unclear whether Charlemagne has anyone specific in mind or is simply asking for one of his barons to be nominated.

198 *Noples and Commibles*: see Index of Proper Names for more geographical detail.

240 *further . . .*: Whitehead perceives a lacuna here; Short supplies text from other manuscripts, adding 'Send one of your barons to him now'.

275 *my kingdom*: ma marche could also refer specifically to a marcher baron, in which case Charles would be manipulating the choice.

302 *grin*: rire can mean 'smile' or 'laugh' in Old French. It is interesting that Ganelon *sees* Roland's reaction.

306 *Now we are sworn enemies!*: 'Jo ne vus aim nïent', literally 'I do not love you at all'. The verb *aimer*, when used in this feudal context, has connotations of mutual respect and protection.

432 *half of Spain as a fief*: it seems that here and in lines 472–3 Ganelon has changed the terms of the pact to appear less favourable; cf. line 224.

516 *gold . . . five hundred pounds*: another possible meaning is that the furs are worth five hundred pounds weight in gold.

520–62 *Thus spoke Marsilie . . . no man alive*: laisses 40–2 are *similaires*: this is a rhetorical device which enables the poet to focus on one important event employing incremental repetition with variation to nuance its meaning; see Introduction.

541 *lances and spears*: it is unclear whether lances and spears (*espiét*) are consistently considered distinct in the text: here the words may denote different weapons or be synonyms. Cf. line 2074. It might be tempting to think that a lance was used couched in order to unseat an opponent (as it was later in the Middle Ages), whereas a spear was used as a projectile, but this is also not always clear from the text either. Furthermore, visual evidence (e.g. the Bayeux Tapestry) shows knights doing both. We have always translated *lance* as 'lance', but have translated *espiét* as both 'spear' and 'lance' depending on context. Both weapons have an *hanste* ('shaft'), on which see the note to line 1204.

604 *without a sworn oath*: from this point on in our translation, italics indicate where a lacuna in Whitehead's edition has been filled by Short's text.

617–41 *Now a pagan...his boot*: laisses 48–50 constitute *laisses parallèles*, in which similar actions are narrated in a parallel way (see Introduction).

618 *bring up*: for Short *lever* means 'stood as godparent', but we have preferred a less precise meaning, cf. line 1563.

736 *Charles is still sleeping*: Charles has two sets of dreams in the *Roland*, cf. laisses 185–6, both of which are prophetic and interpreted as warnings from God. This first pair points to Ganelon's betrayal of Charlemagne through Roland's death at Rencesvals (symbolized by his lance) and the consequent trial of Ganelon back in Aix (where the boar represents Ganelon, the leopard Pinabel, and the hound Thierry). However, at this point in the narrative the symbolism is not clear, nor is the outcome evident, and the dreams function primarily to give a sense of foreboding.

788 *my family's name*: geste can refer to deeds, stories of heroic deeds, a person's or family's reputation, and even lineage; see Introduction.

849–50 *almaçors...sons of the counts*: these terms designate high-ranking pagans (see Glossary).

870 *Durestant*: this has not been identified, but the meaning seems to be from the Pyrenees to the Moorish border (see Jenkins, 73).

888a–b *[If I find Roland...the fourth]*: extra lines suggested by Short to fill an obvious lacuna in the Oxford manuscript.

1015 *The pagans are wrong and the Christians are right*: this famous line could be read as Roland's credo, with which he attempts to justify all his actions.

1093–6 *Roland is brave...fighting to the death*: these famous lines emphasize the valour of both knights and their excellence as vassals. They also have complementary attributes: Roland is a fighter, while Oliver is a tactician.

1132 *Proclaim your mea culpa*: confess your sins.

1204 *With his lance level*: much critical ink has been spilt on the meaning of *pleine sa hanste* and the expression has been variously interpreted as meaning (a) that the shaft of a lance or spear is still intact; (b) that an opponent has been knocked off his horse 'a lance's length'; (c) that the shaft of the lance is being held level in order to unseat an opponent with one clean blow (presumably a feat requiring great strength and skill). We are persuaded by this last interpretation.

1297 *Gautier*: *Gaulter* in the manuscript is not Gautier del Hum and some critics have emended to Oton, who is the companion of Berenger

1386–7 *I neither know… the swifter*: Short suggests that these two lines make more sense after line 1380.

1428–9 *Mont Saint-Michel… Wissant harbour*: cf. note to line 152. Although the geography is not entirely clear, as Seinz could be Saintes or Xanten, what is implied is that the whole country is rocked by exceptional weather.

1490 *This warhorse*: a possible source for the description of Turpin's horse in the lines that follow is Isidore of Seville.

1531 *carbuncle*: see lines 627–33, where there is no mention of a carbuncle, although Whitehead implies that some text is missing from the earlier passage.

1569 *pact with Count Ganelon*: see lines 617–26.

1570 *mangons*: in line 621 the coins are implausibly embedded in the sword but here they seem to be separate.

1653 *The dreadful battle*: we have followed Whitehead's *laisse* numbering of 125a here; although the Oxford scribe has copied these two *laisses* continuously, in Whitehead's view the original poet intended them to be separate.

1724 *bravery by definition is not folly*: this interpretation is proposed by Karen Pratt in 'Reading Epic through Romance: The *Roland* and the *Roman de Thèbes*', in Marianne Ailes, Philip Bennett, and Karen Pratt (eds.), *Reading Around the Epic: A Festschrift in Honour of Wolfgang van Emden* (London: King's College London, 1998), 101–27.

1782 *race*: gent here could mean either 'race' or 'army'.

1926 *lives*: we follow Short's reading cors here, taken from other manuscripts.

2002 *challenge*: in medieval law an attack would be treacherous if not preceded by an open challenge. This is an argument used by Ganelon in his trial.

2074–5 *So they throw… assegais*: we have accepted Short's reading since Whitehead's solution results in an incomplete line.

2250 *crossed his fair white hands*: it is unclear in the original whether Turpin has crossed his own hands, or whether Roland has repositioned them.

2503–4 *the lance… wounded on the cross*: this may be a reference to the 'discovery' of the spear of Longinus in Antioch in 1098.

2529 *dream*: in this second pair of prophetic dreams, Charles is warned of the impending attack by Baligant, whose forces are represented by extreme weather and dangerous exotic animals. Charles's combat with the lion clearly represents his single combat with the emir, but the outcome is unclear. The second dream echoes *laisse* 57; Ganelon is the bear cub, his kinsmen the thirty bears, and Thierry is the hound who attacks the largest bear (Pinabel). Again, the result of the judicial combat is not foretold.

2558 *the Ardennes*: cf. line 728. Geographical locations in dreams help to pin down the time in the future when the events prophesied will take place.

2667 *holds court*: the term *plaider* covers legal and political matters.

3220 *men from Butentrot*: many of the peoples listed here and in the following *laisses* are fictitious.

3243 *Ugleci*: a Slavic tribe.

3298 *Precious*: the name of Baligant's sword.

3686 *mangons*: cf. line 621 and see note to line 1570.

3694 *God under all His names*: the recitation of all the names for God in the different classical languages was considered to bring good luck.

3716 *my kingdom*: *marches* here probably does not have the specific meaning of 'border country'.

3792 *fell at his feet*: Jenkins (p. 264), argues that this is a legal formula meaning 'accepted with thanks'.

3829 *him*: *le* could refer either to Roland or to the *servise* he owed Charles.

3919 *Driving...forehead*: we have based our translation on the emended text of Brault even though the scribe appears to have copied the second hemistich twice.

3959 *Traitors bring death on themselves and others*: a proverbial expression.

4002 *Here ends the ancient tale that Turoldus relates*: 'Ci falt la geste que Turoldus declinet' has been translated in numerous ways which reflect critics' views that Turoldus was either a poet, scribe, or jongleur. We have opted for a general term for *declinet* which covers all these possibilities. Alternatively, *que* may be a conjunction rather than a relative pronoun, thus giving rise to the meaning 'because Turoldus is in decline/growing weak'. Turoldus has not been identified.

DAUREL AND BETON

4 *the boy, Beton*: Beton is referred to throughout the poem as an *enfan*, which can mean, depending on context, 'baby', 'infant', 'child', 'boy', 'lad', 'young man'.

125 *'Companion, you will die because of this gift'*: the text reads 'per sela dona vos convenra morir'. *Dona* here is ambiguous: it could be a form of *domna* ('lady'), but it more obviously means 'gift'. Note that Charlemagne has not yet mentioned his sister. Cf. lines 138 ('Per aqueta molher molra el a dolor') and 155 ('per cesta dona vos vendra destu[r]bier'), which echo this line.

139 *Charlemagne, the Bavarian*: the reference to Charles as a Bavarian is unusual, though he is given the epithet in one other *chanson de geste*. See

Kimmel, 205. Labelling Charlemagne thus may enhance the sense of how alien he is to an Occitan-speaking audience.

195–6 *Celebrating joyfully … lofty fortress*: the text reads 'A molt gran joia intro al paimen | Redon la viala e l'ausor mandamen.' There is some uncertainty over the precise meaning of *paimen*, *viala*, and *mandamen* (see Kimmel, 206 and Lee, 106). The adjective *ausor* is often used to describe palaces in *Daurel*, but here context suggests a distinction between *paimen* and *mandamen*. That a *mandamen* is some kind of fortress is supported by other sources.

257 *France*: used here with the restrictive sense of 'royal territories', which is to say more or less the present-day Île-de-France.

368 *Ardennes forest*: the text seems quite realistic in its relative positioning of Poitiers, Bordeaux, Paris, and Agen. Monclar is clearly on the Atlantic coast on the same level as Poitiers. The Ardennes, Antona, and Aspremont, on the other hand, seem more part of what Kimmel calls 'the conventionalized geography of the *chanson de geste*' (p. 39).

379 *spaulder*: a piece of armour that protects the shoulder. Metal spaulders were a fourteenth-century innovation, so what is almost certainly meant here is some kind of protection made from leather.

428 *holy communion using leaves*: knights about to die on the battlefield are given the last rites by their fellow warriors in this way in *chansons de geste* and other archaic texts.

434 *Take my heart … eat some of it*: this line has elicited a range of interpretations; see Lee, 188. Are we perhaps to infer that Guy will absorb some of Bovis's virtues? Or does Bovis envisage some extreme form of incorporation whereby the two companions will become as one?

531 *Saint Hilary's church*: Saint-Hilaire remains one of the main churches in Poitiers to this day.

614 *Tie this traitor … dust*: Ermenjart imagines a punishment for Guy similar to that of Ganelon in the *Roland*.

622–3 *mighty king … money*: these lines play on the semantic range of *ric* in Occitan, the primary meaning of which is 'powerful' (hence 'mighty duke' here and elsewhere for *lo ric duc* and 'mighty king' for *ric rey*), but with overtones too of 'rich' and 'wealthy'.

629–31 *give me a knight … comfort to my heart*: Ermenjart is asking Charlemagne to give her a champion to challenge Guy in a judicial combat.

633 *ordinary knight*: on the semantic range of *po[e]statz*, the word at the end of the line, see Kimmel, 214.

669 *destined to misery from birth*: see similar formula in line 622.

687 *evening*: Kimmel (p. 215) thinks *lo ses* means 'senses', but this does not seem phonologically possible. Lee translates as 'agli alloggi', citing an analogy from troubadour poetry, but her translation would require a preposition. Our translation is conjectural and based on context.

701 *an island*: literally a gravel bank.

721 *elephant seal*: the manuscript reading (*lo leo* 'the lion') is emended by Kimmel to *lo loc*, but as Lee points out (p. 189), this is not possible at the rhyme. We follow Lee's translation.

722 *The walls... doors*: this line may be corrupt.

1025 *you will be taken care of*: 'seres be noirgatz', literally 'you will be nourished/brought up well'. The poet is playing on the meaning of the verb *noirir*.

1026 *henceforth we are sworn foes*: 'ja mai no·us puec amar': it is hard not to suspect a deliberate echo of the *Roland* here, and of Ganelon's declaration to Roland, 'jo ne vus aim nïent' (line 306).

1065 *her godson*: cf. lines 349–55 where we learn that Bovis had had Daurel's son baptized.

1087 *She falls from the tower*: at this stage, the text merely describes her falling, but it is made clearer later (line 1176) that she has thrown herself from the top of one of the towers.

1182–3 *great lands... dishonour*: the rhyme word in line 1182 is *honor*, meaning both 'fief' and 'honour'. The rhyme word in lines 1183 and 1189 (*dessonor*) is playing on this double meaning.

1195–6 *land of Babylon... port*: a medieval reader would probably have understood Babylon to be Cairo. In the *Roland*, Baligant also hails from Babylon, see line 2614. The port of Cairo is Alexandria.

1215 *the greatest king there has ever been*: a striking assertion, given that Daurel has just mentioned Charlemagne's court. Yet the possibility that Charlemagne is inferior to a foreign king is also raised in *Charlemagne's Journey*.

1288 *They sharpen... blows*: the line is problematic in the manuscript: 'Guio bos brans per los grans colps donar'. The problem is that the meaning of the verb *guiar* is unclear. We translate it as a form of (or possibly a misreading of) *agujar*, 'to sharpen'. See the notes in Kimmel, 221 and Lee, 191.

1299 *How you saw... Monclar*: 'Qu·us vos lai fairit los de Monclar'. Kimmel, 221 describes the line as obscure and reads *fairit* as a form of *ferir*; he is followed in this by Lee, who nonetheless says she is perplexed. We are taking *fairit* as a form or misreading of *faidit*.

1402 *Within the walls... water*: 'Lains an aigua molis, freis e corens'. The line is problematic on two counts: first the exact sense of *molis* is unclear; secondly *freis* is the result of an emendation (from *foreis*). The literal meaning of *aigua molis* would seem to be 'mill water' (*molis* = mill). Both Kimmel (p. 223) and Lee (p. 192) relate the expression here to Catalan *aiguamoll*, which is an evaporation pool, and therefore stagnant. But it seems unlikely that those in the castle would be pleased to have stagnant water. 'Mill water' is obviously running water.

1443–4 *however well…down to size*: these lines are obscure; see Kimmel, 222–3 and Lee, 192. We follow Kimmel in seeing here gaming imagery, but the image in line 1444 (*talhar*) is not one of 'fleecing' as he suggests.

1677–8 *Do not allow…wrong*: 'Per vostre sen no·us volhatz capdelar | Mas per lo mieu, no·i poiretz pecar'. *Sen* in line 1677 more literally means wisdom.

1751 *tumble*: there is a pun here on the 'tumbling' of a knight from his horse, and the 'tumbling' of a minstrel performing acrobatics.

1985 *They all start to…*: from this point the manuscript has lacunae before breaking off. Some text has been supplied in italics.

2083 *He wants her to keep her name*: this marks a deliberate contrast with other Saracen princesses or queens like Bramimunde in the *Roland* or Gui-bourc/Orable in the *Prise d'Orange* from the *Guillaume* cycle.

CHARLEMAGNE'S JOURNEY TO
JERUSALEM AND CONSTANTINOPLE

50 *chivalry*: barnez could mean chivalry or a group of barons.

65 *Bernard of Brusban…Bertram*: these men are Charlemagne's peers in the *Journey*, who later indulge in boasting. Berin is also called Gerin.

80 *iron-tipped ash staffs…pilgrim scrips*: the point is that they are kitted out as pilgrims rather than as Crusaders, although the presence of warhorses in the next line is rather incongruous.

86 *France*: probably a reference to the Île-de-France.

95 *companies*: we use 'companies' rather than 'bands' because we think there are ironic military overtones here.

100–8 *Île-de-France…Jerusalem, an ancient city*: critics have been left bewildered by the poet's geography here, which may be precise (although scholars are not able to interpret all of the items with confidence) or a product of his imagination, in which case any attempt at identification of real geographical locations would be futile. A summary of critical opinion is to be found in Burgess (Garland edn., 1998), 54. Tyssens reorders the lines (100, 101, 105, 106, 102, 103, 104, 107, etc.) so that the elements of the journey make more sense geographically, but we have retained the original order.

102 *that most hated race*: a reference to the Saracens?

103 *the great river at Lycia*: or Laodicea on the river Lycus, or perhaps *a la liee* describes the way the river was crossed, by tying planks together?

104 *Croiz Partie*: the region of the cross is perhaps the Holy Land, although Croatia has also been suggested.

106 *Romania*: this may be the Byzantine Empire or the part of it lying on the Adriatic coast. Tyssens has Asia Minor.

107 *God was crucified*: adopting the usual Trinitarian view, the poet conflates God and Christ here; cf. line 115.

111 *proud*: *feres* could mean fierce or proud; in a battle context fierce is more appropriate, but here it is unclear whether the author has a negative or positive attitude towards these warlike pilgrims.

114 *dedicated to the Paternoster*: there is a church by this name in Jerusalem, dedicated to the Lord's Prayer.

117 *hidden and enclosed*: Tyssens thinks that *ben seelee e close* refers to its sturdy construction; others think that the seat is sealed off or concealed, but Charles seems to have no problem noticing it, and sitting upon it!

127 *baptismal rivers*: we wonder if this is a reference to the image of Christ being baptized in the Jordan.

136 *baptized*: *lever* refers to the action of godparents who offer the child for baptism; cf. *Roland*, lines 618 and 1563.

142–3 *albs...copes*: liturgical vestments; albs are long white garments worn under the cloak-like cope.

158 *Charlemagne*: although the manuscript reads 'Charles', editors emend this to 'Charlemaigne', since this is the moment when the patriarch gives him his famous epithet, which he bears from then on.

177–8 *chalice...silver dish*: the chalice and the Paschal dish also feature in Grail literature.

208 *the Latin church*: the church of Saint Mary Latin was reputed to have been built by Charlemagne for western pilgrims.

260 *Monteles...Abilant*: some critics attempt to locate these places, while others see them as imaginary. Again, the poet's sense of geography is somewhat vague.

263 *eagles*: thought to be a reference to decorative elements on top of buildings.

265–6 *white...wild briar*: in accordance with the assonance of the original we are following Aebischer's emendation of *beaus* to *blans*, and in the following line *glazaus* to *aiglens*.

288 *They support a golden seat suspended*: we follow the emendation 'Une chaiere sus tienent d'or sozpendant' suggested by Eduard Koschwitz in later editions of his *Karls des Grossen Reise nach Jerusalem und Constantinopel: ein altfranzösiches Heldengedicht* (Heilbronn: Henninger, 1883–).

363 *He did not give a fig*: literally 'a glove', but this is an expression of minimal value.

367 *the great monuments of Crescentius of Rome*: Crescentius was thought to have built Hadrian's mausoleum in Rome.

446 *the counts and the marquises began to boast*: these boasts are in jest and may parody the exaggerated claims made by epic heroes before battle.

537 *links...straw*: there is a pun here on expressions of minimal value containing the terms 'link' and 'straw'.

571 *the hour of None*: a monastic hour equivalent to 3 p.m.

581 *hat*: we presume the hat makes Aimer invisible.

725 *She ... gave him her word*: there is a line in the manuscript following this one, struck through either by the original scribe or a later prudish one, which makes the whole scene much more risqué: 'That night the count did not do it to her more than thirty times!' Oliver is able to fulfil his boast even if he does not have sex with the king's daughter, as long as she vouches for it. If, however, this line is original, it undermines Oliver's courtliness, asserted ironically by the narrator.

737 *My lord ... pleases you*: this line is written in the margin of the manuscript and is omitted by Burgess and Tyssens but retained by Aebischer; consequently the latter's line numbering rejoins that of scholars who include the struck through line after 725.

746 *brocade hangings*: *neiles de paile* has received much critical discussion. We have opted for something plausible, influenced by Tyssens's suggestion.

780 *ancient pine*: some critics prefer the reading *pui autif* (lofty hill), but we have opted to translate the manuscript reading *pin antif*, which provides the comic image of Charles and his men up a tree.

814 *Charlemagne is an excellent warrior and leader of men*: see line 28, where the queen in fact admitted this!

GLOSSARY

almaçor a Saracen honorific title

almandine a precious stone like a garnet

amirafle a Saracen honorific title

assegais pole weapons used for throwing or hurling, usually a light spear or javelin made of wood and pointed with iron

bezant a Byzantine gold coin

boss the central, raised part of a shield, often decorated

brocade a rich silk fabric with raised patterns

buckler a shield

byrnie a protective leather tunic covered in chain mail

carbuncle a bright red, luminous gem

citole medieval stringed instrument of the lute family, precursor of the cittern

coif a cap worn under a helmet; sometimes a chain mail protection for the head and neck

crozier a staff carried by a bishop

emir a Saracen honorific title equivalent to emperor

fief a piece of land given to a vassal in return for military service and advice

hauberk a coat of chain mail

hilt the handle of a sword

lighter a flat-bottomed boat

march frontier land, though the term can signify land in general

mea culpa confession of sins

mangon a gold coin

mark a gold coin

oliphant a horn made out of an elephant's tusk

palfrey a docile horse often ridden by women

pommel the decorative end of a sword's hilt, often spherical

quillon either of the ends of the crosspiece of a sword

rote any of several stringed medieval musical instruments, with a soundboard, and either bowed or plucked

sable the precious fur of a marten

scrip a pilgrim's leather satchel with a shoulder strap

sorrel a chestnut colour, usually to describe a horse

trebuchet a catapult used for siege warfare

vassal a knight who serves his lord in return for a fief and protection

viol musical instrument with five, six, or seven strings, and played with a bow

ventail a removable flap of mail worn across the face and chin

INDEX OF PROPER NAMES

Note: references are to line numbers in the texts.

Abilant (hills of): *Journey* 260

Abiram, a biblical character: *Roland* 1215

Abisme, a Saracen knight: *Roland* 1470, 1498

Acelin, a Frankish count: *Roland* 172, 2882

Ademar, Duke Bovis's valet: *Daurel* 93, 99, 1091, 1093, 1094, 1126, 1157, 1289, 1293, 1319, 1334, 1348, 1352, 2074, 2125, 2142, 2150

Aëlroth, Marsilie's nephew: *Roland* 1188

Africa: *Roland* 1593

Agen: *Daurel* 201

Aicelina/Aicelineta, Beton's wet nurse: *Daurel* 716, 724, 733, 783, 807, 855, 934, 2034, 2035

Aimer, one of Charlemagne's twelve peers: *Journey* 64, 579

Aimeri (of Narbonne), father of William of Orange and Bernard of Brusban: *Journey* 739, 765

Aix (Aix-la-Chapelle, Aachen): *Roland* 36, 52, 135, 188, 435, 478, 726, 1409, 2556, 2667, 2860, 2917, 3696, 3706, 3734, 3744, 3873, 3945, 3984

Alexander (the Great): *Journey* 366

Alexandria, Egypt: *Roland* 408, 463, 2626

Alfrere, a Saracen city or country: *Roland* 1915

Almace, Turpin's sword: *Roland* 2089

Almaris, a Saracen king: *Roland* 812

Alphaïen, a Saracen knight: *Roland* 1554

Amborre of Oluferne, a Saracen knight: *Roland* 3297, 3549

Anjou, province of France: *Roland* 106, 2322, 2883, 2945, 2951, 3093, 3535, 3545, 3938

Anseis, one of Charlemagne's twelve peers and companion of Samson: *Roland* 105, 796, 1281, 1599, 2188, 2408

Antelme of Mayence (Mainz), a Frankish knight: *Roland* 3008

Antioch, Holy Land: *Journey* 49

Antona, location uncertain: *Daurel* 6, 31, 32, 56, 69, 81, 113, 127, 1168, 1322, 1674, 1818, 1953

Apollo, viewed as one of the Saracen trinity of gods: *Roland* 8, 417, 2580, 2697, 2712, 3268, 3490

Apulia, the heel of Italy: *Roland* 371, 2328

Aquitaine: *Roland* 2325

Araby: *Roland* 2282, 2810, 2980, 3331, 3473, 3555

Ardennes, forest of: *Roland* 728, 2558; *Daurel* 288, 293, 368

Argoille, a Saracen land: *Roland* 3259, 3474, 3527

Argonne, wooded area in Champagne-Ardenne: *Roland* 3083, 3534

Aspremont, Alpes-Maritimes: *Daurel* 10, 57, 60, 311, 535, 933, 1330, 1378, 2075

Astor, a Frankish knight: *Roland* 796

Aude, Oliver's sister and Roland's betrothed: *Roland*, 1720, 3708, 3717, 3723

Austorie, a Frankish duke: *Roland* 1625

Auvergne: *Roland* 3062, 3796

Babylon (Cairo): *Roland* 2614; *Daurel* 1195, 1694

Balaguer, a fortress in Catalonia: *Roland* 63, 200, 894

Baldise-la-Longue, a Saracen land: *Roland* 3255

Baldwin, Ganelon's son: *Roland* 314, 363

Balide-la-Forte, a Saracen town: *Roland* 3230

Baligant, emir of Babylon: *Roland* 2614, 2654, 2686, 2725, 2769, 2788, 2802, 2827, 2979, 3130, 3135, 3155, 3180, 3184, 3201, 3295, 3324, 3373, 3497, 3513, 3551, 3600

Barbamouche, Climborin's horse: *Roland* 1534

Basan, a Frankish messenger killed by Marsilie: *Roland* 208, 330, 490

Basbrun, one of Charlemagne's officers: *Roland* 3952, 3956

Bascle, a Saracen land, perhaps Blakia in Macedonia: *Roland* 3474

Basil, Saint: *Roland* 2346

Basilie, a Frankish messenger killed by Marsilie: *Roland* 208, 330, 490

Bavaria: *Roland* 2327, 3028, 3977; *Journey* 101

Beatrice, Daurel's wife: *Daurel* 1000

Beaune, a town in Burgundy: *Roland* 1892

Belferne, a Saracen land: *Roland* 812

Berenger, one of Charlemagne's twelve peers: *Roland* 795, 1304, 1624, 2187, 2405; *Journey* 63, 540

Berin (also called Gerin), one of Charlemagne's twelve peers: *Journey* 63

Bernard of Brusban, son of Aimeri of Narbonne and one of Charlemagne's twelve peers: *Journey* 65, 553, 764, 771

Bertram, son of Bernard of Brusban, nephew of Ernaut of Gironde and one of Charlemagne's twelve peers: *Journey* 65, 94, 327, 565, 591

Bertran, Daurel's son: *Daurel* 1165, 1290, 1301, 1308, 1310, 1332, 1343, 1360, 1365, 2076, 2122

Bertran, Guy's squire: *Daurel* 65

Besançon: *Roland* 1429

Besgun, Charlemagne's cook: *Roland* 1818

Beton: *Daurel* 4, 281, 298, 316, 322, 414, 438, 509, 624, 653, 738, 748, 765, 772, 777, 781, 822, 832, 911, 941, 971, 1009, 1010, 1024, 1034, 1090, 1097, 1102, 1116, 1125, 1141, 1156, 1172, 1260, 1273, 1279, 1323, 1404, 1406, 1414, 1419, 1424, 1430, 1437, 1453, 1471, 1480, 1487, 1508, 1523, 1533, 1543, 1553, 1558, 1562, 1564, 1586, 1599, 1625, 1629, 1641, 1667, 1684, 1686, 1696, 1702, 1724, 1727, 1737, 1746, 1748, 1751, 1756, 1760, 1774, 1822, 1844, 1848, 1853, 1868, 1876, 1882, 1903, 1919, 1930, 1932, 1937, 1942, 1949, 1969, 1980, 1992, 2016, 2019, 2035, 2051, 2056, 2060, 2067, 2069, 2089, 2122, 2163, 2169

Bevon, a Frankish knight: *Roland* 1891

Bire, a fortress near Granada?: *Roland* 3995

Blancandrin: *Roland* 23, 24, 47, 68, 88, 122, 368, 370, 377, 392, 402, 413, 414, 464, 503, 506

Blaye (Gironde), burial place of Roland and Oliver: *Roland* 3689, 3938

Bordeaux: *Roland* 1289, 1389, 3684; *Daurel* 136, 200, 1674

Bovis (d'Antona): *Daurel* 6, 26, 31, 36, 45, 56, 70, 75, 93, 111, 113, 127, 134, 145, 171, 174, 220, 239, 275, 289, 317, 432, 491, 1817, 1821, 1822, 2012

Bramimunde, Marsilie's queen: *Roland* 634, 2576, 2595, 2714, 2734, 2822, 3636, 3655, 3680, 3990

Brigal, a place in Saracen lands: *Roland* 889, 1261

Brittany: *Roland* 2322

Bruise, a Saracen land: *Roland* 3245

Burel, a Saracen knight: *Roland* 1388

Burgundy: *Roland* 2328; *Journey* 100

Butentrot, a Saracen land: *Roland* 3220

Brunas Vals (Dark Valleys): *Daurel* 361, 1294

Calabria, Italy: *Roland* 371

Califerne, a Saracen city or land: *Roland* 2924

Canabeus, King of Floredee, Baligant's brother: *Roland* 3312, 3429, 3499

Cappadocia, Turkey: *Roland* 1614; *Journey* 48

Capuel, King of Cappadocia: *Roland* 1614

Carcassonne, a town in Languedoc: *Roland* 385

Carthage: *Roland* 1915

Castel de Sorence, Pinabel's place of origin (*see also* Sorence): *Roland* 3783

Castel del Valfunde, a Saracen fortification, Blancandrin's home: *Roland* 23

Cazmarine, perhaps Camariñas, on the coast north-west of Compostela: *Roland* 956

Charles/Charlemagne: *Roland* 1, 16, 28, 52, 70, 81, 94, 156, 158, 180, 218, 274, 298, 317, 354, 370, 418, 430, 460, 470, 488, 522, 529, 538, 547, 549, 551, 560, 562, 566, 578, 597, 599, 643, 655, 703, 718, 724, 731, 736, 740, 755, 765, 823, 833, 841, 871, 883, 905, 915, 929, 939, 951, 970, 1052, 1060, 1071, 1100, 1127, 1172, 1179, 1195, 1207, 1234, 1241, 1254, 1350, 1403, 1407, 1422, 1560, 1703, 1714, 1727, 1732, 1757, 1766, 1788, 1829, 1842, 1859, 1907, 1928, 1949, 1959, 1973, 2017, 2091, 2103,

2114, 2117, 2133, 2145, 2149, 2242,
2281, 2308, 2318, 2334, 2353, 2362,
2380, 2402, 2429, 2454, 2457, 2476,
2505, 2513, 2525, 2532, 2546, 2569,
2579, 2621, 2658, 2667, 2681, 2721,
2732, 2740, 2750, 2755, 2793, 2807,
2809, 2837, 2846, 2855, 2874, 2877,
2891, 2892, 2897, 2944, 2952, 2974,
2982, 3006, 3014, 3031, 3035, 3066,
3092, 3132, 3145, 3171, 3179, 3187,
3197, 3234, 3277, 3287, 3303, 3314,
3328, 3329, 3359, 3367, 3375, 3443,
3446, 3451, 3494, 3515, 3536, 3543,
3554, 3565, 3579, 3589, 3595, 3603,
3605, 3608, 3612, 3649, 3669, 3676,
3695, 3711, 3720, 3728, 3743, 3750,
3777, 3807, 3815, 3845, 3851, 3862,
3891, 3903, 3935, 3947, 3994; *Daurel*
38, 42, 55, 72, 132, 139, 151, 156, 162,
412, 416, 546, 594, 1214, 1648, 1819,
1821, 1847, 2140, 2165; *Journey* 1, 17,
30, 39, 41, 51, 91, 112, 118, 123, 128,
130, 151, 158, 166, 182, 190, 203, 228,
245, 250, 275, 298, 300, 303, 307, 320,
333, 342, 362, 365, 385, 392, 396, 400,
419, 445, 451, 453, 485, 494, 504, 602,
623, 629, 638, 643, 652, 662, 673, 674,
679, 683, 700, 731, 735, 752, 762, 772,
780, 783, 791, 795, 799, 802, 809, 811,
814, 816, 838, 857, 858, 864

Chartres: *Journey* 654

Cheriant, a Saracen land, Kairouan in
Tunisia?: *Roland* 3208

Chernuble of Muneigre, a Saracen lord:
Roland 975, 984, 1310, 1325

Cherubin (angel): *Roland* 2393

Cize, a mountain pass in the Pyrenees:
Roland 583, 719, 2939

Clarbonne, a Saracen land: *Roland* 3259

Clarïen, a Saracen messenger: *Roland*
2670, 2724, 2771, 2790

Clarifan, brother of Clarïen, a Saracen
messenger: *Roland* 2670

Clarin of Balaguer, a Saracen knight:
Roland 63

Climborin, a Saracen peer: *Roland* 627,
1528, 1539

Commibles, a town in Spain or Portugal,
perhaps Coimbra: *Roland* 198

Constantine: *Journey* 366

Constantinople: *Roland* 2329; *Journey* 47,
262, 816

Cordoba, a town in southern Spain:
Roland 71, 97

Corsablix, a Saracen king: *Roland* 885, 1235

Crescentius (of Rome): *Journey* 367

Croiz Partie, perhaps Croatia: *Journey* 104

Daniel, biblical prophet: *Roland* 2386, 3104

Dapamort, a Lycian king: *Roland* 3205,
3216

Dathan, a biblical character: *Roland* 1215

Daurel: *Daurel* 4, 83, 84, 90, 101, 103,
113, 169, 204, 208, 348, 353, 520, 651,
661, 827, 833, 838, 846, 853, 855, 859,
871, 877, 879, 884, 895, 925, 950, 956,
969, 981, 984, 986, 1016, 1018, 1022,
1026, 1041, 1047, 1051, 1070, 1080,
1090, 1011, 1116, 1141, 1152, 1165,
1172, 1173, 1179, 1195, 1201, 1206,
1212, 1221, 1222, 1232, 1254, 1255,
1258, 1279, 1412, 1422, 1547, 1577,
1580, 1587, 1601, 1602, 1625, 1628,
1633, 1641, 1778, 1786, 1792, 1800,
1811, 1846, 1858, 1871, 1884, 1887,
1899, 1903, 1913, 1921, 1924, 1929,
1932, 1941, 1943, 1948, 1963, 1971,
1974, 1978, 1980, 1982, 1988, 2010,
2012, 2014, 2046, 2056, 2069, 2097

Daurelet, Daurel's baby son: *Daurel* 355

Denis, Saint: *Roland* 2347

Denmark: *Roland* 749, 1489, 3033, 3856,
3937; *Journey* 63, 519

Dijon: *Roland* 1892

Droün, a Frank and uncle of Gautier del
Hum: *Roland* 2048

Dun, a small town in the Midi-Pyrénées,
France: *Journey* 406

Durendal, Roland's sword: *Roland* 926,
988, 1055, 1065, 1079, 1120, 1324,
1339, 1462, 1583, 1870, 2143, 2264,
2304, 2316, 2344, 2780

Durestant, a place in the Pyrenees:
Roland 870

Ebram, a treacherous fisherman: *Daurel*
780, 808, 811, 820, 821, 825, 834, 861,
901, 919, 2021, 2043

Ebro, river in northern Spain: *Roland*
2465, 2642, 2728, 2758, 2798

Engeler of Bordeaux, one of
Charlemagne's twelve peers: *Roland*
1289, 1389, 1537, 1546, 2407

England: *Roland* 372, 2332

Erimena, the emir's daughter: *Daurel* 1411, 1867, 1869, 2084

Ermenjart, Charlemagne's sister and Bovis's wife: *Daurel* 173, 176, 227, 290, 385, 498, 593, 682, 737, 1045, 1050, 1092, 1827, 2000

Ernaut (of Gironde), son of Aimeri of Narbonne and one of Charlemagne's twelve peers: *Journey* 64, 566

Escababi, a Saracen knight: *Roland* 1555

Escremiz of Valterne, a Saracen knight: *Roland* 931, 1291

Espaneliz, a Saracen lord: *Roland* 2648

Esperveres, a Saracen knight: *Roland* 1388

Estamarin, a Saracen knight: *Roland* 64

Estorgant, a Saracen knight: *Roland* 940, 1297

Estramarit, a Saracen knight: *Roland* 941, 1304

Esturgus, a Saracen knight: *Roland* 1358

Ethiopia: *Roland* 1916

Eudon, a Frankish knight: *Roland* 3056

Eudropin, a Saracen knight: *Roland* 64

Faldrun of Pui, a Saracen knight: *Roland* 1871

Falsaron, Marsilie's brother: *Roland* 879, 1213

Flanders: *Roland* 2327

Floredee, a Saracen land: *Roland* 3312

Flurit, a Saracen king: *Roland* 3211

France: *Roland* 16, 36, 50, 94, 109, 116, 135, 167, 177, 187, 360, 422, 447, 470, 488, 573, 694, 702, 706, 726, 755, 804, 808, 829, 835, 857, 938, 969, 972, 989, 1054, 1064, 1090, 1161, 1168, 1194, 1210, 1123, 1423, 1695, 1734, 1861, 1927, 1985, 2017, 2311, 2337, 2379, 2431, 2455, 2556, 2579, 2661, 2681, 2732, 2773, 2909, 2928, 2935, 3084, 3089, 3188, 3234, 3315, 3334, 3422, 3443, 3579, 3615, 3673, 3706, 3765, 3976; *Daurel* 42, 115, 170, 257, 734, 766, 1213; *Journey* 58, 66, 76, 86, 100, 151, 161, 214, 217, 233, 306, 327, 406, 654, 679, 711, 786, 798, 855, 857

Frisia, a coastal region in modern Netherlands: *Roland* 3069, 3700

Fronde, a Saracen land: *Roland* 3260

Gabriel, the archangel: *Roland* 2262, 2390, 2395, 2526, 2847, 3610, 3993

Gaifier, a Frankish duke: *Roland* 798

Gaignun, Marsilie's horse: *Roland* 1890

Galatia, a place known for its silk: *Roland* 2973

Galicia, a province in north-western Spain: *Roland* 1476, 3073

Galne, a town in northern Spain: *Roland* 662

Ganelon: *Roland* 178, 217, 233, 277, 280, 296, 303, 319, 322, 332, 336, 337, 342, 358, 366, 375, 381, 396, 402, 413, 415, 425, 443, 456, 468, 496, 499, 509, 512, 518, 520, 529, 544, 557, 563, 567, 580, 582, 606, 616, 619, 625, 628, 632, 647, 659, 665, 668, 674, 721, 743, 749, 760, 769, 835, 844, 1024, 1147, 1406, 1457, 1529, 1569, 1759, 1770, 1816, 3704, 3735, 3748, 3751, 3757, 3762, 3780, 3786, 3792, 3800, 3809, 3827, 3829, 3847, 3895, 3904, 3932, 3949, 3963, 3969, 3973

Garmalie, the Saracen land of the Gamara?: *Roland* 1915

Gascony: *Roland* 172, 819, 1537

Gauseran, one of Beton's vassals: *Daurel* 2125, 2157

Gautier, a Frankish knight: *Roland* 1297

Gautier del Hum, a Frankish lord: *Roland* 800, 803, 807, 809, 2039, 2047, 2059, 2067, 2076

Gebuïn, a Frankish knight: *Roland* 2432, 2970, 3022, 3469

Gemalfin, a Saracen knight: *Roland* 2814, 3495

Geoffrey, a knight of Monclar: *Daurel* 1366

Geoffrey of Anjou, Charlemagne's standard bearer: *Roland* 106, 2883, 2945, 2951, 3093, 3535, 3545, 3806, 3819, 3938

Gerard of Roussillon, one of Charlemagne's twelve peers: *Roland* 797, 1896, 2190, 2409

Gerer, one of Charlemagne's twelve peers: *Roland* 107, 174, 794, 1269, 1380, 1623, 2186, 2404

Gerin, one of Charlemagne's twelve peers: *Roland* 107, 174, 794, 1261, 1379, 1618, 1623, 2186, 2404; (also called Berin): *Journey* 602

Germany: *Roland* 3038, 3977

Giles, Saint: *Roland* 2096

Gironde, a river and area in south-western France: *Roland* 3688; *Journey* 566

Godselme, a Frankish knight: *Roland* 3067

Goliath: *Journey* 424

Gormon, a Muslim king: *Daurel* 1688, 1694, 1763

Gramimund, Valdabrun's horse: *Roland* 1571

Grandonie, a Saracen prince: *Roland* 1613, 1636

Greece: *Journey* 47, 105

Grossaille, a Danish king killed previously by Turpin: *Roland* 1488

Guarlan, a Saracen knight: *Roland* 65

Guinemant, a Frankish count: *Roland* 3014, 3348, 3360, 3464

Guinemer, Ganelon's uncle: *Roland* 348

Guitume, a place near Constantinople: *Journey* 261

Guiun of Saint-Antoine, a Frankish knight: *Roland* 1624

Guy: *Daurel* 3, 8, 14, 22, 46, 58, 61, 65, 106, 111, 124, 137, 154, 163, 172, 180, 185, 189, 218, 225, 240, 246, 263, 274, 299, 311, 313, 320, 324, 328, 336, 370, 378, 388, 395, 418, 420, 429, 440, 443, 447, 453, 474, 476, 481, 482, 483, 499, 533, 534, 544, 550, 559, 595, 601, 617, 634, 636, 648, 686, 736, 760, 818, 819, 823, 826, 827, 850, 860, 863, 900, 901, 909, 924, 942, 948, 954, 970, 978, 983, 985, 1018, 1024, 1026, 1034, 1038, 1046, 1140, 1155, 1158, 1162, 1169, 1171, 1281, 1296, 1304, 1321, 1329, 1335, 1352, 1353, 1354, 1370, 1371, 1372, 1377, 1384, 1397, 1654, 1658, 1672, 1824, 1829, 1843, 1907, 1938, 1939, 1940, 1946, 1948, 1951, 1965, 1969, 2002, 2007, 2011, 2051, 2061, 2093, 2101, 2112, 2168, 2174

Halteclere, Oliver's sword: *Roland* 1363, 1463, 1550, 1953

Haltilie, an unidentified place in Spain whose name suggests height: *Roland* 209, 491

Hamon of Galicia, a Frankish knight: *Roland* 3073

Henry, nephew of Richard the Old: *Roland* 171

Herman of Thrace, a Frankish duke: *Roland* 3042

Holy See, the: *Roland* 377

Homer: *Roland* 2616

Hugo the Strong, King of Greece and Constantinople: *Journey* 46, 283, 302, 303, 310, 323, 329, 394, 397, 401, 419, 437, 444, 454, 466, 471, 478, 483, 533, 559, 563, 567, 584, 590, 601, 620, 628, 642, 660, 670, 682, 692, 753, 764, 778, 785, 800, 802, 807, 810, 817, 822, 838, 845, 852

Hum, place in France: *Roland* 803, 2039, 2067

Hungary: *Journey* 101

Imphe, an unidentified Christian land: *Roland* 3996

Ireland: *Roland* 2331

Ivoire, one of Charlemagne's twelve peers: *Roland* 1895, 2406

Ivon, one of Charlemagne's twelve peers: 1895, 2406

Jangleu, a Saracen knight: *Roland* 3507, 3508

Jericho: *Roland* 3228; *Journey* 242

Jerusalem: *Roland* 1566; *Journey* 69, 108, 154, 204, 308

Jesus/Christ: *Roland* 339; *Daurel* 172, 263, 327, 435, 476, 481, 482, 483, 499, 724, 739, 817, 841, 934, 940, 1040, 1192, 1818, 1946; *Journey* 170, 187, 674, 676, 790

Joiuse, Charlemagne's sword: *Roland* 2501, 2508, 2989

Jonah, biblical prophet: *Roland* 3101

Joüner, a Saracen knight: *Roland* 67

Jozeran of Provence: *Roland* 3007, 3023, 3044, 3067, 3075, 3113, 3535

Juliana, Bramimunde's Christian name: *Roland* 3986

Jupiter: *Roland* 1392

Jurfaleu (the Blond), Marsilie's son: *Roland* 504, 1904, 2702

Justin of Val-Ferree, a Saracen knight: *Roland* 1370

Laon, Frankish city now in Aisne region of France: *Roland* 2097, 2910

Latin church (in Jerusalem): *Journey* 208

Lazarus, Saint: *Roland* 2385; *Journey* 164

Levant, the: *Roland* 67

Lombardy, region of northern Italy: *Roland* 2326

Lorain, a Frankish knight: *Roland* 3022, 3469

Lorraine, a region of north-eastern France: *Roland* 3077, 3700; *Journey* 101

Louis, Charlemagne's son: *Roland* 3715

Lycia, Turkey: *Journey* 103

Machiner, a Saracen knight: *Roland* 66

Maëlgut, a Saracen knight: *Roland* 2047

Maine, a French province: *Roland* 2323

Malbien, a Saracen knight: *Roland* 67

Malcud, a Saracen king: *Roland* 1594

Malduit, Marsilie's treasurer: *Roland* 642

Malpalin of Narbonne, a Saracen knight: *Roland* 2995

Malpramis, Baligant's son: *Roland* 3176, 3184, 3200, 3201, 3369, 3421, 3498

Malprimis of Brigal, a Saracen lord: *Roland* 884,1261

Malprose, a Saracen land inhabited by giants: *Roland* 3253, 3285

Malquïant, Saracen, son of King Malcud: *Roland* 1594

Maltet, Baligant's spear: *Roland* 3152

Maltraïen, a Saracen king: *Roland* 2671

Malun, a Saracen knight: *Roland* 1353

Marbrise, an unidentified city in Spain: *Roland* 2641

Marbrose, an unidentified city in Spain: *Roland* 2641

Marcule, a Saracen knight: *Roland* 3156

Marganice, the caliph and Marsilie's uncle: *Roland* 1914, 1943, 1954

Margarit of Seville, a Saracen count: *Roland* 955, 1310, 1311

Marmorie, Grandonie's horse: *Roland* 1615

Marose, a Saracen land: *Roland* 3257

Marsilie: *Roland* 7, 10, 62, 78, 89, 125, 144, 181, 196, 201, 222, 235, 245, 276, 288, 299, 414, 424, 438, 441, 452, 485, 495, 504, 512, 520, 563, 580, 601, 603, 610, 618, 647, 680, 686, 848, 860, 873, 874, 880, 891, 900, 908, 911, 919, 933, 943, 1150, 1188, 1214, 1447, 1449, 1467, 1479, 1563, 1669, 1730, 1889, 1905, 1913, 2570, 2592, 2612, 2638, 2674, 2700, 2726, 2741, 2755, 2770, 2778, 2795, 2808, 2827, 2831, 3644, 3773

Marsonne, an unidentified place in Spain: *Roland* 2994

Mary (the Virgin):*Roland* 1473, 2303, 2348, 2938; *Daurel* 437, 672; *Journey* 187, 207

Maseus, a fairy: *Journey* 430

Matthew, a Saracen knight: *Roland* 66

Maurienne, a valley in Savoy, south-eastern France: *Roland* 2318

Mayence (Mainz): *Roland* 3008

Michael, Saint, the archangel: *Roland* 2394

Milceni, a Slavonic people: *Roland* 3221

Miles, a Frankish count: *Roland* 173, 2433, 2971

Mohammed: *Roland* 8, 416, 611, 853, 868, 921, 1336, 1667, 1906, 2590, 2696, 2711, 3233, 3267, 3491, 3552, 3641

Monclar: *Daurel* 87, 209, 355, 527, 655, 882, 930, 949, 1038, 1057, 1070, 1103, 1142, 1149, 1171, 1285, 1299, 1379, 1388, 1405, 1652, 1674, 1676, 1898, 1899

Monjoie, Charlemagne's war cry and oriflamme's name: *Roland* 1181, 1234, 1260, 1350, 1378, 1525, 1974, 2151, 2510, 3092, 3095, 3300, 3565, 3620

Monteles, a location en route for Constantinople: *Journey* 260

Mont Saint-Michel: *Roland* 1428

Moriana, a city on the Ebro in the province of Burgos: *Roland* 909

Muneigre, perhaps Los Munegros near Saragossa or Monegrillo on the Ebro: *Roland* 975

Murgleis, Ganelon's sword: *Roland* 346, 607

Naimon, a Frankish duke and Charlemagne's counsellor: *Roland* 230, 246, 673, 774, 831, 1767, 1790, 2417, 2423, 2882, 2944, 3008, 3113, 3023, 3036, 3044, 3061, 3068, 3075, 3113, 3423, 3432, 3444, 3452, 3455, 3544, 3621, 3937; one of Charlemagne's twelve peers: *Journey* 62, 531

Narbonne, a French town in Languedoc-Roussillon: *Roland* 2995, 3683

Nevelon, a Frankish count: *Roland* 3057

Nineveh, King of: *Roland* 3103

Noples, a town in Spain, perhaps Napal in diocese of Barbastro: *Roland* 198, 1776

Normandy: *Roland* 2324

Occian by the desert, a Saracen land: *Roland* 3246, 3286, 3474, 3517, 3526

Ogier (of Denmark) one of Charlemagne's twelve peers: *Roland* 170, 749, 3033, 3531, 3544, 3546, 3856, 3937; *Daurel* 146; *Journey* 63, 518

Oliver, one of Charlemagne's twelve peers and Roland's companion: *Roland* 104, 176, 255, 324, 546, 559, 576, 586, 672, 793, 903, 936, 947, 964, 1006, 1017, 1026, 1028, 1039, 1049, 1082, 1093, 1099,

1112, 1145, 1170, 1224, 1274, 1313, 1316, 1345, 1351, 1365, 1367, 1395, 1412, 1456, 1512, 1545, 1554, 1671, 1680, 1692, 1698, 1700, 1705, 1715, 1719, 1740, 1866, 1938, 1945, 1952, 1965, 1978, 1990, 2003, 2010, 2017, 2201, 2207, 2216, 2403, 2514, 2776, 2792, 2963, 3016, 3186, 3690, 3755, 3776; *Daurel* 140, 2161; *Journey* 61, 404, 484, 693, 708, 712, 714, 722, 824, 853, 856

Oluferne, a Saracen land or city, Aleppo?: *Roland* 3297

Orange, a town in Provence: *Journey* 62, 326, 507

Orient, the: *Roland* 401, 558, 3594

Oton, one of Charlemagne's twelve peers: *Roland* 795, 2187, 2405

Oton, a Frankish marquis: *Roland* 2432, 2971, 3058

Outremer: *Roland* 3156, 3507

Palermo, town in Sicily: *Roland* 2923

Paris: *Daurel* 73, 109, 545, 2149; *Journey* 36, 60, 654, 862

Passecerf, Gerer's horse: *Roland* 1380

Paternoster (church of): *Journey* 114

Persia: *Journey* 48

Peter, Saint: *Roland* 921, 2346, 3094; *Journey* 181, 326

Pinabel, Ganelon's kinsman: *Roland* 362, 3783, 3788, 3797, 3838, 3885, 3892, 3899, 3906, 3915, 3926, 3928, 3950

Pine, perhaps the district in which the monastery of San Juan de la Peña was located: *Roland* 199

Poitiers: *Daurel* 135, 175, 585, 1044, 1673, 1862, 1875, 1987, 1990, 2022, 2063, 2152

Poitou, a French province: *Roland* 2323

Precious, Baligant's sword and pagan war cry: *Roland* 3146, 3298, 3471, 3564

Priamun, a Saracen knight: *Roland* 65

Primes, a Saracen land: *Roland* 967

Provence: *Roland* 2325, 3007, 3916

Pui, a Saracen location: *Roland* 1871

Rabel, a Frankish count: *Roland* 3014, 3348, 3352

Rainier, a Frankish duke, father of Oliver: *Roland* 2208

Rembalt, a Frankish knight: *Roland* 3073

Rencesvals: *Roland* 892, 901, 912, 923, 934, 944, 963, 985, 2225, 2398, 2483, 2516, 2716, 2791, 2854, 2855, 3412

Rheims: *Roland* 173, 264, 2077, 2083, 2433, 3058

Rhône, river in France: *Roland* 1626

Richard the Old (Richard, Duke of Normandy): *Roland* 171, 3050, 3470

Riquier, one of Guy's knights: *Daurel* 1366

Roland, Charlemagne's nephew: *Roland* 104, 175, 194, 254, 277, 286, 292, 302, 303, 322, 355, 382, 387, 392, 404, 473, 557, 575, 581, 585, 593, 596, 605, 613, 615, 623, 630, 656, 663, 672, 707, 743, 751, 761, 766, 777, 782, 783, 792, 801, 803, 843, 866, 888a, 893, 902, 914, 923, 935, 947, 963, 986, 1008, 1020, 1026, 1051, 1053, 1059, 1062, 1070, 1073, 1088, 1093, 1099, 1106, 1110, 1145, 1152, 1196, 1288, 1321, 1338, 1360, 1368, 1376, 1394, 1413, 1437, 1456, 1512, 1545, 1558, 1580, 1591, 1629, 1638, 1642, 1671, 1680, 1691, 1702, 1713, 1722, 1731, 1740, 1752, 1753, 1761, 1768, 1774, 1777, 1785, 1795, 1804, 1815, 1837, 1846, 1851, 1869, 1875, 1883, 1897, 1922, 1932, 1964, 1975, 1978, 1989, 1998, 2001, 2006, 2018, 2022, 2024, 2035, 2044, 2054, 2056, 2066, 2086, 2099, 2107, 2118, 2122, 2124, 2134, 2152, 2157, 2162, 2166, 2176, 2184, 2200, 2207, 2215, 2222, 2233, 2246, 2259, 2273, 2280, 2284, 2297, 2312, 2338, 2355, 2366, 2375, 2397, 2475, 2513, 2701, 2720, 2775, 2779, 2792, 2863, 2875, 2887, 2898, 2909, 2916, 2933, 2962, 3012, 3016, 3109, 3120, 3182, 3185, 3709, 3719, 3758, 3771, 3775, 3802, 3827, 3871; *Daurel* 130, 277, 558, 2137, 2161; *Journey* 61, 232, 276, 307, 469, 484

Romagna, a region in Italy: *Roland* 2326

Romaine, the oriflamme's previous name: *Roland* 3094

Romania: *Journey* 106

Rome: *Roland* 639, 921, 2998; *Journey* 367

Roussillon, a hill in Burgundy: *Roland* 797, 1896, 2189, 2409

Runers, Vale of, land of Oliver's father: *Roland* 2209

Saint-Antoine: *Roland* 1624

Saint-Denis, town and abbey near Paris: *Roland* 973; *Journey* 1, 86, 863

Saint Hilary, church in Poitiers: *Daurel* 531, 749, 2085

Saint Romain, church: *Roland* 3693

Saintes, town in south-western France: *Roland* 1428

Saltperdut, Malqüiant's horse: *Roland* 1597

Samson, one of Charlemagne's twelve peers: *Roland* 105, 1275, 1574, 1580, 2188, 2408

Samuel, perhaps the tsar of the Bulgarians: *Roland* 3244

Saragossa: *Roland* 6, 10, 211, 245, 253, 299, 310, 406, 476, 677, 852, 996, 1407, 1526, 2462, 2570, 2598, 2617, 2645, 2673, 2689, 2752, 2762, 2768, 2818, 2833, 3635, 3650, 3660, 3676

Satan: *Roland* 1268

Saxony: *Roland* 2330

Scotland: *Roland* 2331

Seurin, Saint, bishop of Bordeaux: *Roland* 3685

Seville: *Roland* 200, 955

Siglorel, a Saracen knight and magician: *Roland* 1390

Simeon, Saint: *Journey* 163

Solomon, Temple of: *Roland* 1567

Sorel, Gerin's horse: *Roland* 1379

Sorence, Pinabel's land: *Roland* 3783, 3915

Spain: *Roland* 2, 59, 197, 224, 409, 432, 472, 666, 697, 703, 824, 826, 848, 869, 907, 910, 1021, 1029, 1081, 1083, 1745, 1847, 2058, 2119, 2165, 2266, 2367, 2376, 2445, 2610, 2636, 2660, 2703, 2721, 2747, 2787, 2832, 2900, 2913, 3089, 3705, 3752, 3985; *Journey* 230

Stephen, Saint: *Journey* 165

Strymonis, a Saracen land: *Roland* 3258

Suatilie, a Saracen land: *Roland* 90

Sylvester, Saint: *Roland* 3746

Tachebrun, Ganelon's horse: *Roland* 347

Tedbald of Rheims, one of Charlemagne's barons: *Roland* 173, 2433, 2970, 3058

Tencendur, Charlemagne's horse: *Roland* 2993, 3342, 3622

Tervagant, one of the Saracen trinity of gods: *Roland* 611, 2468, 2589, 2696, 2712, 3267, 3491

Thierry, Duke of Argonne: *Roland* 3083, 3534

Thierry, brother of Geoffrey of Anjou: *Roland* 2883, 3806, 3818, 3843, 3850, 3871, 3892, 3896, 3899, 3916, 3924, 3929, 3934, 3939

Thrace (in modern Bulgaria and Turkey): *Roland* 3042

Timozel, a Saracen knight: *Roland* 1382

Torleu, a Persian king: *Roland* 3204, 3216, 3354

Tortosa, a town in Catalonia: *Roland* 916, 1282

Tudela, a town on the Ebro in Navarre: *Roland* 200

Turgis of Tortosa, a Saracen count: *Roland* 916, 1282, 1358

Turoldus, the poet or transmitter of the text: *Roland* 4002

Turpin, archbishop and one of Charlemagne's twelve peers: *Roland* 170, 264, 1124, 1243, 1393, 1483, 1504, 1605, 2077, 2083, 2130, 2137, 2169, 2242, 2963; *Journey* 87, 202, 494, 828

Tyre, a town in Lebanon known for its purple dye and costly fabrics: *Daurel* 112

Valdabrun, a Saracen peer: *Roland* 617, 1562

Vale of Runers, land of Oliver's father: *Roland* 2209

Valence, a town in south-eastern France: *Roland* 1626

Valencia, a Spanish port: *Roland* 998

Val-Ferree, a Saracen land: *Roland* 1370

Val-Fuït, a Saracen region: *Roland* 3239

Val-Marchis, a Saracen land: *Roland* 3208

Val-Metas, a Saracen land: *Roland* 1502

Val-Peneuse, a Saracen land: *Roland* 3256

Val-Sevree, a Saracen land: *Roland* 3313

Val-Tenebros, a Saracen land: *Roland* 2461

Val-Terne, probably Valterra on the Ebro: *Roland* 199, 931, 1291

Veillantif, Roland's horse: *Roland* 1153, 2032, 2127, 2160, 2167

Viana, city in Galicia or Vienne in France?: *Roland* 997

Virgil: *Roland* 2616

Viterbo, Italian city and province: *Roland* 2991

Vivian, Christian King of Imphe: *Roland* 3996

William of Blaye, one of Charlemagne's barons: *Roland* 3938

William of Orange, son of Aimeri of Narbonne: *Journey* 62, 326, 507, 739, 744

Wissant, French port on the north coast: *Roland* 1429

The Oxford World's Classics Website

www.worldsclassics.co.uk

- Browse the full range of Oxford World's Classics online

- Sign up for our monthly e-alert to receive information on new titles

- Read extracts from the Introductions

- Listen to our editors and translators talk about the world's greatest literature with our Oxford World's Classics audio guides

- Join the conversation, follow us on Twitter at OWC_Oxford

- Teachers and lecturers can order inspection copies quickly and simply via our website

www.worldsclassics.co.uk

American Literature

British and Irish Literature

Children's Literature

Classics and Ancient Literature

Colonial Literature

Eastern Literature

European Literature

Gothic Literature

History

Medieval Literature

Oxford English Drama

Philosophy

Poetry

Politics

Religion

The Oxford Shakespeare

A complete list of Oxford World's Classics, including Authors in Context, Oxford English Drama, and the Oxford Shakespeare, is available in the UK from the Marketing Services Department, Oxford University Press, Great Clarendon Street, Oxford OX2 6DP, or visit the website at www.oup.com/uk/worldsclassics.

In the USA, visit www.oup.com/us/owc for a complete title list.

Oxford World's Classics are available from all good bookshops. In case of difficulty, customers in the UK should contact Oxford University Press Bookshop, 116 High Street, Oxford OX1 4BR.

French Decadent Tales
Six French Poets of the Nineteenth
   Century

HONORÉ DE BALZAC **Cousin Bette**
Eugénie Grandet
Père Goriot
The Wild Ass's Skin

CHARLES BAUDELAIRE **The Flowers of Evil**
The Prose Poems and Fanfarlo

DENIS DIDEROT **Jacques the Fatalist**
The Nun

ALEXANDRE DUMAS (PÈRE) **The Black Tulip**
The Count of Monte Cristo
Louise de la Vallière
The Man in the Iron Mask
La Reine Margot
The Three Musketeers
Twenty Years After
The Vicomte de Bragelonne

ALEXANDRE DUMAS (FILS) **La Dame aux Camélias**

GUSTAVE FLAUBERT **Madame Bovary**
A Sentimental Education
Three Tales

VICTOR HUGO **Notre-Dame de Paris**

J.-K. HUYSMANS **Against Nature**

PIERRE CHODERLOS DE **Les Liaisons dangereuses**
LACLOS

MME DE LAFAYETTE **The Princesse de Clèves**

GUILLAUME DU LORRIS **The Romance of the Rose**
and JEAN DE MEUN

A SELECTION OF   **OXFORD WORLD'S CLASSICS**

GUY DE MAUPASSANT	**A Day in the Country and Other Stories**
	A Life
	Bel-Ami
PROSPER MÉRIMÉE	**Carmen and Other Stories**
MOLIÈRE	**Don Juan and Other Plays**
	The Misanthrope, Tartuffe, and Other Plays
BLAISE PASCAL	**Pensées and Other Writings**
ABBÉ PRÉVOST	**Manon Lescaut**
JEAN RACINE	**Britannicus, Phaedra, and Athaliah**
ARTHUR RIMBAUD	**Collected Poems**
EDMOND ROSTAND	**Cyrano de Bergerac**
MARQUIS DE SADE	**The Crimes of Love**
	Justine
	The Misfortunes of Virtue and Other Early Tales
GEORGE SAND	**Indiana**
MME DE STAËL	**Corinne**
STENDHAL	**The Red and the Black**
	The Charterhouse of Parma
PAUL VERLAINE	**Selected Poems**
JULES VERNE	**Around the World in Eighty Days**
	Journey to the Centre of the Earth
	Twenty Thousand Leagues under the Seas
VOLTAIRE	**Candide and Other Stories**
	Letters concerning the English Nation
	A Pocket Philosophical Dictionary

ÉMILE ZOLA

L'Assommoir
The Belly of Paris
La Bête humaine
The Conquest of Plassans
The Fortune of the Rougons
Germinal
The Kill
The Ladies' Paradise
The Masterpiece
Money
Nana
Pot Luck
Thérèse Raquin

A SELECTION OF   **OXFORD WORLD'S CLASSICS**

	Eirik the Red and Other Icelandic Sagas
	The Kalevala
	The Poetic Edda
LUDOVICO ARIOSTO	Orlando Furioso
GIOVANNI BOCCACCIO	The Decameron
GEORG BÜCHNER	Danton's Death, Leonce and Lena, and Woyzeck
LUIS VAZ DE CAMÕES	The Lusiads
C. P. CAVAFY	The Collected Poems
MIGUEL DE CERVANTES	Don Quixote
	Exemplary Stories
CARLO COLLODI	The Adventures of Pinocchio
DANTE ALIGHIERI	The Divine Comedy
	Vita Nuova
J. W. VON GOETHE	Elective Affinities
	Erotic Poems
	Faust: Part One and Part Two
	The Sorrows of Young Werther
JACOB and WILHELM GRIMM	Selected Tales
E. T. A. HOFFMANN	The Golden Pot and Other Tales
HENRIK IBSEN	An Enemy of the People, The Wild Duck, Rosmersholm
	Four Major Plays
	Peer Gynt
FRANZ KAFKA	The Castle
	A Hunger Artist and Other Stories
	The Man who Disappeared (America)
	The Metamorphosis and Other Stories
	The Trial
LEONARDO DA VINCI	Selections from the Notebooks
LOPE DE VEGA	Three Major Plays

A SELECTION OF   **OXFORD WORLD'S CLASSICS**

FEDERICO GARCIA LORCA   **Four Major Plays**

MICHELANGELO   **Life, Letters, and Poetry**
BUONARROTI

ROBERT MUSIL   **The Confusions of Young Törless**

PETRARCH   **Selections from the Canzoniere and
Other Works**

LUIGI PIRANDELLO   **Three Plays**

RAINER MARIA RILKE   **Selected Poems**

J. C. F. SCHILLER   **Don Carlos and Mary Stuart**

JOHANN AUGUST   **Miss Julie and Other Plays**
STRINDBERG

A SELECTION OF   **OXFORD WORLD'S CLASSICS**

LUDOVICO ARIOSTO	**Orlando Furioso**
GIOVANNI BOCCACCIO	**The Decameron**
LUÍS VAZ DE CAMÕES	**The Lusíads**
MIGUEL DE CERVANTES	**Don Quixote de la Mancha** **Exemplary Stories**
CARLO COLLODI	**The Adventures of Pinocchio**
DANTE ALIGHIERI	**The Divine Comedy** **Vita Nuova**
GALILEO	**Selected Writings**
J. W. VON GOETHE	**Faust: Part One and Part Two**
FRANZ KAFKA	**The Metamorphosis and Other Stories** **The Trial**
LEONARDO DA VINCI	**Selections from the Notebooks**
LOPE DE VEGA	**Three Major Plays**
FEDERICO GARCIA LORCA	**Four Major Plays** **Selected Poems**
NICCOLÒ MACHIAVELLI	**Discourses on Livy** **The Prince**
MICHELANGELO	**Life, Letters, and Poetry**
PETRARCH	**Selections from the Canzoniere and** **Other Works**
LUIGI PIRANDELLO	**Three Plays**
RAINER MARIA RILKE	**Selected Poems**
GIORGIO VASARI	**The Lives of the Artists**

A SELECTION OF   **OXFORD WORLD'S CLASSICS**

ANTON CHEKHOV
About Love and Other Stories
Early Stories
Five Plays
The Princess and Other Stories
The Russian Master and Other Stories
The Steppe and Other Stories
Twelve Plays
Ward Number Six and Other Stories

FYODOR DOSTOEVSKY
Crime and Punishment
Devils
A Gentle Creature and Other Stories
The Idiot
The Karamazov Brothers
Memoirs from the House of the Dead
Notes from the Underground and
    The Gambler

NIKOLAI GOGOL
Dead Souls
Plays and Petersburg Tales

MIKHAIL LERMONTOV
A Hero of Our Time

ALEXANDER PUSHKIN
Boris Godunov
Eugene Onegin
The Queen of Spades and Other Stories

LEO TOLSTOY
Anna Karenina
The Kreutzer Sonata and Other Stories
The Raid and Other Stories
Resurrection
War and Peace

IVAN TURGENEV
Fathers and Sons
First Love and Other Stories
A Month in the Country

	Late Victorian Gothic Tales
	Literature and Science in the Nineteenth Century
JANE AUSTEN	Emma
	Mansfield Park
	Persuasion
	Pride and Prejudice
	Selected Letters
	Sense and Sensibility
MRS BEETON	Book of Household Management
MARY ELIZABETH BRADDON	Lady Audley's Secret
ANNE BRONTË	The Tenant of Wildfell Hall
CHARLOTTE BRONTË	Jane Eyre
	Shirley
	Villette
EMILY BRONTË	Wuthering Heights
ROBERT BROWNING	The Major Works
JOHN CLARE	The Major Works
SAMUEL TAYLOR COLERIDGE	The Major Works
WILKIE COLLINS	The Moonstone
	No Name
	The Woman in White
CHARLES DARWIN	The Origin of Species
THOMAS DE QUINCEY	The Confessions of an English Opium-Eater
	On Murder
CHARLES DICKENS	The Adventures of Oliver Twist
	Barnaby Rudge
	Bleak House
	David Copperfield
	Great Expectations
	Nicholas Nickleby

CHARLES DICKENS	**The Old Curiosity Shop**
	Our Mutual Friend
	The Pickwick Papers
GEORGE DU MAURIER	**Trilby**
MARIA EDGEWORTH	**Castle Rackrent**
GEORGE ELIOT	**Daniel Deronda**
	The Lifted Veil and Brother Jacob
	Middlemarch
	The Mill on the Floss
	Silas Marner
EDWARD FITZGERALD	**The Rubáiyát of Omar Khayyám**
ELIZABETH GASKELL	**Cranford**
	The Life of Charlotte Brontë
	Mary Barton
	North and South
	Wives and Daughters
GEORGE GISSING	**New Grub Street**
	The Nether World
	The Odd Women
EDMUND GOSSE	**Father and Son**
THOMAS HARDY	**Far from the Madding Crowd**
	Jude the Obscure
	The Mayor of Casterbridge
	The Return of the Native
	Tess of the d'Urbervilles
	The Woodlanders
JAMES HOGG	**The Private Memoirs and Confessions of a Justified Sinner**
JOHN KEATS	**The Major Works**
	Selected Letters
CHARLES MATURIN	**Melmoth the Wanderer**
HENRY MAYHEW	**London Labour and the London Poor**

A SELECTION OF **OXFORD WORLD'S CLASSICS**

WILLIAM MORRIS — **News from Nowhere**

JOHN RUSKIN — **Praeterita**
Selected Writings

WALTER SCOTT — **Ivanhoe**
Rob Roy
Waverley

MARY SHELLEY — **Frankenstein**
The Last Man

ROBERT LOUIS STEVENSON — **Strange Case of Dr Jekyll and Mr Hyde
and Other Tales**
Treasure Island

BRAM STOKER — **Dracula**

W. M. THACKERAY — **Vanity Fair**

FRANCES TROLLOPE — **Domestic Manners of the Americans**

OSCAR WILDE — **The Importance of Being Earnest
and Other Plays**
The Major Works
The Picture of Dorian Gray

ELLEN WOOD — **East Lynne**

DOROTHY WORDSWORTH — **The Grasmere and Alfoxden Journals**

WILLIAM WORDSWORTH — **The Major Works**

WORDSWORTH and
COLERIDGE — **Lyrical Ballads**